"My whole purpose with this boat has been to resist "advice" to rebuild, etc. Percy Coverdale might have built fast but he built strong. What he made has lasted unlike many of Landfall's USA-built sisters. The boat builders of Battery Point cannot ever be regarded as just manual labourers, they filled the space between craftsmen and artists."

Mike Strong (January, 2017)
Owner of *Landfall,* built by Percy Coverdale and launched in 1935.

Purdon and Featherstone's Battery Point yard (circa 1960s).
Courtesy Tasmanian Archive and Heritage Office.

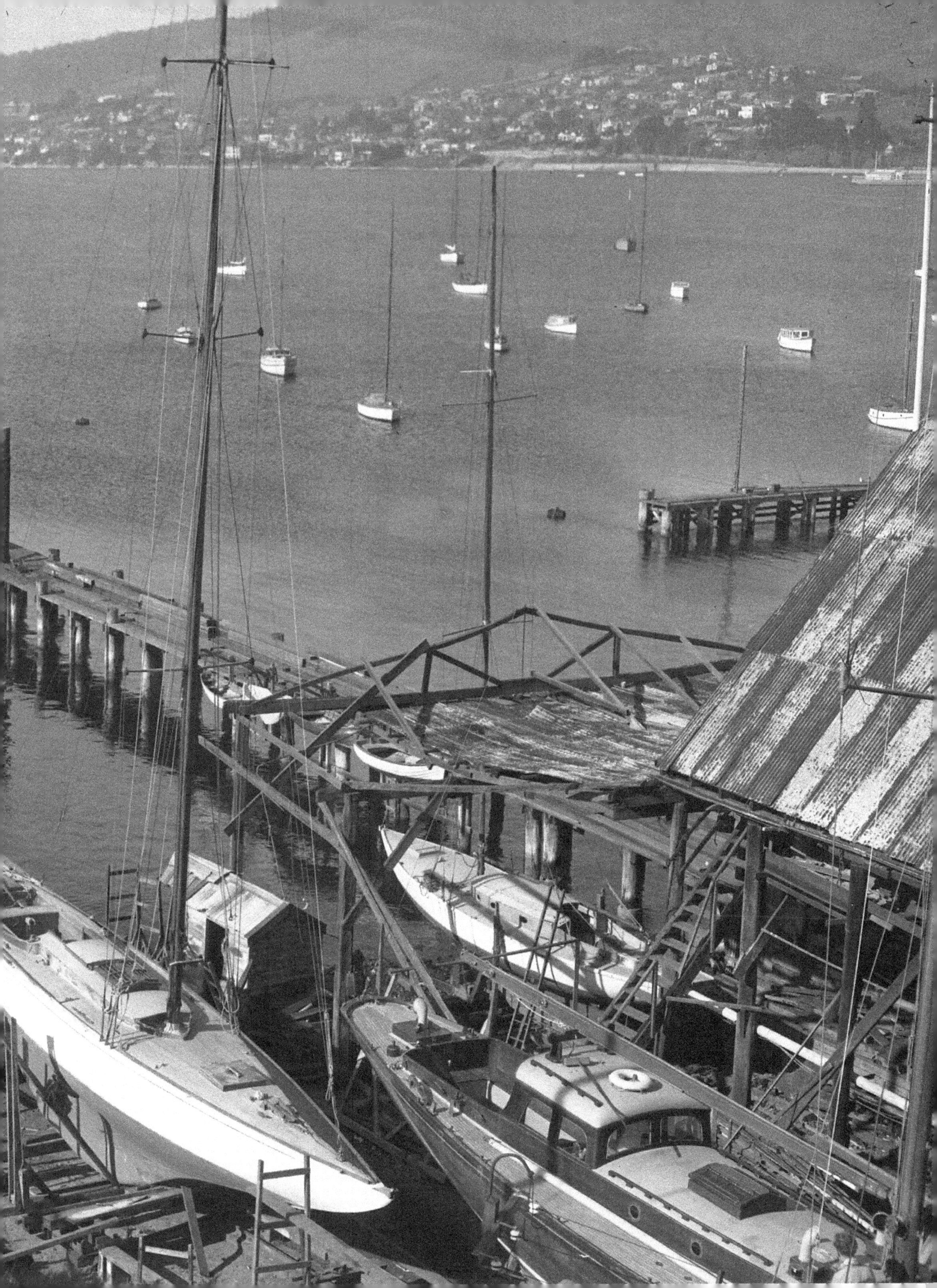

Peter Creese (left) and Max Creese (right) on board *Seaman*.
Courtesy Darryl Ridgeway.

Industrious, Innovative, Altruistic:

The 20th Century Boat Builders of Battery Point.

Nicole Mays

Hardcover printed in 2018

First published in 2017 by Navarine Publishing

GPO Box 2178, Hobart, Tasmania 7001

Copyright © Nicole Mays

Design and layout by Nicole Mays

Printed by IngramSpark

Enquiries should be made to the author at nicmays@gmail.com

ISBN: 978-0-9923660-5-6

A catalogue record for this book is available from the National Library of Australia

NATIONAL LIBRARY OF AUSTRALIA

Front cover images

Ketch *Swift* at Battery Point. Courtesy Maritime Museum of Tasmania.

Sharpies under construction at Taylor Brothers. Courtesy Maritime Museum of Tasmania.

Fishing boat *Marie Laure* under construction. Courtesy Jock Muir Family Collection.

Yacht *Mistral IX* under construction. Courtesy Guy Rex Collection (Suzanne Rex).

Back cover image

Sam Purdon working at Battery Point. Courtesy Sam Purdon.

Background image

Plans of *Sandra* by Max Creese. Courtesy Sandra Wilson.

To Owen and Liam, "Oh, the places you will go!"

Charlie Lucas' Battery Point boatyard (circa 1920s).
Courtesy Living Boat Trust.

Contents

Acknowledgements

I would like to thank the following individuals for their input, encouragement, edits and/or advice: Joel Geoghegan, Owen Geoghegan, Liam Geoghegan, Robyn Mays, John Allport, Bill Batt, Kenn Batt, Mary Brewer, Graeme Broxam, Peter Creese, Bill Foster, Colin Grazules, Harry Hale, Peter Higgs, Jenny Keyes, Peter Keyes, John Lucas, Greg Muir, John Muir, Philip Muir, Ross Muir, Russell Pocock, Mick Purdon, Sam Purdon, Suzanne Rex, Mike Strong, Jan Taylor, Barry Wilson, Sandra Wilson, Carol Wise, and Rona Hollingsworth and staff at the Maritime Museum of Tasmania.

Members of the "Battery Point Boat and Ships" Facebook group are to be thanked for their assistance in piecing together facets of the information contained herein, as well as for their unfailing interest and enthusiasm in the Battery Point boat and slip yards.

Additionally, thank you to all the individuals and organisations who graciously provided photographs, including the Living Boat Trust, the Maritime Museum of Tasmania and the Tasmanian Archive and Heritage Office, and in particular Colin Grazules, the Muir and Pilkington families, and Suzanne Rex.

Acronyms, Abbreviations and Measurements

ACT - Australian Capital Territory
ci - Cubic inch
ft - Feet
hp - Horsepower
in - Inches
Jr - Junior
lb - Pound
LWL - Length on waterline
NSW - New South Wales
NT - Northern Territory
NZ - New Zealand
Sr - Senior
TAS - Tasmania
UK - United Kingdom
USA - United States of America
VIC - Victoria
WA - Western Australia

Sloane St

umpeter St

ent
St

Marine Terrace

Derwent Ln

well St

Napoleon St

rrace

Aerial View of the Battery Point boat and slip yards (2016).
Courtesy Goggle Maps.

Bill Price and John Lucas at Battery Point (1976).
Courtesy Maritime Museum of Tasmania.

Foreword

After a lifetime associated with Tasmania's boat builders, shipwrights, shipbuilders, ship repairers and marine surveyors, it gives me great pleasure to write this foreword. Nicole has put a mighty effort into writing this book, her second in a series highlighting the craftsmanship of the state's boat builders, particularly those who worked at Battery Point.

I feel privileged to have known many of the boat builders mentioned in this book, including Percy Coverdale; Norm Taylor; Charles Lucas; Ernest "Jock" Muir; Max Creese; Clyde, Keith and Richard Featherstone; and of course the characters who worked for them. Men such as Henry "Chook" Newman; R. W. R. "Mick" Smith; John "Jack" Hansen; Max, Wally and Don Muir; Bill Foster; Alan Cracknell; David Wardrop; Ray Kemp; Jack "Turk" Bridge; Barry Wilson; Brian Freeman; Bob Laughlin; Ken Owens; Alan Whitton; Geoff Maddock; and Hughie Auld, to name just a few. Many have passed on but their legacy lives in the magnificent vessels turned out from the Battery Point yards.

Tasmania has been very lucky to have had the best boat builders working with the best timbers; wonderful timbers such as the famous Huon, celery top and King Billy pines, along with eucalypts like stringybark, swamp and blue gum. The quality of these timbers is second to none and the reason why many of the craft built at Battery Point are still sailing as well today as the day they were built. In fact boats built at Battery Point can be traced all over the world. The 8 metre class *Erica J*, for example, built at Battery Point by Max Creese and launched in 1949, is now based in England and recently finished second in an 8 metre event on the Solent.

Nicole Mays' remarkable effort in researching and writing the stories of these men and their vessels highlights the impact that Battery Point has had on the state's maritime history, one of Tasmania's first industries, as well as how linked this quaint suburb of Hobart remains to the boat and slip yards located along Napoleon Street.

John Lucas

(April, 2017)

Top and Bottom: Views of the Battery Point boat and slip yards (2016).
Courtesy author's private collection.

Introduction

This book details the history and legacy of the 20th century boat builders of Battery Point, near Hobart in Tasmania. It overlaps somewhat with the first volume I wrote on the area's boat and ship yards, *Spirited, Skilled and Determined - The Boat and Ship Builders of Battery Point: 1835 – 1935*. Yet this manuscript goes beyond the reach of the previous volume by extending the discussion to run the entire breadth of the 20th century. There are also some minor updates, including the addition of several vessels built between 1900 and 1935 that were inadvertently omitted from the first volume.

The dawn of the 20th century precipitated a new generation of boat builders at Battery Point. The discussion begins with talented and well-known Hobart waterfront identities Charles (Charlie) Lucas and Albert "Tucker" Abel. Both were enterprising boat builders. Charlie Lucas' sole passion was boat building. He spent nearly 60 years working at Battery Point during which time he was involved with the construction of more than 60 boats.

Working at yards nearby were Henry Featherstone, Thomas (Tom) Purdon, William Lucas and Percival (Percy) Coverdale. Together Purdon and Featherstone dominated the steam ferry landscape, launching eight ferries in eight years between 1905 and 1913. The pair also built ketches for the local timber and fishing trades. Following Tom Purdon's retirement in 1919, Henry Featherstone persevered, launching the schooner *Leprena* and the ketch *Terralinna* in 1922. The 1930s saw Henry Featherstone's sons join the firm, duly entrusted to carry on their family's maritime heritage. William Lucas, the son of pioneer Battery Point shipbuilder John Lucas, also continued his family's legacy, establishing a yard at Battery Point in 1904. The doyen of Hobart's boat builders, Percy Coverdale, purchased William Lucas' yard in 1914 where he famously eked out a living until the early 1960s.

The years surrounding World War II were a pivotal time for the Battery Point boatyards. Charlie Lucas, Tucker Abel, Henry Featherstone and Tom Purdon retired and/or passed away, their yards taken over by up-and-coming boat builders and designers, including Taylor Brothers, Ernest "Jock" Muir and Maxwell (Max) Creese. In the decades that followed, brothers Donald "Sam" and Allan "Mick" Purdon joined the collective, as did William (Bill) Foster.

Through triumph and tragedy the 20th century boat builders of Battery Point extended the tradition of those who had worked the yards before them. Like their predecessors they were as equally spirited, skilled and determined. Many of the men grew up near the yards, spending their free time nipping at the heels of mentors, as well as participating in model yacht club and junior sailing events. Several attended the Battery Point Trade School during their final year of primary school and went on to learn the craft of boat building through apprenticeship. Others built boats in their backyards during spare hours. Some even established boatyards after starting careers in other trades. Singularly and collectively these men were innovative, industrious and altruistic. Though the last boat built at Battery Point was launched some years ago, the legacy of Battery Point's 20th century boat builders continues in the yards that are still in operation, as well as in the more than 470 wooden vessels they built, of which at least one quarter remain in existence.

Historical Context

Since its establishment in the initial years of Hobart's founding, Battery Point has been an eclectic suburb — a patchwork of industry and commercial activities interspersed with grand mansions, terraced houses and working class cottages. Situated along part of its shore, off Napoleon Street and at one time along the waterfront at the bottom of Finlay Street, are the boat and ship building yards that lay claim to a history rich with industry, entrepreneurism, competitiveness and camaraderie.

The earliest of Battery Point's shipbuilders were William Williamson and John Watson. The former established a yard at the bottom of Finlay Street in 1835, the latter established a yard along Napoleon Street in 1839. Both men arrived in Tasmania in the early 1830s and both were experienced shipwrights from the United Kingdom. In the 13 and 16 years, respectively, that William Williamson and John Watson spent at Battery Point they collectively launched more than 20 schooners, eight barques and three brigs. Many of these vessels played important roles in the development of intercolonial and trans-Tasman trades, while others became pioneers of international trade and were among the first Tasmanian built vessels to arrive in Asia, Europe and South America. Some of the vessels built by William Williamson and John Watson also were the first locally built craft to be employed in the whaling industry.

In 1846 Peter Degraves, the patriarch of the Cascade Brewery empire, established a shipyard at Battery Point in the vicinity of William Williamson's Finlay Street yard. One of Tasmania's wealthiest and more powerful businessmen, his determination and resolve culminated in construction of the largest vessel built in Australia at the time, the 562 ton *Tasman*, launched in March 1847. Together with his son Henry, Peter Degraves continued to oversee the building of larger vessels at Battery Point up until his death in 1853, primarily barques and schooners destined for intercolonial and international trades and/or the whaling industry.

Also in the late 1840s Joseph Risby and Jacob Chandler, both boat builders, established yards along Napoleon Street near John Watson's shipyard. The Risby family's yard was the first commercial boatyard in operation at Battery Point. In the succeeding years a slew of boats were built, many of which were prominent in local whaleboat races and regattas, while others were exported to the mainland. In 1858 Joseph Risby opted to forgo boat building in lieu of his rapidly expanding timber milling and export business; the enterprise made lucrative by the mainland gold rush. Significantly, the company he created would remain in operation for 135 years.

Like the Risby family, Jacob Chandler was a prolific builder of whaleboats, particularly those used for racing. He also built many boats for Hobart's watermen. Yet the evolution of the maritime industry in the 47 years Jacob Chandler spent at Battery Point saw him transition to the building of fishing boats and passage boats, the latter for use in transporting goods, produce and timber from ports in the Huon, D'Entrecasteaux Channel and Ralphs Bay to Hobart. The building of the first four steam ferries for the O'May Brothers, for use in Derwent passenger services, is another highlight of Jacob Chandler's long career. All up he built over 170 vessels at Battery Point.

The early 1850s saw James Mackey (in partnership with Thomas Cullen and his brother David Mackey) establish a shipyard along Napoleon Street just north of Jacob Chandler's yard. Having learned the craft of shipbuilding from John Watson, the trio built many successful intercolonial and coastal schooners and ketches, and also furnished vessels for the New Zealand coastal trade. When his partners retired, James Mackey continued on with the firm, including launching the steamer *Warrentinna* in 1883. Distinguished as the longest serving shipbuilder at Battery Point, in 1903, after 51 years of employment, James Mackey passed on the reins to his nephew Henry Featherstone.

Left: The Hobart wharf (likely in the 1870s) showing two vessels built at Battery Point. Second from left is the 283 ton barque *Runnymede*, launched from John Watson's Napoleon Street yard on 21 March 1849. On the far right is the 230 ton barque *Lady Emma*, launched on 16 December 1848 from the Degraves family's yard at Battery Point (near Finlay Street) and built under the superintendence of John Ross (who later operated his own yard at Battery Point). Courtesy Tasmanian Archive and Heritage Office.

Likely the earliest photo of the Napoleon Street boat and ship yards in existence (circa 1860).
Courtesy Tasmanian Archive and Heritage Office.

NS 73 |1|2

John Ross, another of Battery Point's colonial shipbuilders, established a yard in the vicinity of Finlay Street, just south of Peter Degraves' shipyard, in the early 1850s. In 1854 he took a calculated risk by installing Tasmania's first patent slip at a cost of £20,000. Capable of accommodating vessels up to 1,500 tons, the slip began operation the following year and proved to be a boon not only for John Ross personally but also for Hobart's maritime community and associated commercial enterprises. In 1866 John Ross relocated the patent slip to a Napoleon Street shipyard. All told he spent 20 years working at Battery Point, notably building several large barques and ships, as well as four schooners. Many of these vessels were prominent in intercolonial and international trades.

The late 1850s saw John Lucas, one of John Watson's protégés, begin operating a shipyard along Napoleon Street in partnership with Robert Jeffrey. Primarily involved in the repair, overhaul, cleaning, refit and alteration of vessels, the building of new vessels supplemented the pair's income. Between 1858 and 1883, 17 vessels were built, including nine schooners and two barques. Later in his career John Lucas diversified his expertise by designing and building several of Hobart's more successful recreational and racing yachts.

Charles Miller joined the ranks of the Battery Point boat builders during the 1850s, eventually succeeding Joseph Risby at his Napoleon Street yard. Charles Miller spent the next 31 years building over 100 boats, including 27 whaleboats, many for interstate or New Zealand customers. Like Jacob Chandler, Charles Miller also built vessels for the developing river and coastal trades.

Battery Point from Dunkley's Point (now the site of Wrest Point Casino), Sandy Bay (circa 1870s).
Courtesy Tasmanian Archive and Heritage Office.

Another who honed the craft of boat building through apprenticeship at Battery Point was George Whitehouse. Yet his tenure as a boat builder, operating a yard in partnership with his brother William in the 1870s through to 1883, was superseded by his involvement in the regional steamer trade. In this enterprise George Whitehouse heralded the Tasman Peninsula passenger service at a time when regional steam communication and passenger services to this area were in their infancy.

Lachlan "Lark" Macquarie also operated a boatyard at Battery Point from 1875 where he was involved in the building of smaller racing boats, particularly gigs and skiffs, many of which were successful at local regattas and in rowing club races. Following ten years of operation Lark closed his yard, opting to travel the state building new vessels to order and undertaking repair work.

The 1880s saw the relocation from the Huon region of Robert Inches who became one of Battery Point's most revered shipwrights. Between 1882 and his untimely death in 1904 he built at least 19 vessels, including nine yachts and five ketches.

Overall, there were upwards of 30 boat and ship builders who operated commercial yards at Battery Point in the 19th century, beginning in 1835. During this 65-year period more than 630 vessels were built, including over 215 whaleboats, pleasure boats and waterman boats; 95 ketches, schooners and passage boats; 25 fishing boats; 45 yachts; and 23 barques, brigs and ships. This book details the next stage of Battery Point's maritime history, chronicling the 20th century boat builders and the vessels they built. The story begins with Charlie Lucas.

The barque *Genevie M. Tucker* on the slipway at Kennedy's Battery Point yard (January 1890).
Courtesy Tasmanian Archive and Heritage Office.

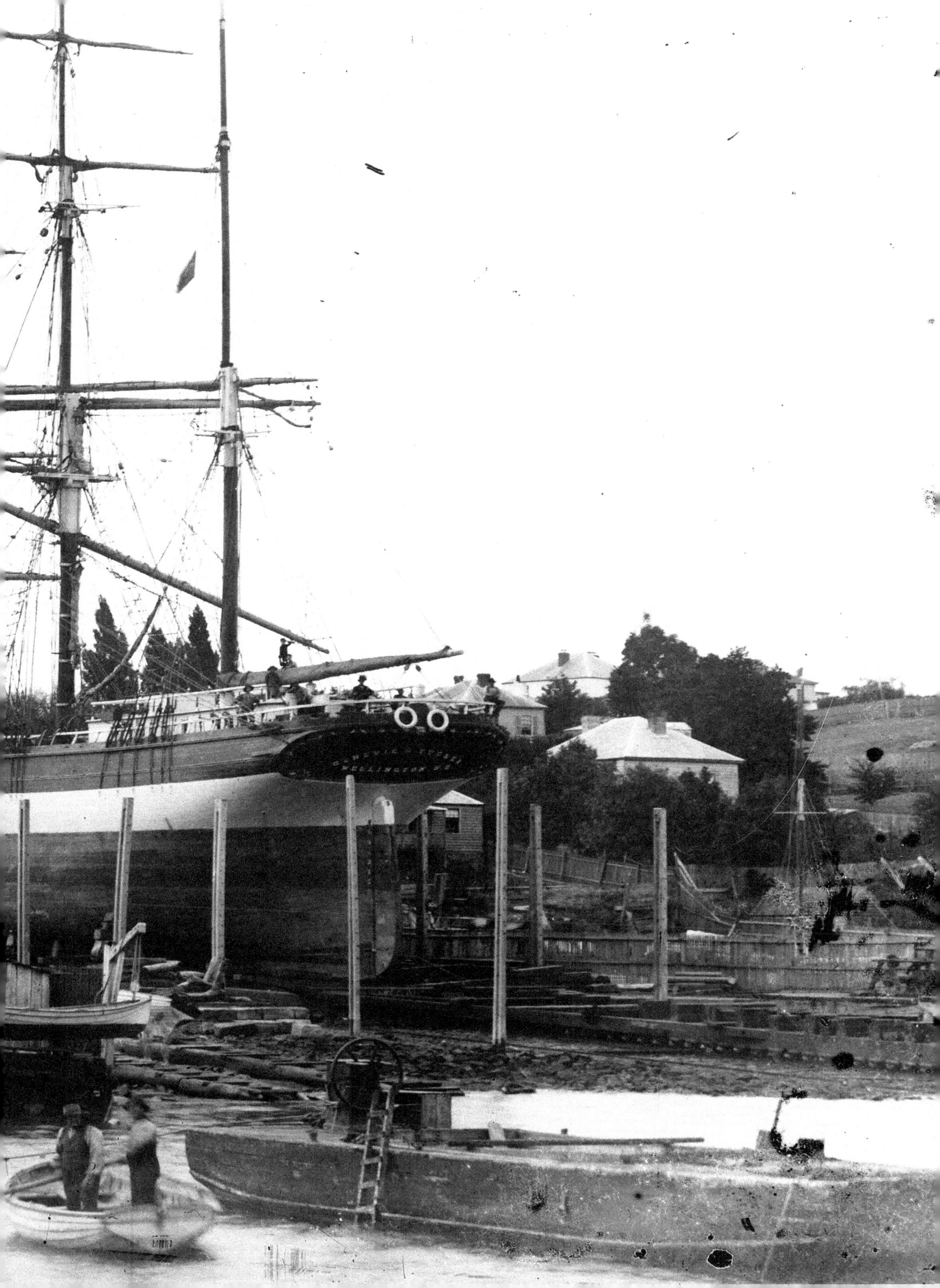
WELLINGTON N.Z.

Charles (Charlie) Lucas

**The product of a rural community and the son of a blacksmith, Charlie Lucas'
determination and inherent talent for boat building saw him relocate to Battery Point
in the early 1880s where he was apprenticed to shipbuilder Robert Inches. Admired for
his tenacious, humble and determined persona, it was here that Charlie Lucas operated
his own boatyard between 1899 and 1936, building many stalwarts of Tasmania's
maritime past, including the one-design class of yachts and the Forster Cup sensations
Tassie, *Tassie Too* and *Tassie III*. Yet Charlie Lucas also built more than 60 commercial and
recreational boats in the time he spent at Battery Point, over one third of which remain
in existence. A relentless work ethic combined with an altruistic nature saw Charlie
Lucas continue working at Battery Point up until his death in 1946 at the age of 82, a
decade after the sale of his yard to Taylor Brothers.**

Charles (Charlie) Lucas was born at Sorell,
Tasmania, on 18 July 1864 to Charles Lucas
and Jane Bird. A blacksmith by trade from
Huntingdonshire, England, Charles (Sr) had
arrived in Hobart in 1841 on board the *Lord
Lyndoch* having been sentenced to 15 years
transportation for assault and robbery. Four years
later Jane Bird, a 19-year old housemaid from
Manchester, England, arrived in Hobart on board
the *Lloyds* having been sentenced to seven years
transportation for stealing a dress.

During their sentences Charles Lucas (Sr) and Jane
Bird both married; Charles to Bridget Blenkinsop
and Jane to Thomas Blackmore, with the two
couples establishing themselves in the Sorell area.
Following the death of her husband in 1860, Jane
Bird formed a relationship with Charles Lucas (Sr)
with three children born to the couple between
1861 and 1864, the last of which was Charlie Lucas.

Though not married the status of Charles Lucas (Sr) and Jane Bird's relationship does not appear to have affected the couple's standing in the local community. Charles (Sr) was noted as
a blacksmith in the 1860s and remained in this profession until his death in 1902. His partner
Jane became a successful and respected storekeeper of Sorell. The couple eventually married in
1885.

Apprenticeship

Albeit from the rural community of Sorell and with no apparent maritime heritage in either of his parents' families, Charlie Lucas developed an interest in boat building from an early age and as a young lad successfully built a 30 ft fishing boat. In his teens Charlie found employment locally as a house carpenter. However, he soon realised that his passion was on the waterfront and it was to Battery Point that Charlie Lucas ventured, where he could combine his carpentry skills with a maritime-related career.

In the early 1880s, and likely at an age several years more mature than his peers, Charlie Lucas was apprenticed to Robert Inches at Inches' Battery Point shipyard. In the years that followed Charlie was involved with the building of many notable yachts and ketches, including the *Lughretta*, *E. H. Purdon*, *Vendetta* and *Lillie May*. It was also during this period that Charlie Lucas became involved in yachting, competing locally in the *Nancy Lee* and later the *Tiger*.

Building a Reputation

Upon completing his apprenticeship Charlie Lucas remained employed at Robert Inches' shipyard, progressing to more senior roles. By the early 1890s he was receiving notable mentions in the local press for his handiwork. In late 1892, Charlie Lucas was noted as rebuilding Olaf Hedberg's 35 ft (21 ft waterline) yacht *Viking* which had been badly damaged by fire. Designed by Alfred Blore, with the work undertaken at Robert Inches' yard, the vessel was launched in January 1893. In November 1897 Charlie Lucas launched another yacht for the 21 ft (waterline) size class, the *Caress*. The vessel was built to the order of Percy Lovett to a design by Alfred Blore.

Viking. Courtesy Tasmanian Archive and Heritage Office.

A Yard of His Own

Having built up his reputation, by mid-1899 Charlie Lucas left the employ of Robert Inches and established his own boatyard at Battery Point. Located next door to his former employer, the yard was previously in the possession of John Watson and John Lucas, among other celebrated shipbuilders. John Watson had established his yard on the property in 1839 and remained there until 1855, launching 13 schooners, six barques and one brigantine during the period. John Lucas operated his shipyard at the site between 1856 and 1872 at which time he relocated next door to a yard previously in the possession of John Ross.

The First Vessels

The first vessel built by Charlie Lucas at his Battery Point boatyard was the inaugural 21 ft (waterline) "one-design" class yacht *Caprice*. Launched on 29 November 1899, the vessel was designed by Alfred Blore and built to the order of E. H. Webster (of the A. G. Webster and Woolgrowers family), Hobart's most vocal ambassador for a one-design class of yachts.

The second vessel built by Charlie Lucas at his newly-established yard was the 43 ft fishing boat *Blanche*. Built to the order of Oscar Thompson, the vessel was launched on 15 October 1900, just under a year following the launch of *Caprice*. Though a departure from his three previous builds, which were all yachts, the *Blanche* was the fourth vessel Charlie Lucas built to a design by Alfred Blore.

The 62 ft ketch *Enterprise*, launched in early 1902, was the next vessel off the stocks at Charlie Lucas' yard. Built to the order of Harry Purdon, who was also the vessel's designer, the *Enterprise* was the first flat-bottomed scow-like ketch to be built in Tasmania and was intended for the Huon timber trade.

On 18 August 1902, a few months following completion of the *Enterprise*, the 40 ft fishing boat *Ethel* was launched from Charlie Lucas' boatyard. Built to the order of a "prominent fisherman," this particular vessel had a modified spoon-like bow and was considered yacht-like in appearance. Finally, in late November 1902, Charlie Lucas completed the *Neva*, a 15 ft dinghy built to the order of H. Risby.

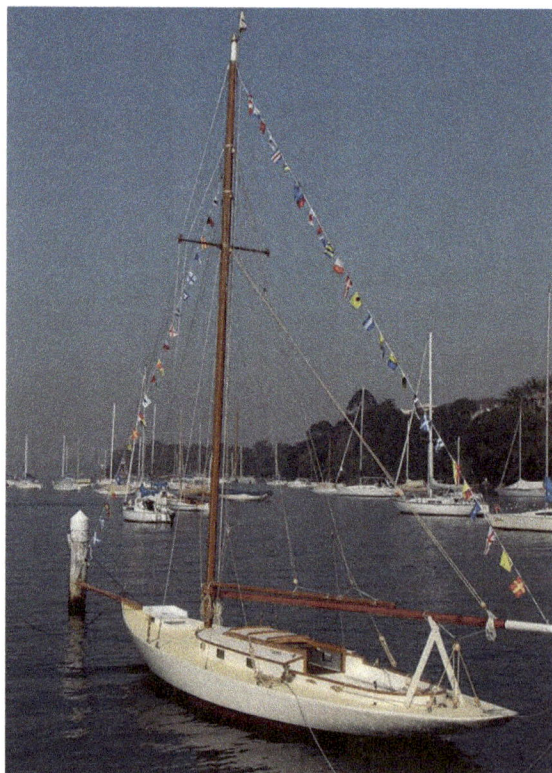

Caprice (2016).
Courtesy Ben Stoner.

Enterprise.
Courtesy Tasmanian Archive and Heritage Office.

In early 1903 Charlie Lucas launched the 44 ft yacht *Athena,* built to the order of McLain Brothers of Bass Strait's Clarke Island. Later that year, on 10 December, the 60 ft ketch *Alma* was launched, built to the order of J. Sward and intended for the Huon and Channel trade.

In mid-1904, likely owing to the success of the *Enterprise*, Charlie Lucas was asked to build another flat-bottomed scow for the coastal trade. The 80 ft *Heather Belle,* built to the order of Henry Heather of Hobart, was launched on 17 May 1905, construction having been somewhat delayed by the unavailability of timber. During the interim Charlie built the 28 ft cruising yacht *Diamond*. This particular vessel was commissioned by F. N. Clarke who had only recently sold his William Fife designed racing yacht *Fairlie III*. The *Diamond* was launched in late 1904.

Five Boats Built in Two Years

Throughout 1905 and 1906 demand for new boats continued to be high. In addition to the *Heather Belle*, Charlie Lucas launched at least two vessels in 1905 and five in 1906. The two boats launched in 1905 were both motor launches, among the first of their type built in Tasmania. At 30 ft in length, the *Wanda* was built to the order of Percy Evans of Lindisfarne and launched on 5 October 1905. The *Palmer*, also 30 ft in length, was built to the order of E. H. Webster and launched in December of that year.

The first of the five boats launched from Charlie Lucas' yard in 1906 was a small vessel built for a syndicate of Tasmanian fishermen for use on the Great Lake. The boat was conveyed by the mail train from Hobart to Campbell Town in March 1906. A few months later Charlie Lucas launched the 41 ft auxiliary yacht *Falcon*, built to the order of Arthur A. Smith based on a design by Alfred Blore. The vessel was fitted with a 12 hp New Jersey City standard engine. Two yacht hulls of 40 ft and 33 ft, respectively, were completed by Charlie Lucas in June 1906 and advertised for sale in the local press. Both were deemed suitable for installation of an engine. Finally, on 21 November 1906, the 48 ft cruising yacht *Alcides* was launched, built to the order of Alfred Oldmeadow. Noted to be the largest yacht yet built in Hobart, the *Alcides* was jointly designed by Charlie Lucas and Alfred Oldmeadow based on an American-style cruiser.

More Yachts and Ketches

Continuing a successful collaboration, the next vessel launched by Charlie Lucas was the 53 ft cruising yacht *Spindrift*, built to the order of E. H. Webster to a design by Alfred Blore based on plans prepared by Camper and Nicholson of Gosport, England. Described as one of the finest vessels to grace Tasmanian waters, the yacht was launched on 2 November 1907. Slightly longer than the *Alcides,* the *Spindrift* also claimed the title of the largest yacht yet built in Hobart. However, it was a bittersweet period for Charlie Lucas and his family. Tragically eight days following the *Spindrift's* launch, his 15-year old son Eric was drowned in a boating accident on the Derwent.

Top: *Palmer* (2016). Courtesy Richard Blundell.
Middle (Left): Launch of *Heather Belle*. Courtesy *Weekly Courier*, 27 May 1905.
Middle (Right): *Falcon*. Courtesy *Illustrated Tasmanian Mail*, 17 April 1929.
Bottom: (Left) Launch of *Alcides*. Courtesy *Weekly Courier*, 22 December 1906.
Bottom: (Right) Launch of *Spindrift*. Courtesy *Weekly Courier*, 7 November 1907.

Top: One-design yacht under construction at Charlie Lucas' yard. Likely V*anity*.
Courtesy *Tasmanian Mail,* 3 August 1911.
Middle: The newly lengthened bow of the *Vanity* receiving surface treatment from W. T. Gibson, F. Berriman,
P. Murphy and W. Young. Courtesy *Illustrated Tasmanian Mail,* 13 October 1932.
Bottom (Left): *Curlew*. Courtesy *Tasmanian Mail*, 16 March 1911.
Bottom (Right): *Gannet*. Courtesy *Tasmanian Mail*, 23 November 1911.

In mid-1908 Charlie Lucas received an order from a prominent Victorian yachtsman to build a cruiser larger than the recently completed *Spindrift*. Three months into the build, however, the order was cancelled. It is possible that the order was placed by William Oliver of Melbourne who instead opted to purchase *Spindrift* after the vessel was sailed to Victoria in October 1908. It was an unfortunate predicament for Charlie Lucas. Not only was he left with a partially built vessel, but he had also turned down several orders during the interim. Still, Charlie Lucas likely gained notoriety within the Victorian yachting fraternity when *Spindrift* arrived in Melbourne.

Owing to the cancelled order the only vessel built by Charlie Lucas in 1908 appears to have been a 36 ft yawl-rigged cruising yacht. Fitted with a centreboard, this particular vessel was launched on 4 December 1908.

In 1909 Charlie Lucas returned to constructing commercial vessels, having been engaged to design and build a shallow draught ketch for Edwin Young of Rokeby. He was also noted as having received orders for a fishing boat and motor launch, though work was somewhat stymied by a lack of availability of local timber, most of it being exported overseas.

Intended for the local produce and firewood trade, Edwin Young's 54 ft ketch *Boronia* was launched in July 1909, built of Tasmanian blue gum. In late December 1909 Charlie Lucas completed the 36 ft yawl-rigged yacht *Diadem* for his own use. The yacht made her debut at the Shipwrights Point Regatta on 1 January 1910 and was active in local races for a year before being transferred to Sydney. The next boat off the slipway was the 25 ft motor boat *Dorothy*, built to the order of E. Linnell of Franklin and launched in May 1910. In the months that followed Charlie Lucas completed the 37 ft fishing boat *Gladys*, built to the order of John Parker, and the 41 ft fishing boat *Aone*, built to the order of L. Maizey.

One-Design Class

The year 1910 was particularly busy for Charlie Lucas. Early in the year E. H. Webster, continuing his decades-long quest for the implementation of a local one-design class of yacht, had tasked Alfred Blore with developing plans based on a design by W. Hand (Jr), a well-known American boat designer. He also offered a handsome sum of prize money to entice local yachtsmen to build the boats. E. H. Webster's persistence paid off and in May 1910 orders were placed with Charlie Lucas for the construction of three one-design yachts. Principal dimensions of the class were 21 ft waterline, 33 ft overall, with an extreme beam of 9.1 ft and a draught of 4.6 ft. Other design features included a lead keel of 3,100 lbs, a 21 ft mainsail host, a 20.5 ft boom and a 16.5 ft gaff. Blue gum was to be used for the keel, stem and sternpost, with half-inch Huon pine used for the planking. Expected costs were around £180.

The resulting three vessels — *Spindrift*, *Pandora* and *Curlew* — were launched from Charlie Lucas' yard in late 1910 and early 1911. First came *Spindrift*, built to the order of E. H. Webster and launched on 17 October 1910. Next came *Pandora*, built for David Barclay (Jr) and launched ten days later. Finally, on 23 February 1911, came *Curlew*, built for the trio of P. C. Douglas, John W. Tarleton and H. W. Knight.

Canobie in Western Australia. Courtesy Owen Stacy.

Meticulously crafted with Charlie Lucas' care and precision, the one-design class was an instant success, providing a much needed boost to the Royal Yacht Club of Tasmania's racing repertoire. As such, it was not long before an order for a fourth yacht was received. This particular vessel, *Vanity*, was launched from Charlie Lucas' yard on 2 November 1911, built to the order of W. F. Darling, G. S. Crisp and Dr Ireland. A fortnight later Charlie completed a fifth one-design yacht, *Gannet*, built to the order of Charles Shannon of Geelong, Victoria.

Another one-design class yacht, *Pilgrim*, was built by E. A. Jack in Launceston and launched in December 1911. Identical in design to those built by Charlie Lucas, this particular vessel was built to the order of E. H. Webster with the intention of reinvigorating the North Versus South Challenge Cup. Capitalising on interest generated for the one-design class, however, Webster sold *Pilgrim* part-way through construction to O. R. Tinning of Hobart.

A sixth one-design class yacht built by Charlie Lucas, *Canobie*, was launched on 31 October 1912. This vessel was also built to the order of E. H. Webster but, like *Pilgrim*, was sold part-way through construction to A. J. Cotton of Kettering.

Consistent with E. H. Webster's vision, Tasmania's one-design class of yachts dominated the racing circuit well into the next decade, not only winning local sailing races and regattas but also the annual 100 mile race around Bruny Island and the North Versus South Challenge Cup. Remarkably, the Royal Yacht Club of Tasmania's 1913 race around Bruny Island saw the first four vessels, all one-design yachts, finish the course within 35 seconds of one another. Equally remarkable, over 100 years later, all six of the one-design yachts built by Charlie Lucas remain in existence, as well as the E. A. Jack built *Pilgrim*.

Pre World War 1

In addition to building the one-design class of yachts, the years leading up to World War I were busy for Charlie Lucas. The 36 ft double-ender fishing boat *Georgie*, built to the order of George Chambers, was launched on 21 June 1911.

In winter 1912 Charlie Lucas was noted as having in the course of construction a 35 ft motor launch, built to the order of C. R. Davies of *The Mercury* newspaper. This particular vessel, *Risdon*, was launched on 28 September 1912, built to a design by J. E. Saunders from the Isle of Wight, England. Around this time Charlie was also noted as having 20 yachts and motor launches slipped and undergoing winter overhaul at his yard.

The next boat off Charlie Lucas' slipway was the 26 ft motor boat *Sealark*. Launched in early to mid-1913, the vessel was built to the order of Arthur E. Risby of the famed Risby Timber Company (and son of Joseph Risby, late boat builder of Battery Point). In January 1914 Charlie completed a 26 ft four-oared whaleboat, built to the order of Tom Dunbabin of Bream Creek. Historically named *Marie Laure*, the boat received a modern makeover in that a square stern allowed for an engine to be installed. 1914 also saw Charlie Lucas finish two more motor launches. These were the 25 ft *Kelvin*, built to the order of A. Pretyman, and the 37 ft *Hermione III*, built to the order of G. A. Roberts. Both were regular competitors in local motor boat races for many years.

Above (Top): *Risdon*. Courtesy *Tasmanian Mail*, 17 October 1912.
Above (Bottom): *Sealark*. Courtesy *Tasmanian Mail*, 26 February 1914.
Opposite: *Curlew*. Courtesy Maritime Museum of Tasmania.

The War Years

The years during World War I were lean ones for Charlie Lucas and his peers. Only a small number of vessels were built in Hobart, yachting took a backseat to war efforts, and times were sombre. Of the few vessels known to have been built by Charlie Lucas during this period, all were fishing boats. These include the 40 ft *Curlew*, launched in early 1915 and built to the order of Harold Chambers; the 39.9 ft *Ethel,* owned for several decades by Clarence Dear; and the *Beatrice*, built to the order of George Hooper and first noted in the press in July 1916.

Charlie Lucas' Battery Point yard (circa 1908).
Courtesy W. L. Crowther Library, Tasmanian Archive and Heritage Office.

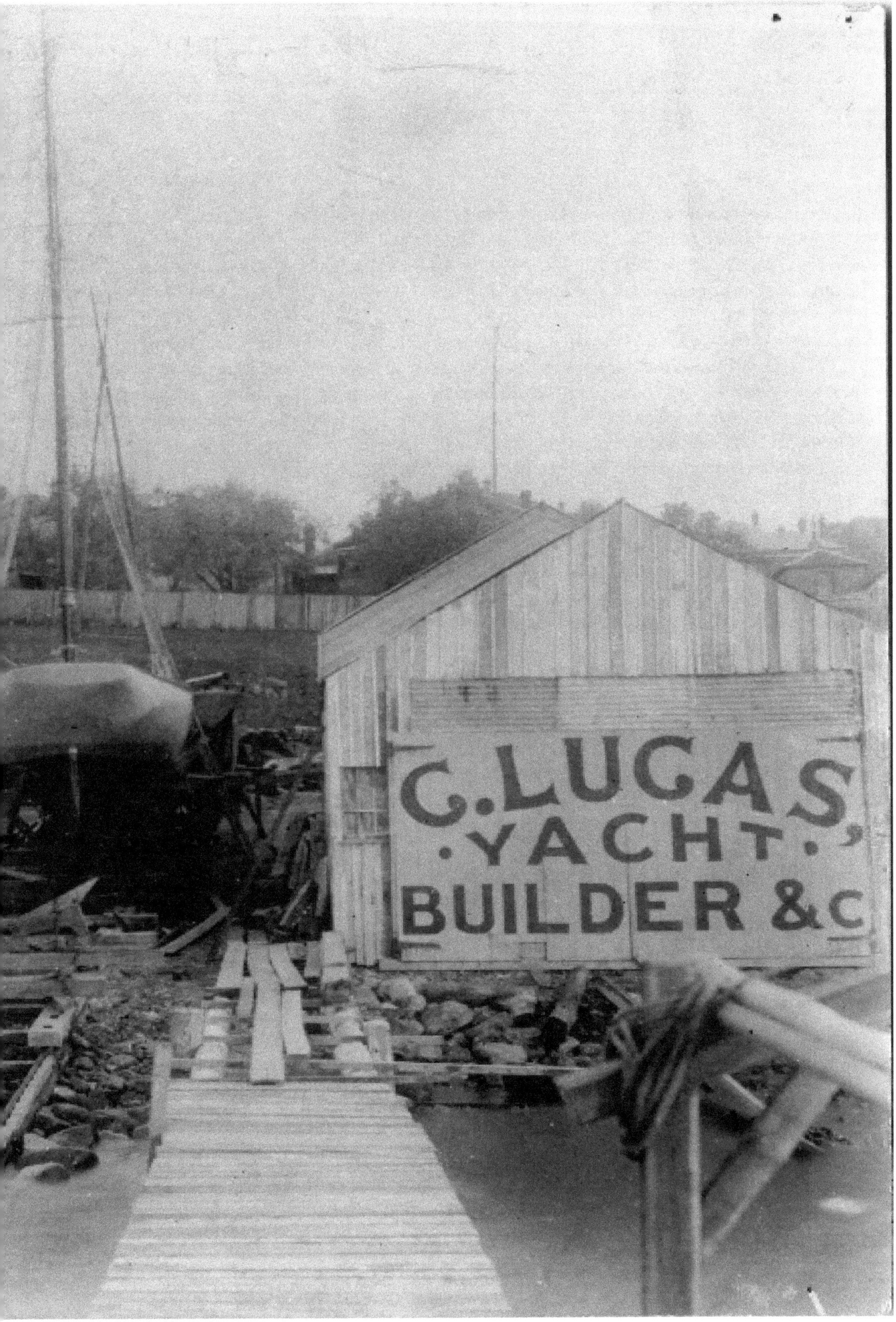
C. LUCAS,
·YACHT·
BUILDER &C

Speculation

With little prospect for new recreational boat orders during the War years, Charlie Lucas instead opted to build yachts and motor boats on speculation. In January 1916, for example, he advertised a "new, comfortable cruising yacht" for sale. In March 1918 two motor boats were advertised for sale (one 21 ft, the other 25 ft).

Towards the end of World War I Charlie Lucas began building the cruising yacht *Molly Hawk*. Built to the order of Sir Herbert Nicholls to a design by Fred Goeller (Jr) that was first published in 1913, the vessel's hull was partly constructed down the Channel and brought up to Battery Point where Charlie completed the work. Following the launch in December 1918, one of *Molly Hawk*'s first outings was to a picnic held at Bellerive for soldiers. The vessel was one of 45 boats volunteered to transport 250 recently returned ANZACs to the event.

Post World War I

Continuing to undertake slip and repair work and build boats on speculation, in late 1919 Charlie Lucas was noted as assisting in the transport of the 45 ft motor launch *Governor Newdegate* (ex *Blanche*) to the Great Lake on behalf of her new owner, the Hydro Electric Department. In May of the following year Charlie Lucas advertised the fishing boat *Dulcie* for sale at his yard. Built on speculation, by 1922 this particular vessel was owned by the Spaulding family of the Tasman Peninsula.

Another boat built by Charlie Lucas during this period was the *Diana*, first noted in the local press in January 1920 after competing in the fishing boat race at the Hobart Regatta. The vessel's owners were listed as Messrs Steele and Parker and she was stated to have been "C. Lucas' ex-yacht."

On 28 October 1920 the 41 ft yacht *Valkyrie* was launched. Built on speculation, though purchased part-way through completion by O. R. Tinning, the vessel was constructed of Huon pine and designed by Charlie Lucas.

During the early 1920s Charlie Lucas continued to build boats on speculation, several of which were advertised for sale at his yard. These include a four month old 20 ft Huon pine-planked and copper-fastened motor boat hull advertised for sale in March 1922.

In addition Charlie Lucas built the cadet dinghy *Pierette* (notably the first of its type built in Tasmania) to the order of Rex Willing. This particular vessel is first noted on the Derwent in March 1924. In July of that same year Charlie Lucas launched a 36 ft yacht built on speculation.

21 ft Restricted Class and the Forster Cup

Thankfully the slow period of the 1920s did not last with Tasmania's involvement in the national competition for 21 ft restricted class vessels, the Forster Cup, precipitating another highlight of Charlie Lucas' long and extraordinary career. In the final months of 1924, following the adoption of plans by W. P. "Skipper" Batt (developed in conjunction with Alfred Blore and John W. Tarleton) for a Tasmanian-built yacht to compete in the 1925 Forster Cup, the Royal Yacht Club of Tasmania's committee hurriedly approached local and interstate builders to construct the vessel, needing it to be completed in only a matter of weeks. After initially declining due to other commitments, Charlie Lucas changed his mind. However, it was on the proviso that the cruiser he was building to the order of E. H. Webster be completed first.

Named *Spindrift II* (though registered as *Spumedrift*), E. H. Webster's cruiser was launched on 9 December 1924. Less than ten days later, the keel of Tasmania's Forster Cup contender, *Tassie*, was laid. The vessel was launched in under four weeks, on 17 January 1925. Thankfully experienced help was at hand with skilled Finnish boat builder Ivar "Chips" Gronfors working with Charlie Lucas to build both *Spindrift II* and *Tassie*.

Having completed *Tassie* just in time for the start of the Forster Cup, the actual staging of the event in Hobart was another busy period for Charlie Lucas and his employees, with the rigging of interstate vessels taking place at his Battery Point yard. The Tasmanian and interstate vessels were also stored at the yard between heats. Additionally, Charlie Lucas' slip was noted as the location where a jib and new rudder were fitted to one of the Victorian boats, and where final preparations to vessels were made ahead of the race series.

Launch of *Spindrift II* on 9 December 1924. Courtesy Jock Muir Family Collection.

Tassie. Courtesy Tasmanian Archive and Heritage Office.

Following the conclusion of the 1925 Forster Cup, astoundingly won by *Tassie*, a large crowd gathered at Charlie Lucas' yard to celebrate. A few days later, as the interstate teams prepared to leave, Charlie was graciously thanked by all involved because in the words of Major Campbell of Victoria, "Nothing was too much for him to do." Grateful for his efforts, Charlie Lucas was also honoured by the Royal Yacht Club of Tasmania who presented him with a silver model of the *Tassie* at its annual presentation night.

Back to Business

With the success of the *Tassie* under his belt, Charlie Lucas next built a cruising yacht with a raised deck on speculation. The vessel was completed in late 1925 having been purchased by M. Weston. During 1925 Charlie Lucas and Chips Gronfors also received an order for a motor boat from John E. Reid of Newcastle, New South Wales, a good friend of Gronfors. Launched on 9 December 1925, the 35 ft *Moani* was intended for cruising and fishing on Lake Macquarie and had been designed and planned by Chips Gronfors. Constructed solely of Tasmanian wood, with no expense spared, Gronfors delivered *Moani* to Sydney, the vessel secured by cradle on board the deck of the *SS Kanna*.

Tassie Too. Courtesy Jock Muir Family Collection.

Following completion of the *Moani,* in 1926 Charlie Lucas launched the *Lialee,* a 48 ft fishing boat built to the order of Ernest Parker of Dunalley. However, with orders for new boats still somewhat subdued several boats, either built on speculation or refurbished, were advertised for sale at his boatyard between 1926 and 1928. These include a 10 ft dinghy advertised for sale in December 1926; the fishing boat *Janet* and the motor launch *Osprey,* both advertised for sale in August 1927; and a 10 ft Huon pine dinghy advertised for sale in February 1928.

1928 Forster Cup

In 1927 Charlie Lucas and Chips Gronfors continued their involvement with the hotly contested Forster Cup. Following the success of *Tassie* — the 21 ft restricted class vessel built at a cost significantly less than her interstate competitors, of immediately available materials, and in a hurry — Charlie Lucas was tasked by the Royal Yacht Club of Tasmania with building a second boat to represent Tasmania at the national event. Again designed by Skipper Batt, with assistance from Alfred Blore and John W. Tarleton, the new vessel was launched from Charlie Lucas' boatyard on 26 November 1927 and named *Tassie Too.* Much to the chagrin of the mainland states, the vessel won the 1928 Forster Cup, held in Sydney, with her kin *Tassie* finishing second.

More Boats

Following the success of *Tassie Too* at the 1928 Forster Cup, Charlie Lucas once again teamed up with Alfred Blore, this time to design and build a cabin cruiser to the order of H. C. Millington. Appropriately named *H. C. M*, the 26 ft vessel was launched in August 1928. Obviously satisfied with the builder though not the vessel, H. C. Millington advertised the *H. C. M* for sale in January 1929 and soon after placed an order with Charlie Lucas for a larger motor boat. The 32 ft *Wanderer* was launched in December 1929 and remained in Millington's possession for several decades.

1928 also saw another familiar collaboration with E. H. Webster ordering a new yacht from Charlie Lucas, built to the specifications of the newly-coined Derwent class which Webster had recently established on the Derwent. The *Sprite* was launched later that year, joining the ranks of several Derwent class yachts built by Percy Coverdale at Battery Point, including *Imp* and *Pixie*.

The following year, in June 1929, Charlie Lucas was noted as building a B class yacht to the order of Rowley Vautin who was returning to local yacht racing after an absence of some 20 years. Designed by Skipper Batt, the 26 ft bulb-finned *Anitra* was launched on 2 November 1929.

1930 Forster Cup

With the intention of continuing Tasmania's national domination of the 21 ft restricted class, in October 1929 the Royal Yacht of Tasmania's committee approved construction of a third boat to represent the state at the 1930 Forster Cup to be held in Victoria. Based on a model by Skipper Batt, with P. C. Douglas tasked with drafting the plans, the vessel's design was stated to be "almost exactly midway between the *Tassie* and *Tassie Too*." With Charlie Lucas once again tasked with building the vessel, *Tassie III* was launched from his boatyard on 21 December 1929 in front of a large crowd.

The 1930s

The launch of *Tassie III* coincided with the start of a world-wide depression, with unemployment in Australia reaching a peak of 32 per cent in mid-1932. Fortunately, the financial crisis seems to have affected slipwork at Charlie Lucas' yard very little. There was, however, a marked slow-down in the number of commissions received. One new order that did come through during this period was from Jack Forsyth for a 31 ft cruising yacht. This particular vessel, named *Margaret*, was designed by Charlie Lucas and launched on 11 October 1930.

One of the last vessels Charlie Lucas is known to have built at his yard, the cruiser *Spindrift*, was launched four years after the *Margaret*. Fittingly built to the order of E. H. Webster, the 42 ft yacht was launched on 2 October 1934, nearly 24 years to the day that Charlie launched E. H. Webster's original one-design class yacht *Spindrift*.

Launch of *Tassie III*.
Courtesy Tasmanian Archive and Heritage Office.

Spindrift.
Courtesy Guy Rex Collection (Suzanne Rex).

Additional Income

Like most of his peers, activities at Charlie Lucas' yard throughout his career were supplemented by the slipping, repair, overhaul and alteration of vessels. He also received income from the storage of boats, particularly yachts over winter. The weeks before the opening of the yachting season were commensurately busy, with much time and effort spent getting yachts ready for racing.

Charlie Lucas also leased or provided (in-kind) space at his yard to fellow boat builders and employees. For example, on 25 April 1928 the fishing boat *Ralphs Bay* was launched from his yard. She was built to the order of J. Elliott by Fred Coverdale, brother of Battery Point boat builder Percy Coverdale. The 40 ft yawl-rigged boat was intended for the oyster and scallop industries.

Retirement?

The last vessel Charlie Lucas built prior to retirement was the *Saona*, a 40 ft cruiser built to the order of Morton Weston of Austins Ferry to a Philip L. Rhodes design. Launched in early 1936, she was later purchased by Len Nettlefold.

In August 1936 Charlie Lucas sold his Battery Point yard to Norm and Athol Taylor (operating as Taylor Brothers). Shortly thereafter, in recognition of his many professional achievements, E. H. Webster made a presentation to members of the Royal Yacht Club of Tasmania on Charlie Lucas' career stating, "He had become an institution which was of the greatest service to yachtsmen." Later that year the Motor Yacht Club of Tasmania paid tribute to Charlie Lucas, presenting him with a silver-mounted walking stick. Now in his early 70s, however, Charlie Lucas did not remain idle for long. The work ethic that had driven his entire career refused to yield.

Following Athol Taylor's tragic drowning in April 1937, Charlie Lucas returned to his former boatyard. Seven years later, in 1944, and by now 80 years old, Charlie Lucas was still actively working with Norm Taylor, stating in the press that as long as he enjoyed good health he would continue to build boats. "There is nothing like work to keep you fit," he added. Continuing apace Charlie Lucas was also actively involved in the Shiplovers Society during this period, and designed the cruising yacht *Tunis* (built by owner E. F. Smith at Southport and launched in January 1946).

Death

Charlie Lucas continued working at Taylor Brothers' Battery Point yard up until his death. He died on 24 August 1946, aged 82, at a private hospital in Hobart. He was buried at Cornelian Bay Cemetery. His wife Annie had died at their residence, 5 Bath Street, Battery Point, the year prior, on 16 January 1945. Charlie was survived by two daughters (Gladys and Florence) and a son (Reginald). His eldest daughter (Ethel) had died in 1929 at the age of 43. A son (Eric) had drowned in 1907 at the age of 15.

WELL-KNOWN HOBART SHIPBUILDER DIES

PROMINENT Hobart shipbuilder and yachtsman for more than 50 years, Mr Charles Lucas died at a private hospital in Hobart on Saturday. He was in his 83rd year.

MR LUCAS was born at Sorell in 1864 and as a lad built a 30ft sailing boat. He was building boats before he learned the trade with the late Mr Robert Inches at Battery Pt.

Upwards of 50 years ago he started his own yard next to that of Inches, and from it he launched the ketches Alma and Boronia, and the better known Heather Belle and Enterprise.

Two of the first boats he owned and used for cruising were the Elephantus and Tiger. Subsequently he built various boats of different designs, and which he used himself for pleasure cruises on the East Coast and down the Channel.

Outstanding among his noteworthy building successes was the construction of the three "Tassies," which won fame in the interstate Forster Cup contests.

Older yachtsmen will remember Mr Lucas when he was in charge of Mrs Wilson's cruising yacht Lughrata.

Among the yachts he built were Alcides, Spindrift II., Spindrift (now Weene), Pandora, Curlew, Vanity, Canobie, Anitra, Roma, Caprice, Caress, and Falkyre. He also built the Derwent class yacht Sprite for Mr E. H. Webster.

Fishing boats he constructed were Beatrice, Athena, Gladys, Lialee, Blanche, Ethel, Diana, Dulcie, and Curlew. He also built the motor yachts Falcon, Risdon, Sealark, Wanderer, Kelvin, and Diamond.

Last yacht he built was the Saona for the late Mr W. Weston, and now owned by Mr L. Nettlefold.

In 1944 when he attained his 80th birthday, he was the guest of honour at a function at the RYCT and the recipient of a presentation from members.

He is survived by his wife, and a son, Mr R. J. Lucas.

His funeral will take place at Cornelian Bay this morning.

Mr Charles Lucas, former Hobart shipbuilder, at the job which he did so well for more than 50 years.

The Mercury, **Monday 26 August 1946.**

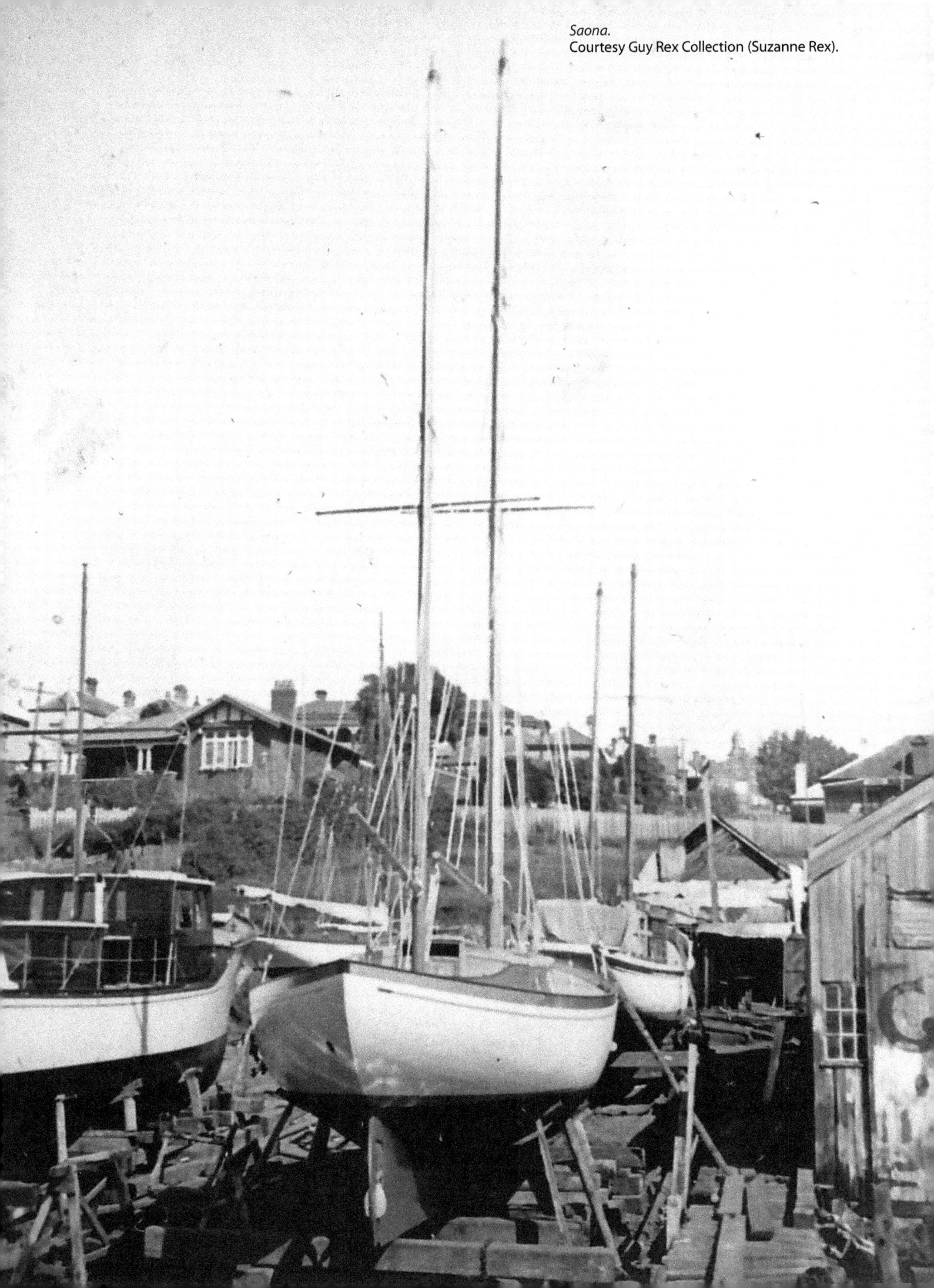

Saona.
Courtesy Guy Rex Collection (Suzanne Rex).

Hermione III (2017).
Courtesy Ian Roberts.

Vessels Built by Charlie Lucas and Employees at Battery Point (1893 – 1936).

1893. *Viking*. Yacht. 35 x 8.3 x 6.3 ft. Initially built by Olaf Hedberg and James Jolly at Hedberg's Brisbane Street (Hobart) residence. Designed by Alfred Blore. Badly damaged by fire in November 1892, just prior to completion. Rebuilt by Charlie Lucas and J. Ludgrove at Robert Inches' Battery Point yard and launched in January 1893. Subsequently owned by Mark Stump, E. Boon and E. O. Sward. In existence up until recently.

1897. *Caress*. Yacht. 33 x 21 ft (LWL). Built to the order of Percy Lovett to a design by Alfred Blore and launched in November 1897. A successful racing yacht on the Derwent for many years. Transferred to Launceston and by 1910 owned by H. Shepherd. Spent several decades sailing with the Tamar Yacht Club. Advertised for sale in April 1938 by owner W. H. Park. Last noted when advertised for sale in Launceston in September 1945.

1899. *Caprice*. Yacht. 32 x 8.5 x 4.5 ft. Inaugural 21 ft (LWL) one-design class yacht built to the order of E. H. Webster to an Alfred Blore design. Launched on 29 November 1899. Sold to A. E. Starkey of Sydney, NSW, in October 1901. Purchased by A. M. Doudney of North Sydney in December 1907. Purchased by R. G. Smith in December 1913. Between 1922 and 1928 owned by Arthur J. Stone. Then owned by brothers Harry and John Pfeiffer, and several decades later passed to Harry's son Tony. Proudly remains in the Pfeiffer family's possession, now under ownership of a third generation. Recently converted back to her original rig.

1900. *Blanche*. Fishing boat. 43 x 9.8 x 4 ft. Built to the order of Oscar Thompson to an Alfred Blore design. Launched on 15 October 1900. Subsequently purchased by the Spaulding family of the Tasman Peninsula. By the 1950s owned by Gordon Johnson of Nubeena. Wrecked off Droughty Point in the River Derwent, TAS, on 25 September 1965, having blown off her mooring at Battery Point where she was awaiting the installation of a new engine.

1902. *Enterprise*. Ketch. 62.2 x 18.2 x 5.1 ft. Built to the order of Harry Purdon who was also the designer. Involved in local and coastal trade for many decades under several owners, including Gorringe Brothers and Henry Jones and Company. Featured in the movie "For the Term of His Natural Life" in 1926. In the 1950s used to transport night soil from Glenorchy to Storm Bay. In the 1970s purchased by Bill Price. Later sold to Bill Bailey for shore-based preservation at the Sea Life Centre in Bicheno, TAS. Broken up in July 2009.

1902. *Ethel*. Fishing boat. 40 x 10 x 4 ft. Built to the order of a local fisherman and launched on 18 August 1902. Completely wrecked on 3 March 1913 near the entrance to Table Cape, TAS, having snapped her tiller during a squall. Owners (M. Splane and E. Etchell, who had only recently purchased the vessel) managed to make it to safety in the vessel's dinghy.

1902. *Neva*. Dinghy. 15 ft. Built to the order of H. Risby to compete in Derwent Dinghy Sailing Club events in the "Boxie" class. Launched in November 1902 on the afternoon of her first race. Lengthened in mid-1910 by 6 ft (by Charlie Lucas) and converted to a motor boat; fitted with a 3 hp Regal engine. Sold to Fisher, Bond and Co. in late 1913. Disappears after 1914.

1903. *Athena*. Yacht. 44 x 11 x 4.9 ft. Built to the order of McLain Brothers of Clarke Island, Bass Strait, and launched in early 1903. Owned by McLain Brothers for 18 years then owned by Tom Martyn and converted to a fishing boat. Wrecked off South West Cape, TAS, on 8 January 1959; all hands saved. At the time of loss owned by John Lette.

Vessels Built by Charlie Lucas and Employees at Battery Point (1893 – 1936).

1903. *Alma.* **Ketch.** 60 x 15 x 4.7 ft. Built to the order of J. Sward and launched on 10 December 1903. Involved in the Huon and Channel trade for many years. Sold to a contingent from Cunninghame, VIC, in 1912. Transferred to Sydney, NSW, in July 1915 and involved in coastal trade. Register closed in 1951.

1904. *Diamond.* **Yacht.** 28 ft. Yawl-rigged cruising yacht noted to be almost ready for launching in November 1904. Built to the order of F. N. Clarke. Fitted with a 5 hp Standard engine making her one of the first auxiliary yachts on the Derwent. By September 1908 owned by Robert Cumming. Later owned by the Butler family who maintained possession for several decades. Still in existence; located in northern TAS.

1905. *Heather Belle.* **Ketch.** 80 x 20.7 x 5.7 ft. Built to the order of Harry Heather and launched on 17 May 1905. Employed in the Huon timber trade. Later owned by Holyman Brothers, Henry Jones and Company, and B. J. Boxhall. Transferred to Port Adelaide, SA, in July 1933. Destroyed by fire at Wallaroo, SA, on 17 May 1937; all hands saved.

1905. *Wanda.* **Motor launch.** 30 x 6.2 ft. Built to the order of Percy Evans of Lindisfarne and launched on 5 October 1905. Fitted with a 7.5 hp Lozier petrol engine. Sold to J. Thompson of Geeveston in May 1907 and used to tow wooden barges at Shipwrights Point.

1905. *Palmer (Slave).* **Motor launch.** 30 x 6.3 x 3 ft. Built to the order of E. H. Webster and launched in December 1905. Sold to Lou Rapp of the Huon in 1911. Renamed *Slave*. Later reverted back to *Palmer*. Sold to buyers from VIC in the 1980s. Still in existence. Sighted at Gippsland Lakes, VIC, in 2017.

1906. **Boat.** Built for a syndicate for use on the Great Lake. Conveyed by the mail train from Hobart to Campbell Town in March 1906.

1906. *Falcon.* **Yacht.** 41 x 9 x 4 ft. Built to the order of Arthur A. Smith and launched in July 1906. Designed by Alfred Blore. By 1916 owned by F. H. Oldham. Purchased by the Tasmanian Police Department in December 1937 for use in Bass Strait patrol work. Sold by tender in 1941 to G. H. Evans of Hobart. Converted to a fishing boat in the 1960s. Wrecked on 21 February 1968 off South Cape, TAS; all hands saved. At the time owned by Valentine Stoberl.

1906. **Yacht.** 40 x 6 x 3 ft. Hull advertised for sale in June 1906. Suitable for installation of an engine.

1906. **Yacht.** 33 x 8 x 4 ft. Hull advertised for sale in June 1906. Suitable for installation of an engine.

1906. *Alcides (Hurrica III).* **Yacht.** 48 x 11 ft. Built to the order of Alfred Oldmeadow, who was also the designer, and launched on 21 November 1906. One of the finest yachts on the Derwent during her infant years. Sold to William Oliver of Melbourne, VIC, in March 1913 and renamed *Hurrica III*. Sold again in 1919 to the federal government for use as a defence vessel.

1907. *Spindrift (Hurrica II, Stormy Petrel).* **Yacht.** 53 x 12.5 x 7 ft. Built to the order of E. H. Webster based on a Camper and Nicholson design adapted by Alfred Blore. Launched on 2 November 1907. Sold to William Oliver of Melbourne, VIC, in 1908 and renamed *Hurrica II*. Purchased by S. M. Dempster of NSW in 1912 and renamed *Stormy Petrel*. Sold to Napier Birks of Adelaide, SA, in 1922. Wrecked on 21 December 1937 off Kangaroo Island, SA; all hands saved.

1908. Yacht. 36 x 9.2 x 3.5 ft. Yawl-rigged cruising yacht fitted with a centreboard and built of Huon pine. Equipped with a large cockpit and comfortable cabin. Launched on 4 December 1908.

1909. *Boronia*. Ketch. 54.5 x 14.6 x 4.7 ft. Built to the order of Edwin Young of Rokeby. Designed by Charlie Lucas. Intended for the local produce and firewood trade and launched in July 1909. Purchased by Captain Austin of the Solomon Islands from then owner H. Sward in April 1921. Intended for use trading between local islands. Arrived at Tulagi, Solomon Islands, in July 1921.

1909. *Diadem (Tasma)*. Yacht. 36 x 9.5 x 4.8 ft. Yawl-rigged yacht built by Charlie Lucas for his own use. Debuted at the Shipwrights Point Regatta on 1 January 1910. Active in local races for a year. Sold to George Robertson of Sydney, NSW, arriving in January 1911. Advertised for sale in February 1913. Renamed *Tasma*. Advertised for sale in May 1921 and again in April 1928.

1910. *Dorothy*. Motor boat. 25 x 4.7 ft x 20 in. Built to the order of E. Linnell of Franklin and launched in May 1910. Fitted with 7.5 hp Buffalo engine. Advertised for sale in October 1918. Purchased by L. Lester of Moonah. Advertised for sale in October 1926.

1910. *Gladys*. Fishing boat. 37 ft. Launched in the latter half of 1910, built to the order of John Parker who was unfortunately drowned when swept off the vessel in April 1933 while coming up the River Derwent. Advertised for sale a few months later and throughout 1934. By the 1940s owned by the Young family of Dunalley.

1910. *Aone*. Fishing boat. 40 x 10.5 x 4.6 ft. Built to the order of L. Maizey and launched by mid to late 1910. By 1913 owned by William Burnett. By the 1950s owned by the Sward family. By the 1970s owned by R. J. Burnett. In the early 1990s converted to a motor launch and moored at Kettering. Still in existence; located in northern TAS.

1910. *Spindrift (Weene)*. Yacht. 32.7 x 9.1 x 3.5 ft. First of the one-design class of yacht instigated by E. H. Webster and adapted by Alfred Blore from a W. Hand (Jr) design. Built to the order of E. H. Webster and launched on 17 October 1910. Sold to brothers W. P. "Skipper" and Harry Batt in April 1911 for £165 and renamed *Weene*. Remained in the Batt family's possession up until the 1960s. Subsequently owned by Rex Strong. Later transferred to Sydney, NSW, where she is still in existence, owned by Ben Stoner.

1910. *Pandora*. Yacht. 32.7 x 9.1 x 3.5 ft. Second of the one-design class of yacht instigated by E. H. Webster and adapted by Alfred Blore from a W. Hand (Jr) design. Built to the order of David Barclay (Jr) and launched on 27 October 1910. Transferred to E. Barclay following David Barclay's death in Egypt in August 1916. By 1919, and for several decades following, owned by W. A. Young. Advertised for sale in August 1949. Subsequent owners include J. R. Cairns (1950s), David Short (1970s) and Jeff Briscoe (1990s). Still in existence; located in southern TAS.

1911. *Curlew (Culwulla IV)*. Yacht. 32.7 x 9.1 x 3.5 ft. Third of the one-design class of yacht instigated by E. H. Webster and adapted by Alfred Blore from a W. Hand (Jr) design. Built to the order of P. C. Douglas, John W. Tarleton and H. W. Knight and launched on 23 February 1911. Transferred to Sydney, NSW, in October 1913 having been purchased by Andrew Wilson. In March 1914 sold to Walter M. Marks and renamed *Culwulla IV*. Purchased by Ernest Bent in February 1920. By 1923 owned by Noel Fraser; by 1926 owned by James Hardie; by 1927 owned by Robert F. Graham; by 1942 owned by A. F. and E. M. Graham; by 1950 owned by A. F. and R. P. Graham. Several owners since. Still in existence; recently advertised for sale in QLD.

Vessels Built by Charlie Lucas and Employees at Battery Point (1893 – 1936).

1911. *Georgie.* **Fishing boat.** 36 x 9.5 x 4 ft. Built to the order of George Chambers and launched on 21 June 1911. Advertised for sale in September 1919. By 1931 owned by Cyril Davis of Dover. Wrecked off Mussel Roe Bay, TAS, in June 1966; all hands saved. At the time owned by Clifford Sward.

1911. *Vanity.* **Yacht.** 32.7 x 9.1 x 3.5 ft. Fourth of the one-design class of yacht instigated by E. H. Webster and adapted by Alfred Blore from a W. Hand (Jr) design. Built to the order of W. F. Darling, G. S. Crisp and Dr Ireland and launched on 2 November 1911. Sold to a Mr Watson of Murdunna towards the end of WWI. By October 1919 owned by Angus Cumming. Purchased by Frank Harris and C. Flynn in December 1922; by January 1927 owned by Frank Harris and Claude Cooper; between 1933 and 1938 owned by Frank Harris, Claude Cooper and W. T. Gibson who lengthened her to 34 ft in 1933. Still owned by Harris and Gibson in 1943, and by Harris until April 1949. Owned by A. K. Ward in the 1950s. During the 1970s and 1980s owned by Jim Payne. In 1989 purchased by Paul Howard and transferred to NSW. Subsequently purchased by Peter Nicolsen in 2000. Sold to Rob Virtue in 2005 and fully restored in QLD. Still in existence; located in southern TAS and owned by Rob Virtue.

1911. *Gannet.* **Yacht.** 32.7 x 9.1 x 3.5 ft. Fifth of the one-design class of yacht instigated by E. H. Webster and adapted by Alfred Blore from a W. Hand (Jr) design. Launched on 15 November 1911. Built to the order of Charles Shannon of Geelong, VIC. Sailed with the Royal Geelong Yacht Club up until the 1950s under several owners including Harold Anderson and Jack Fitzgerald. Subsequent owners include K. Holder (1980s) and Bob Major (1990s). Still in existence; purchased by her current owner (Martin Cox) in 2000 and moved to Sydney, NSW, where she underwent restoration.

1912. *Risdon (Kyeema).* **Motor boat.** 35 x 7 x 3.9 ft. Built to the order of C. R. Davies based on a design by J. E. Saunders from the Isle of Wight. Launched in September 1912. Purchased by the Deep Sea Fisheries Commission in 1926. Renamed *Kyeema* and altered by Charlie Lucas and Ivar "Chips" Gronfors to suit patrol work off the TAS coast. Following several decades of service in Bass Strait, Launceston, and later Hobart, sold by tender in July 1945. Has since undergone several changes of ownership and location. Still in existence; located at Lewisham, TAS.

1912. *Canobie.* **Yacht.** 32.7 x 9.1 x 3.5 ft. Sixth of the one-design class of yacht instigated by E. H. Webster and adapted by Alfred Blore from a W. Hand (Jr) design. Built to the order of E. H. Webster but sold part-way through construction to A. J. Cotton of Kettering. Launched on 31 October 1912. Subsequent owners include E. H. Webster (1918 – 1920), E. T. Domeney (1920 - 1930), J. H. Rae (1944 – 1950s), Neil Houston (1980s) and Bruce Anderson (1995 – 2009), among others. Purchased by Owen Stacy and transferred to Perth, WA, in 2009, where she is still in existence, fully restored to her original configuration. Most recently participated in the 2017 Australian Wooden Boat Festival.

1913. *Sealark.* **Motor boat.** 26 x 7 ft. Built to the order of Arthur E. Risby. Following Risby's death, transferred to his son Harry. Sold in 1919 to E. H. Webster and subsequently to W. J. Horlock who retained ownership for several decades. Later purchased by the Geeves family, among others. Still in existence; currently owned by John Allport and located in southern TAS.

1914. *Marie Laure.* **Whaleboat.** 26 ft. Four-oared whaleboat built to the order of Tom Dunbabin of Bream Creek and launched in January 1914. Historically named *Marie Laure*. Fitted with a square stern to allow an engine to be installed. Remained in the Dunbabin family's hands for several generations.

1914. _Kelvin_. Motor launch. 25 x 7 ft. Built to the order of A. Pretyman of Hobart. A regular competitor in local motor boat races for many years. By 1917 and into the early 1930s owned by the Latham family.

1914. _Hermione III_. Motor launch. 37.2 x 9 x 7.6 ft. Built to the order of G. A. Roberts of Hobart and launched on 12 December 1914. A regular competitor in local motor boat races for many years. Sold to the Australian Navy in 1943 and involved in coastal patrol work. Subsequently sold to Tony Chamberlain. Later transferred to VIC. Still in existence; located in Queenscliff, VIC, and owned by Ian Roberts.

1915. _Curlew_. Fishing boat. 40.3 x 10 x 4.5 ft. Launched in early 1915 and built to the order of Harold Chambers who retained ownership for many decades. Still in existence, based at Prince of Wales Bay, TAS. Advertised for sale in early 2017.

1915. _Ethel (Diane B)_. Fishing boat. 39.9 x 10 x 4.7 ft. Likely built to the order of Clarence Dear who retained ownership for several decades. Later owned by Jack Behrens and renamed _Diane B_. Subsequently owned by Terry Chopping. By the late 1960s owned by Keith Cripps and moved to the Tasman Peninsula. Sold in 2004. Still in existence; moored at Kettering, TAS.

1916. Yacht. "New comfortable cruiser". Advertised for sale in January 1916.

1916. _Beatrice_. Fishing boat. > 40 ft. Built to the order of George Hooper of Hobart. For many years involved in the local barracouta trade. Still operating out of Hobart in 1937. Into the 1940s possibly owned by the McKillop Brothers. May have moved to Strahan, TAS.

1918. Motor boat. 21 ft. Advertised for sale in March 1918.

1918. Motor boat. 30 ft. Advertised for sale in March 1918.

1919. _Molly Hawk (Roma)_. Yacht. 35.5 x 10.7 x 3 ft. Built to the order of Sir Herbert Nicholls to a Fred Goeller (Jr) design. By 1930 purchased by W. Robinson and renamed _Roma_. Thereafter purchased by Justice Wilfred Hutchins. Damaged following a collision with the _Cartela_ in April 1943. Salvaged and repaired. Destroyed by arson at Franklin, TAS, in October 2012.

1919. _Diana (Rata, Bronzewing)_. Yacht. 37 x 9.2 x 4.2 ft. Built by Charles Lucas for his own use, likely completed in late 1919. Converted to a fishing boat in early 1920 and operated by several owners in the ensuing decades, including Messrs Steele and Parker. Then owned by Peter Hindrum, and by the 1940s, the Flinders Island Trading Company. Still in existence, renamed _Rata_ in 1995, and more recently _Bronzewing_. Currently based in NSW.

1919. _Dulcie_. Fishing boat. Built on speculation and advertised for sale in May 1920. Purchased by the Spaulding Brothers. Wrecked in September 1929 near New Harbour, TAS; all hands saved. At the time owned by J. Coleman of Hobart.

1920. _Valkyrie (Falkyrie)_. Yacht. 41 x 9.8 x 5 ft. Built on speculation; designed by Charlie Lucas. Purchased prior to completion by O. R. Tinning. Launched on 28 October 1920. Renamed _Falkyrie_ in the early 1930s. Sold to A. Greig of Melbourne, VIC, in October 1934 following Tinning's death, sailing with the Royal Geelong Yacht Club for several years, and then with the Royal Brighton Yacht Club. Wrecked on 19 December 1978 in VIC with the loss of one life.

Vessels Built by Charlie Lucas and Employees at Battery Point (1893 – 1936).

1922. Motor boat. 20 x 6.8 ft. Hull advertised for sale in March 1922. Huon pine, four months old.

1924. *Pierette*. Cadet dinghy. 12 x 5 ft x 14 in. Built to the order of Rex Willing in early 1924. Advertised for sale in November 1929. Purchased by G. and J. Bailey. By 1931 owned by M. P. C. Festing. Advertised for sale in October 1934. In 1935 owned by Rex Creese and in 1937 by Alan McGuire.

1924. Yacht. 36 ft. Built on speculation and launched in July 1924. Subsequently advertised for sale and purchased by James Bingham Maycock who died shortly thereafter. Subsequent history unknown.

1924. *Spindrift II (Spumedrift)*. Yacht. 44 x 10 x 6 ft. Built to the order of E. H. Webster to a design by Alfred Blore and launched on 9 December 1924. Sailed to Sydney, NSW, in September 1926 and sold a few years later to J. Wira. By the early 1960s owned by Neil and Toni O'Brien of Brisbane, QLD.

1925. *Tassie*. Yacht. 25 x 7.5 ft. 21 ft restricted class yacht designed by Skipper Batt with assistance from Alfred Blore and John W. Tarleton. Built by Charlie Lucas and Chips Gronfors. Launched on 17 January 1925. Represented TAS in numerous Forster Cup, finishing first in 1925, 1926, 1927 and 1929. Transferred to Jack Joyce of Hobart, one of the vessel's original shareholders, in February 1932. Sold to T. Geary of Williamstown, VIC, in 1936. Remained in VIC for several decades. Believed to have been destroyed in the 1960s.

1925. Yacht. Cruiser. Built on speculation and purchased by M. Weston. Noted in the press as having a raised deck and nearing completion in November 1925. Fitted with a 12 hp Kermath engine.

1925. *Moani*. Motor boat. 35 x 9 x 5.2 ft. Built by Charlie Lucas and Chips Gronfors to the order of John E. Reid of Newcastle, NSW; a friend of Gronfors. Designed and planned by Gronfors. Launched on 9 December 1925 and subsequently transferred to Sydney on board the *SS Kanna*. Remained in the Reid family's possession for many years. Still in existence; currently moored at Pittwater, NSW.

1926. *Lialee*. Fishing boat. 48 x 12.5 x 6 ft. Built to the order of Ernest Parker of Dunalley and launched in October 1926. Intended for employment in the crayfish industry. In use well into the 20th century.

1927. *Tassie Too*. Yacht. 25 x 7.5 ft. 21 ft restricted class yacht built by Charlie Lucas and Chips Gronfors to a design by Skipper Batt (assisted by Alfred Blore and John W. Tarleton). Launched on 27 November 1927. Competed in numerous Forster Cups, finishing first ten times (1928, 1934, 1936, 1937, 1939, 1947, 1948, 1949, 1950 and 1952); a feat unmatched by any other vessel. Raffled in 1955 to Sam Good of Launceston. Later transferred to Melbourne, VIC, and owned by Doug and Cyril Eastgate, and then Rod Fulton. In the early 2000s restored by owner Tony Siddons. Still in existence; returned to Hobart, TAS, in September 2017. Owned by "Friends of Tassie Too".

1926. Dinghy. 10 ft. Advertised for sale in December 1926.

1928. Dinghy. 10 ft. Huon pine. Advertised for sale in February 1928.

1928. *Ralphs Bay*. Fishing boat. 40 x 12 x 5 ft. Built by Fred Coverdale to the order of J. Elliott at Charlie Lucas' boatyard and launched on 25 April 1928. Intended for the oyster and scallop industries. Noted to be active on the Derwent into the 1950s, for many years owned by the Whitton family.

1928. *H. C. M.* Motor boat. 26 x 8.5 ft. Built to the order of H. C. Millington and launched in August 1928. Designed by Alfred Blore. Advertised for sale in January 1929. Sold and likely renamed.

1928. *Sprite*. Yacht. 24.5 x 6.8 x 4 ft. Derwent class yacht built to the order of E. H. Webster and launched in late 1928. Designed by A. C. Barber and P. C. Douglas. Purchased by H. J. Whelan in October 1932. Sold in October 1935 to a yachtsman from Sydney, NSW, likely W. L. Heather of the Sydney Amateur Sailing Club who sailed a yacht named *Sprite* between 1935-37. Disappears after 1937; possibly sold and renamed.

1929. *Anitra*. Yacht. 26 x 7 ft. B class yacht built to the order of Rowley Vautin and launched on 2 November 1929. Designed by Skipper Batt; uniquely fitted with a bulb fin. Remained in Vautin's hands for several decades. Later owned by the Escott family and then David Hasseltine. Still in existence; located in southern TAS and owned by Harry Hale.

1929. *Wanderer*. Motor boat. 32 ft. Built to the order of H. C. Millington. Launched in December 1929 and remained in Millington's possession for many years. Advertised for sale in 1943. Still in existence; located at Bellerive, TAS, and owned by John McLea.

1929. *Tassie III (Wombat)*. Yacht. 25 x 7.5 x 2.2 ft. 21 ft restricted class yacht designed by Skipper Batt with assistance from P. C. Douglas. Launched on 21 December 1929. Represented TAS in numerous Forster Cups, finishing first in 1931 and 1938. Sold in March 1939 to A. S. Huybers of the Royal Queensland Yacht Club and renamed *Wombat*. Several changes of owners. Later converted to a cruiser. In the 1960s transferred to Lord Howe Island. Subsequent history not known.

1930. *Margaret*. Yacht. 31.8 x 8.5 x 3.5 ft. Built to the order of Jack Forsyth to a design by Charlie Lucas and launched on 11 October 1930. Remained on the Derwent in Forsyth's possession until his death in 1950. Later owned by Jack Levis, subsequently owned by Dick Lane and then Graham Richardson. Still in existence. Located in southern TAS and owned by Libor Sikora.

1934. *Spindrift (Suzanne II)*. Yacht. 42.5 x 9.6 x 6.2 ft. Built to the order of E. H. Webster and launched on 2 October 1934. Sailed to Sydney, NSW, in April 1937 by Percy Coverdale, Neall Batt, Jack Hansen and G. Chamberlain. Purchased by R. A. Terrill and renamed *Suzanne II*. Competed in the 1949 Sydney to Hobart Yacht Race. Still owned by R. A. Terrill in March 1953, though advertised for sale later that year.

1936. *Saona*. Yacht. 40 x 11.6 x 6.3 ft. Built for Morton Weston of Austins Ferry and launched in early 1936. Designed by Philip L. Rhodes. Later owned by Len Nettlefold. Still in existence, moored at Kettering, TAS, and owned by Ben Marris.

Battery Point boatyards (circa 1910).
Courtesy State Library of Victoria.

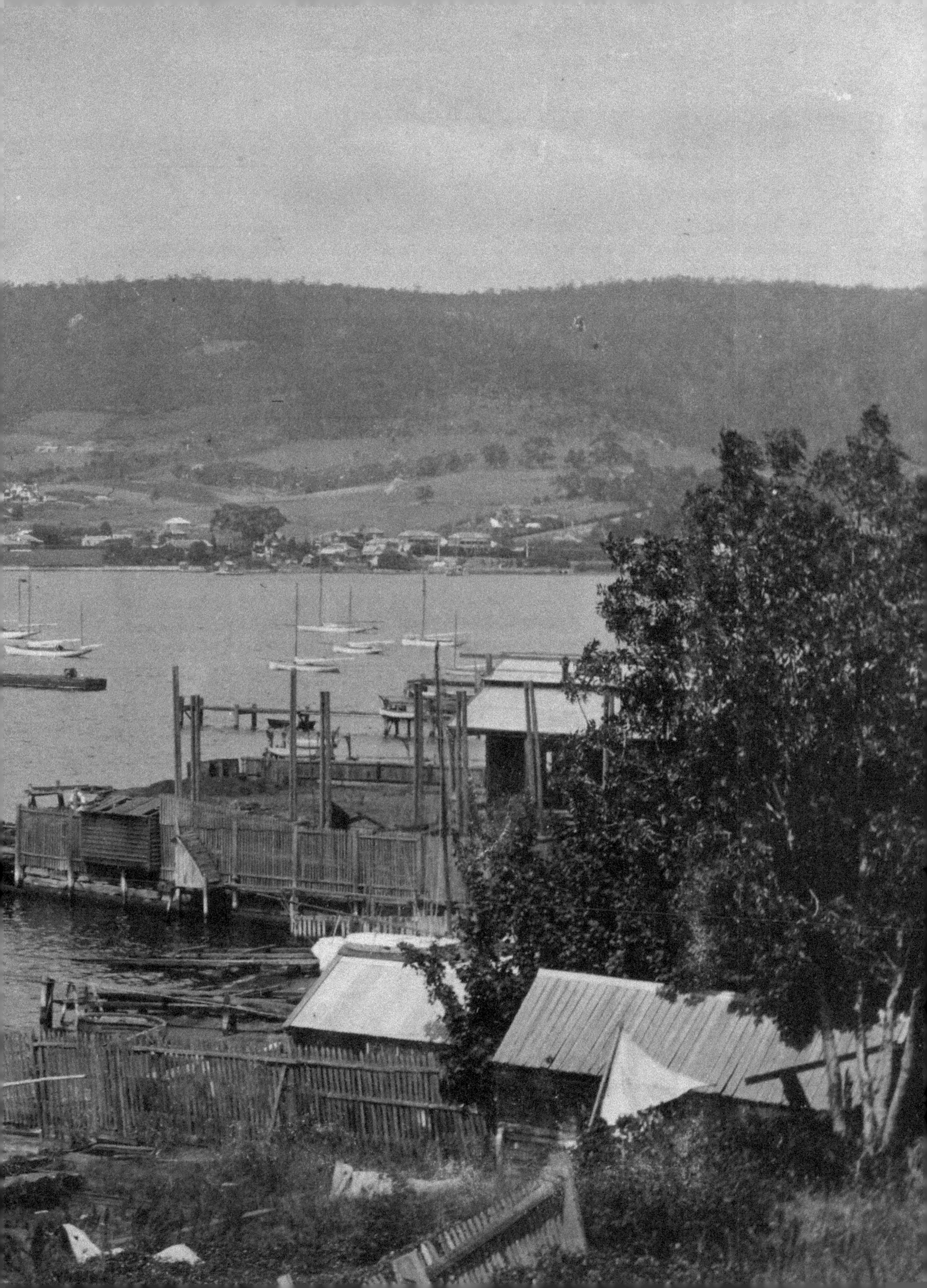

Albert "Tucker" Abel

Hailing from Battery Point, Tucker Abel spent his teenage years learning the craft of boat building from his father who was a local shipwright. In 1897 he established a boatyard at Battery Point on an allotment owned by the Risby family. Here, between 1898 and 1937, Tucker Abel built more than 65 vessels, including 18 motor launches; the building of which became his forte. Diversifying his business interests, three motor launches (the *Blanche*, *Blanche Abel* and *Eva Blanche*) were also built to service Tucker Abel's own River Derwent chartering company, the Royal Blue Motor Launch Line. Unfortunately Tucker Abel's boat building career was interrupted by World War I and a fire at his boatyard in 1917 which destroyed many vessels. Still, Tucker Abel's legacy continues in the vessels he built which remain in existence, including the motor launches *Eva Blanche*, *Waterloo*, *Vera* and *Nancy* (ex *Rowella*).

Albert Arthur Abel, colloquially known as Tucker, was born on 17 November 1871 at Battery Point, the sixth of nine children born to Thomas and Lydia Abel (nee Bayes). Tucker's father was a local shipwright, spending many years working for John Lucas, renowned shipbuilder of Battery Point. The Abel family lived close to the boat and ship yards, in De Witt and later Trumpeter streets.

As a teenager Tucker Abel became active in local yachting circles, first competing in races for boys under 16 years of age. Following, he competed in sailing races in the yacht *Daisy*. During this period Tucker was also learning the craft of boat building from his father.

In June 1894, at the age of 22, Tucker Abel purchased the 21 ft yacht *Hebe*. He successfully sailed the vessel in Derwent Sailing Club events and at various regattas throughout Tasmania before advertising it for sale by auction. The auction proved the first of many Tucker Abel would orchestrate in the ensuing years. Other vessels he auctioned included the yacht *Mischief*, a fishing smack, the 16 ft yacht *Linuet*, and a canoe.

Beginning in February 1897 Tucker Abel began advertising smaller sail boats and canoes for sale at William Bayes' Battery Point boatyard. By September of that year he had taken a lease out on the Risby family's Battery Point yard. Located off Napoleon Street, the site was previously leased to Charles Miller. Continuing his efforts to buy, overhaul and then sell vessels at profit, Tucker Abel advertised various sailing boats, loading boats, dinghies, rowing boats and fishing boats for sale at his new yard, some of which he may have also built.

The First Known Vessels

The first vessels Tucker Abel is known to have built at his yard include a large boat for the schooner *Lemael* and several lightweight pulling boats, all built in 1898; a boat for the pilot station, built in early 1899; and a 15 ft loading boat that was advertised for sale in July 1899. He also continued to advertise sailing and rowing boats for sale, as well as purchase decrepit vessels to salvage metal.

In July 1903 Tucker Abel completed a 15 ft sailing dinghy. In November of that same year he completed several lifeboats for the local river steamers to comply with new Hobart Marine Board regulations. The 14.7 ft boats, considered unsinkable owing to the installation of air-tight copper tanks, were capable of carrying up to nine passengers. Two more lifeboats were built for Purdon and Featherstone's new steamer *Mongana*, launched in July 1905. Also completed towards the end of 1905 was a motor launch, likely the *Phoebe*, which was purchased by Thomas Smart, local waterman, and in service by late January of 1906. The vessel proved to be the first of many motor launches built by Tucker Abel over the next decade.

More Motor Launches

On 13 August 1906 Tucker Abel completed the motor launch *Blanche*, named for his wife and built for his own use. Modelled off Tom Purdon's plan for the steamer *Mongana*, the vessel was constructed of Huon pine, fitted with a 15 hp Frisco Standard oil engine and considered "… the handsomest motor boat yet seen on the Derwent …". At 45 ft, she was also the longest motor launch yet built in Hobart.

With accommodation for up to 81 passengers, commencing in October 1906 Tucker Abel made the *Blanche* available for private charter and excursions. The vessel was also suited to the local angling and tourist trades.

Blanche (later named *Governor Newdegate*) on the Great Lake in 1919.
Courtesy *Weekly Courier,* 13 November 1919.

Tucker Abel's Battery Point boatyard (circa 1910).
Courtesy *Tasmanian Mail*, 6 October 1910.

Following the success of the *Blanche*, Tucker Abel received several orders for motor launches. These include the *Mary*, built to the order of Arthur Davies of Port Cygnet, and the *Petrel*, built to the order of T. Heathorn. Both were launched in late 1907.

1908 proved another busy year for Tucker Abel with the completion of at least six motor launches: *Pixie, Irene, Campania, Bellevue, Palana* and *Berriedale*. The *Pixie* was built to the order of a Mr Chalk, though was later owned by the McAllister family. The *Irene* was built to the order of A. E. Iles, though was later owned by Jack Elliott and involved in the local barracouta trade. The *Campania* was built to the order of Eric Brock for employment on the Coal River. The *Bellevue* was built to the order of J. Eyles of New Town and, like several of her cohorts, competed in local motor boat races for many years. The *Palana* was built to the order of Matthew Fitzpatrick, who for many years served as warden of Port Cygnet, chairman of the Port Cygnet Regatta Association, and commodore of the Port Cygnet Yacht Club. Finally, the *Berriedale* was built to the order of James Davidson of Berriedale.

During this period Tucker Abel also built boats on speculation. For example, a new 30 ft motor launch fitted with an 8 hp engine was advertised for sale at his boatyard in September 1909.

Smaller Vessels

In addition to building motor launches, Tucker Abel completed several smaller vessels between 1907 and 1909. These include three punts built for various owners; a ferry boat named *Derwent*, built to the order of Robert Cracknell, a local waterman; a dinghy for a customer located on Tasmania's east coast; a lifeboat for Purdon and Featherstone's new steamer *Marana*; and a boat to the order of the Strahan Marine Board for use at Macquarie Heads. In late 1909 Tucker completed another lifeboat, this one was for Purdon and Featherstone's new steamer *Reemere*.

Royal Blue Motor Launch Line

The success of Tucker Abel's boat hiring and charter business utilising the *Blanche* soon saw him build a second motor launch. Named *Blanche Abel,* the 42 ft vessel was launched on 17 October 1908 and designed off Purdon and Featherstone's plan for the steamer *Marana*. With accommodation for up to 75 passengers, the *Blanche Abel* was intended for the local tourist and angling trades. Operating under the flag of Tucker's newly-coined Royal Blue Motor Launch Line, the *Blanche Abel* joined the *Blanche* on the Derwent in November 1908.

Just over 18 months later, in July 1910, Tucker Abel petitioned the Hobart Marine Board for permanent berths for his two motor launches at the Hobart wharf, as well as for provision of an office. The Marine Board subsequently agreed that accommodation for the two vessels be provided on the south side of Watermans Dock and that an office be made available nearby.

Continuing to expand his motor launch line, in September 1910 Tucker Abel completed a third vessel, capable of carrying 54 passengers. Named after his late niece, the 35 ft *Eva Blanche* joined the *Blanche* and *Blanche Abel* at Tucker's new Watermans Dock berth in January 1911. During this period Tucker also received approval from the Hobart Marine Board to run charters to Gordon via the Channel ports, including Woodbridge and Bruny Island.

Tucker Abel's motor launch line was well received. In January 1912 he made plans to expand the fleet even further, advertising both the *Blanche* and *Blanche Abel* for sale with the intention of replacing them with a larger 60 ft launch capable of accommodating up to 120 passengers.

The *Blanche* was sold in mid-1912 to E. H. Webster for use as a private launch. However, either by choice or failure to find a suitable buyer, Tucker Abel retained ownership of the *Blanche Abel*. Beginning in February 1913 he employed the vessel on a regular schedule, departing Hobart's wharf for River Derwent tours on Monday, Tuesday, Thursday and Friday afternoons. His other vessel, the *Eva Blanche*, was advertised for daily hire or charter.

Motor launch *Eva Blanche* assisting with the launch of the *Cartela* on 21 September 1912.
Courtesy Tasmanian Archive and Heritage Office.

Two of Tucker Abel's launches at the New Town Regatta. Courtesy *Tasmanian Mail*, 12 March 1914.

Vera.
Courtesy Graeme Norris.

Nancy (ex Rowella).
Courtesy Nell Tyson
(Living Boat Trust).

Additional Boat Orders

In addition to operating his Royal Blue Motor Launch Line, the years leading up to World War I saw Tucker Abel continue to receive orders for small boats and motor launches. For example, in October 1910 he was noted as building a motor launch for a resident of Port Cygnet that was slightly larger than the *Eva Blanche*. In September 1911 Tucker Abel completed the *Palana*, a ferry boat built to the order of Robert Cracknell, by now one of Hobart's oldest watermen. In July 1912 Tucker Abel completed the motor launch *Empire*, built to the order of T. S. Timmins, managing director of the English Amusement Company.

A shortage of skilled labour during this period, however, affected work at all of the Battery Point boatyards, including Tucker Abel's yard. Instead he focussed his energies on the Royal Blue Motor Launch Line, with the *Blanche Abel* and *Eva Blanche* remaining popular.

World War 1

During World War I Tucker Abel was noted as building several more motor launches and dinghies. At least three motor launches, the *Waterloo*, *Vera* and *Rowella*, were built for well-known families of the Huon region. The *Waterloo* was built to the order of the Calvert family of Waterloo and launched in 1914. The *Vera* was launched in 1915, built to the order of Edgar Norris, an orchardist of Glaziers Bay, and named for his only daughter. Finally, the *Rowella* was built to the order of Harry Rowe of Brooks Bay and launched in September 1917. This particular vessel was likely constructed from the hull of a motor launch built by Tucker Abel to the order of W. T. Foreman and advertised for sale in August 1917.

The smaller boats built by Tucker Abel during World War I include the dinghy *Myra Burgess*, built to the order of Harold Burgess, orchardist of the Huon, as a wedding present for his bride Myra Pillings, and the pleasure boat *Lutana*, another boat built to the order of Robert Cracknell, local waterman.

Disastrous Fire

In December 1917 a disastrous fire at Tucker Abel's boatyard resulted in many vessels being destroyed, including several under construction. Amongst them were a nearly complete 40 ft motor launch and a 20 ft motor tender for the fishing boat *Myrtle Burgess*. Also destroyed was 5,000 ft of Huon pine. All told Tucker estimated his loss to be £600. Though insured for £500, his boat building business appears not to have fully recovered.

Post World War I

The end of World War I saw Tucker Abel continue to promote and prioritise his vessel hiring business over his boatyard. Not only were his motor launches made available for private charter and daily excursions but he also used them to augment and, in some cases, take the place of local steamers in the Derwent passenger trade.

The early 1920s saw Tucker Abel continue to operate his Royal Blue Motor Launch Line. He also continued to advertise new dinghies and punts for sale at his boatyard. In efforts to further supplement his income, in 1921 Tucker began selling fresh scallops and oysters on a daily basis, an enterprise he continued for the next 17 years. Initially scallops were sold out of a punt (the ex-yacht *Clutha*) at the Hobart wharf. By the 1930s Tucker was selling scallops directly from his Battery Point boatyard.

More changes were to come. By 1923 Tucker Abel had sold both the *Blanche Abel* and *Eva Blanche*. Following, he became master of the motor launch *Arcadia*, at the time owned by George Rometch.

During the 1920s and into the 1930s Tucker Abel remained involved in the building of smaller craft, such as rowing boats and dinghies, as well as overhaul and repair work. The smaller boats were built both to order and on speculation. This work, combined with his daily shellfish sales during the season, was likely enough to meet his family's needs.

Death

On 16 November 1938, one day before his 67th birthday, Tucker Abel suffered serious head injuries after being knocked down by a car outside the Hobart Town Hall. He died on 11 December 1938 at the Royal Hobart Hospital, less than one month after the accident, and was buried at Cornelian Bay Cemetery. Tucker Abel was survived by his wife Blanche (nee Beard) and their son Douglas "Jack" Abel.

Ex-racing yacht *Clutha* (built at Battery Point by Robert Inches in 1898). Converted to a scallop punt by Tucker Abel in the early 1920s. Courtesy Tasmanian Archive and Heritage Office.

Vessels Built by Tucker Abel and Employees at Battery Point (1898 – 1937).

1898. Boat. Built for the schooner *Lemael*.

1898. Boats (2). "Light and stylish pulling boats," completed in late 1898.

1899. Boat. Built for the pilot station.

1899. Loading boat. 15 ft. Advertised for sale in July 1899.

1903. Dinghy. 15 ft. Sailing dinghy. Advertised for sale in July 1903.

1903. Lifeboats (2). 14.7 x 5.3 ft. Built for local river steamers to comply with Hobart Marine Board regulations. Fitted with air-tight copper tanks to prevent sinking.

1904. Punt. Advertised as lost or stolen in October 1904.

1905. Lifeboats (2). Built for Purdon and Featherstone's steamer *Mongana*.

1905. *Phoebe*. Motor launch. 30 x 7 ft. Likely built on speculation and advertised for sale without a motor in November 1905. Purchased by Thomas Smart and first noted on the River Derwent in late January 1906. Fitted with a 5 hp Standard engine. Employed as a charter vessel for several decades. Advertised for sale in August 1943.

1906. *Blanche (Starling, Brunette, Governor Newdegate, Dolphin)*. Motor launch. 45 x 10 x 4.5 ft. Hull designed off plans for the steamer *Mongana*. Employed on the Derwent for many years as part of Tucker Abel's Royal Blue Motor Launch Line. Sold in June 1912 to E. H. Webster and renamed *Starling*. Sold in 1913 to A. J. Cotton and renamed *Brunette*. Advertised for sale in 1918 and purchased by the Hydro Electric Department for use on the Great Lake, renamed *Governor Newdegate*. By 1927 noted as lying "useless at the southern end of the lake". Sold to Reg Plummer in late 1933 and moved to Ulverstone. Purchased by C. B. Poole in November 1936 for use as a houseboat on the Tamar River and renamed *Dolphin*. Believed to have sank near Swan Bay, TAS.

1907. Punts (3). Built for various owners.

1907. *Mary*. Motor launch. 35 x 9 ft. Built to the order of Arthur Davies of Port Cygnet. Competed in motor boat races and regattas. Remained in the Huon region for several decades, the 1920s spent carting fruit. By the mid-1930s and into the 1940s owned by J. Dalton, licencee of the Dover Hotel. Advertised for sale in September 1945. By the 1950s working as a fishing boat working out of St Helens, TAS. Later moved to Battery Point. Wrecked around 1984 following a lengthy period out of the water.

1907. *Petrel*. Motor launch. 27.5 x 6.5 x 2.7 ft. Built to the order of T. Heathorn, modelled off the *Blanche*. Fitted with a 5 hp engine. Advertised for sale in March 1909. Spent several years competing in local regatta and yacht club events under various owners, including Dr Cummings, T. A. Tabart (Jr) and Messrs Dudley and Saunders.

1908. *Pixie*. Motor launch. 24 ft. Built to the order of a Mr Chalk. By 1912 owned by the McAllister family, competing in local motor boat races with the Derwent Sailing Club.

Vessels Built by Tucker Abel and Employees at Battery Point (1898 – 1937).

1908. *Irene (Irene T)*. **Motor launch.** 35.2 x 9.2 x 4 ft. Built to the order of A. E. Iles. By 1910 owned by Jack Elliot and employed in the barracouta trade, also involved in local motor boat events. Later converted to a licensed fishing boat. Noted to be still afloat in the 1980s, though in a deteriorated state.

1908. *Campania*. **Motor launch.** 30 ft. Built to the order of Eric Brock of Campania. Fitted with a 10 hp Brook engine. For sale in September 1912 and purchased by Webster, Rometch and Duncan Ltd. for use in the local tourist trade. Advertised for sale in May 1914. By 1926 transferred to Launceston and owned by H. Clarke. Active on the Tamar until April 1929 when "half of the motor boat *Campania*" was noted as lying on the fish market wharf following flooding.

1908. *Bellevue (Finsbury)*. **Motor launch.** 32 x 8 ft. Built to the order of J. Eyles of New Town. Fitted with a 15 hp Fairbanks engine. Competed in local motor boat races and made available for charter. Likely remained in the Eyles family's possession until the 1920s. Renamed *Finsbury*. Advertised for sale at Purdon and Featherstone's Battery Point slip in November 1941.

1908. *Palana*. **Motor launch.** Built to the order of Matthew Fitzpatrick of Port Cygnet. Competed in Huon regattas and sailing events for several years. Likely sold following Fitzpatrick's death in 1917. Possibly advertised for sale in Hobart in May 1939.

1908. *Berriedale*. **Motor launch.** 20 ft. Fitted with a 4 hp Regal engine. Built to the order of James Davidson of Berriedale. Used for recreational angling. Involved in local regatta races.

1908. *Derwent*. **Ferry boat.** Built to the order of Robert Cracknell, local waterman.

1908. **Dinghy.** Built to the order of a customer located on the east coast of TAS.

1908. **Lifeboat.** Built for Purdon and Featherstone's new steamer *Marana*.

1908. **Boat.** Built for the Strahan Marine Board for use at Macquarie Heads.

1908. *Blanche Abel*. **Motor launch.** 42 x 9 x 4 ft. Designed off plans for the steamer *Marana*. Employed on the River Derwent for many years as part of Tucker Abel's Royal Blue Motor Launch Line. Sold in the early 1920s. Wrecked at Maria Island, TAS, on 2 August 1925. Salvage and sundries advertised for sale by auction in September 1925.

1909. **Lifeboat.** Built for Purdon and Featherstone's steamer *Reemere*.

1909. **Motor launch.** 30 ft. Fitted with a 8 hp engine. Advertised for sale in September 1909.

1910. *Eva Blanche*. **Motor launch.** 35 x 8.5 x 4 ft. The third vessel built for Tucker Abel's Royal Blue Motor Launch Line. Advertised for sale in late 1922. Sold to A. Hammond of the Huon. By 2006 owned by H. Rodway and moored at Lindisfarne. Still in existence. In 2017, located in southern TAS and owned by Dave Conway.

1910. **Motor launch.** > 35 ft. Built to the order of a resident of Port Cygnet.

1911. *Palana.* **Ferry boat.** Built to the order of Robert Cracknell, local waterman. Competed at the 1922 Sandy Bay Regatta.

1912. *Empire.* **Motor launch.** 18 (LWL) x 7 ft. Huon pine, copper-fastened, seating capacity for 20 passengers. Built to the order of T. S. Timmins, managing director of the English Amusement Company. Participated in local yachting activities and events up until 1917.

1914. *Myra Burgess.* **Dinghy.** 11.3 x 4.6 ft. Built to the order of Harold Burgess, orchardist of the Huon, as a wedding present for his bride Myra Pillings. Believed to be still in existence (Huon region).

1914. *Waterloo.* **Motor launch.** 40 x 10 ft. Fitted with a 10 hp engine. Built to the order of H. D. Calvert of the Huon. Used to convey fruit, as well as for pleasure trips. For sale in 1927 and again in 1929, though likely remained in the Calvert family's hands. Still in existence and based at Beauty Point, TAS. Advertised for sale in May 2017.

1915. *Vera.* **Motor launch.** 35 x 8.5 x 3.5 ft. Built to the order of Edgar Norris, orchardist of Glaziers Bay. Fitted with a Frisco 8 hp engine. Used to cart apples to Port Huon from Glaziers Bay, as well as for pleasure trips. Sold in 1936. Later owned by the Lucas family. Noted in 2006 at Murdunna on the Tasman Peninsula. Still in existence; in April 2017 sighted at Blackmans Bay, TAS.

1916. *Lutana.* **Pleasure boat.** Built to the order of Robert Cracknell, local waterman.

1917. *Rowella (Nancy).* **Motor launch.** 35 x 8.5 x 3.5 ft. Built to the order of Harry Rowe of Brooks Bay. Later owned by Thomas Smart, among others. Renamed *Nancy.* Still in existence. Gifted to the Living Boat Trust of Tasmania and returned to the Huon River in 2010 after undergoing restoration in QLD.

1917. Dinghy. Built to the order of Captain Whitehouse.

1917. Motor launch. 40 x 10 x 4.5 ft. Destroyed by fire just prior to launch.

1917. Motor tender. 20 ft. Built for the fishing boat *Myrtle Burgess.* Destroyed by fire.

1917. Boats (4). Smaller boats. Destroyed by fire just prior to launch.

1920. Boats (6). Huon pine dinghies and punts advertised for sale.

1922. Dinghy. 11 ft. Huon pine. For sale at Tom Purdon's Battery Point boatyard in August 1922.

1923. Dinghies (3). 10, 11 and 12 ft Huon pine dinghies built by Jack Abel. Advertised for sale in late 1923/early 1924.

1929. Dinghy. 10 ft. Advertised for sale in August 1929.

1933. Motor boat. Hull, under construction, advertised for sale.

1934. Dinghy. 10 ft. Advertised for sale in October 1934.

1935 - 1937. Dinghies (16). 9, 9.5, 10 and 11 ft. Advertised for sale.

Aerial view of Battery Point and surrounds, showing the Napoleon Street boat and ship yards (circa early 1920s). Courtesy Queen Victoria Museum and Art Gallery.

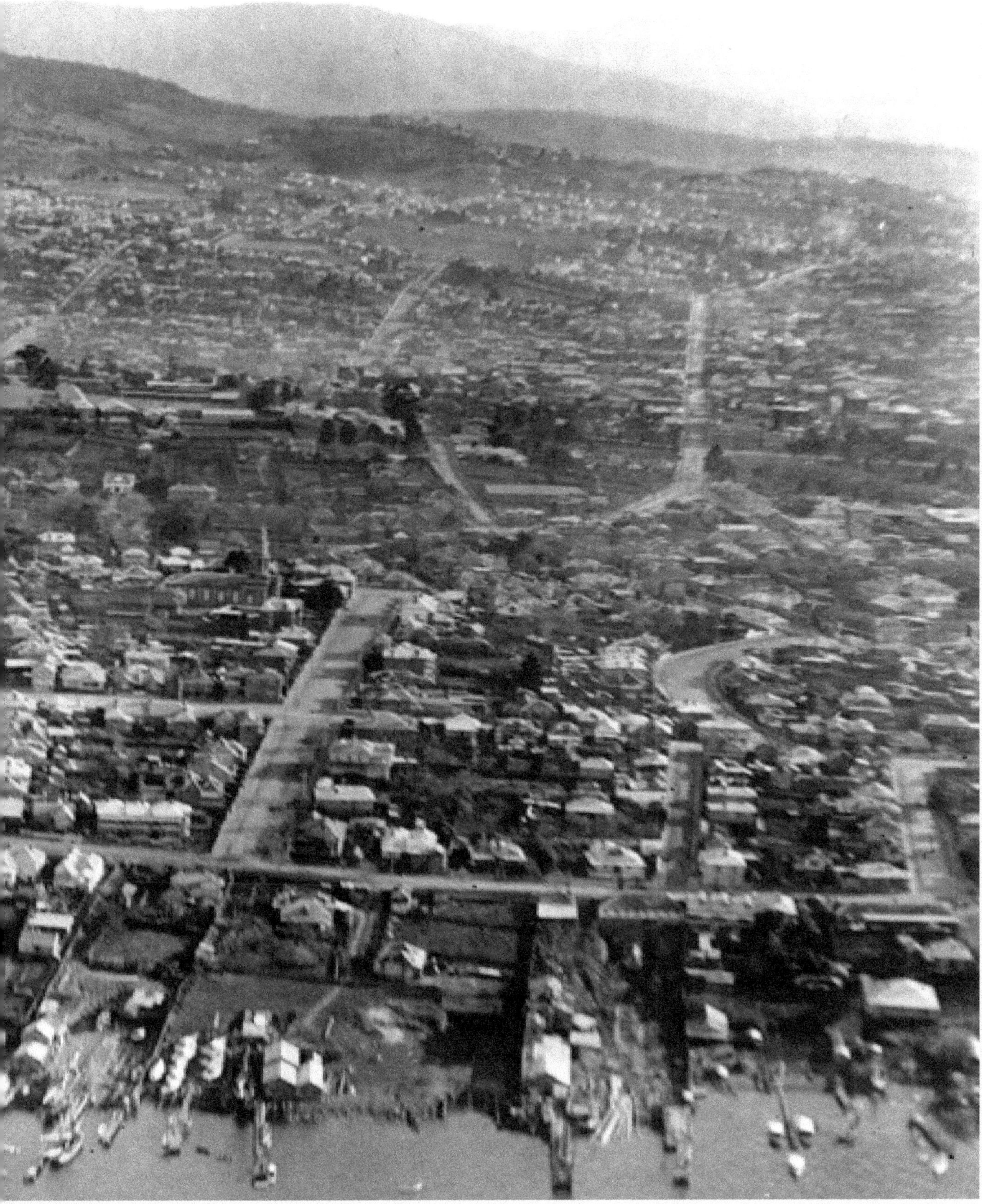

William "Skipper" Batt

From an early age Skipper Batt developed an interest in sailing, precipitated by his involvement with the Derwent Model Yacht Club and his family's home being situated close to the Battery Point slipyards. Though professionally employed as a cooper, in his early 20s Skipper began competing in 15 ft "boxie" dinghies, also designing and building several vessels for this class. In 1911 Skipper and his younger brother Harry purchased the one-design class yacht *Spindrift*, which they renamed *Weene*, both immediately making an impact at the helm of the vessel and winning many coveted titles. Following Skipper Batt's return from Europe at the end of World War I, he and his brother Harry orchestrated a revival of the Derwent Model Yacht Club and were instrumental in Tasmania's success in the interstate competition for the 21 ft restricted class, the Forster Cup. Combined the pair won the event ten times over a 14-year period. From the late 1920s, Skipper Batt also designed and built several smaller vessels at the Batt family's Napoleon Street slip, including cadet dinghies and 16 ft skiffs.

William Percy Batt, from childhood referred to as Skipper, was born on 3 December 1879 at Sandy Bay, the seventh of 11 children born to Henry and Ellen Batt (nee Rose). Sadly his twin brother died at the age of seven months.

Skipper Batt's father was a carpenter and builder by trade and the large Batt family initially lived at King Street in Sandy Bay. By 1870 Henry Batt had purchased a parcel of land at 54-56 Napoleon Street, Battery Point. Given its location, the property was considered a potential site for construction of public baths in 1879, though Henry Batt declined the council's offer of £250.

In 1882 Henry Batt applied to the Hobart City Council for town water to be installed at the Napoleon Street property. By 1888 the Batt family had moved to the site, their house likely built by Henry Batt. In September 1888 Henry received permission from the Hobart Marine Board to lay a small slip along the foreshore at the bottom of the property. In November 1894 he received permission to build a jetty.

Derwent Model Yacht Club

Growing up so close to the water it was inevitable that Skipper Batt would gravitate to aquatic sports. Moreover, his father Henry had been active in local rowing races as a teenager and in the 1890s his uncle, William H. Batt, served on the committees of the Sandy Bay Sailing Club and the Hobart Regatta Association.

The Derwent Model Yacht Club appears to have been Skipper's initial foray into the world of boats. His first model was the *King Billy* which won several cash prizes throughout 1898 and 1899. In fact Skipper Batt was so successful with his models that he won an intercolonial model yacht race in 1899 against a competitor from the Sydney-based Port Jackson Model Yacht Club.

Established in the late 1880s by a collective of 30 of Hobart's more prominent yachtsmen, the objectives of the Derwent Model Yacht Club were to promote the design and racing of models built or carved from scale drawings, and to encourage younger generations to get involved with the sport. Models were 50 inches long and participants followed them around a set course in chaser dinghies. Though club events originally took place from Sandy Bay, by 1898 the club had moved to Robert Inches' Napoleon Street shipyard which was next door to the Batt family's property. Often competing against his brothers, in the early 1900s Skipper Batt continued his success with *King Billy* winning the senior championship five seasons in a row.

Left (Top): The start of a first class model race.
Left (Bottom): The start of the first heat for the Commodore's Prize.
Right: Skipper Batt's *King Billy*, the first class champion model over several seasons beginning in 1899.
All photos courtesy *Weekly Courier,* 9 November 1901.

Dinghy Racing

In 1902 Skipper Batt began successfully competing in dinghy races for 15 ft "boxies" with the Derwent Dinghy Sailing Club. His first dinghy was aptly named *King Billy*. The opening of the 1903/04 yachting season saw two new dinghies built by Skipper Batt competing with the club. These were the *Trucanini* and *Kitty*. The former was designed and built for Skipper Batt's own use, while the latter was built to the order of A. Bingham based on a British design that had been published in *Rudder* magazine in August 1902.

Between 1904 and 1906 Skipper Batt designed and built three more 15 ft "boxie" dinghies at his Battery Point home, all were based on the newly-developed scow principle. These were the *Lallah Rookh*, *Lahloo* and *Lalla Berri*. Launched in January 1904, the *Lallah Rookh* was built for Skipper Batt's own use. He successfully raced the vessel at club events and in local regattas for several years. *Lahloo*, first noted in November 1904, was built for Skipper's younger brother Harry. *Lalla Berri* was built for Skipper Batt's own use and launched in November 1906.

The success of Skipper Batt and his younger brother Harry in the local dinghy class was due to their skill at the helm as well as the workmanship and design of the vessels they built. Skipper Batt's reputation was well-earned within the class both locally and interstate. In October 1907 he built a 14 ft racing dinghy for A. T. Creek of Melbourne. Named *Tasma*, the vessel went on to successfully race with the St Kilda Dinghy Club.

Lahloo and *Lalla Berri* on the River Derwent.
Courtesy Maritime Museum of Tasmania.

Weene

After nearly a decade spent racing 15 ft dinghies, Skipper Batt and his brother Harry purchased the one-design class yacht *Spindrift* from E. H. Webster in April 1911 for £165. Renaming the vessel *Weene*, they continued their success at the helm and were awarded the championship pennant for the one-design class in June 1912. It proved the first of many pennants Skipper and Harry Batt would receive over the ensuing decades. *Weene* was successful in multiple formats; for example, winning the Bruny Island Ocean Race in 1914 and 1915. Extending their involvement to club administration, in late 1915 Skipper Batt was elected to the committee of the Royal Yacht Club of Tasmania. He and his brother Harry would serve numerous roles in the club's administration throughout the following decades.

World War I

As World War I took hold, Skipper Batt's involvement with yachting was reduced. With the intention of enlisting, on 24 October 1916 Skipper Batt entered a training camp at Claremont. Only two weeks prior he had married Myrtle Bisdee at the Church of St James in New Town. On 5 January 1917 a large gathering of yachtsmen took place at the Royal Yacht Club of Tasmania's clubrooms to bid farewell to Skipper Batt. He was presented with a set of Barling pipes, some ammunition in the shape of tobacco, and a vase for his new wife.

Courtesy Jenny Keyes.

Skipper Batt was trained in the Australian Army's field artillery as a gunner. In early January of 1917 he left Tasmania for Maribyrnong, Victoria, where he received further training. Six months later Skipper Batt arrived in England. From there he was sent to France and subsequently Belgium, where Skipper saw active service, though several illnesses and injuries saw him spend time back in England. Skipper Batt returned to Tasmania in September 1919 whereupon he first met his two-year old daughter Ray.

Post World War 1

Once back in Tasmania Skipper Batt immediately returned to sailing *Weene* with his brother Harry. Though *Weene* continued her success in the one-design class, the years following the end of World War I saw interest in the class wane. The War not only affected the ability of vessel owners to find crews to race existing vessels, it also stymied any possibility of new vessels being built to enhance the competition. Instead reclassification of the existing yacht classes by both the Royal Yacht Club of Tasmania and the Derwent Sailing Squadron took place. In 1922 the open and one-design classes were replaced by A, B and C classes. The A class yachts were longer than the one-design yachts such that several of the one-designers (though not *Weene* until 1927) were modified to allow them to successfully compete in the class. Mainstays of the A class during this period included the likes of *Werona, Redpa, Elf, Aotea* and *Crescent II*. The B class featured regulars such as *Bronzewing, Marie Jo, Carita* and *Ventura*.

Model Yacht Club Revival

In winter of 1923 Skipper Batt and his brother Harry orchestrated a revival of the Derwent Model Yacht Club with the goal of fostering the next generation of sailors in the sport, including Harry's young son Neall. Skipper's original model, *King Billy*, by now over 20 years old, again proved a leader in the class. Successfully carrying on the legacy of the Batt family's involvement with the Derwent Model Yacht Club, in August 1923 Neall Batt debuted a new model designed and built by his uncle Skipper. Named *June,* the boat was interestingly built on the lines of the one-design class yachts.

Revived again in the early 1930s, with events taking place from the Batt family's Napoleon Street slip, the next generation of yachtsmen proved as equally tenacious and capable as the last. In addition to Neall Batt, future Battery Point boat builders and nationally recognised blue-water helmsmen involved in Derwent Model Yacht Club activities during this period were Ernest "Jock" Muir and Henry "Chook" Newman.

With an interest in nurturing the development of sailing more generally amongst local lads, in the mid-1920s Skipper and Harry Batt also began training crews to compete in the newly-instituted 12 ft cadet dinghy interstate championship, the Stonehaven Cup. The pair would continue their involvement and encouragement of the cadet dinghy class for many years, particularly through Harry's sons Neall and Ken, and their cohorts.

Top: Pre-race preparations. **Bottom:** The start of a model race.
Courtesy *Illustrated Tasmanian Mail,* 16 August 1923.

Initiation of The Forster Cup

Concurrent with re-invigorating the model yacht club and the 12 ft cadet dinghy class, another movement was taking place within Australia's yachting circles that would prove to be a coup for the Batt brothers: an interstate competition for 21 ft restricted class yachts. In the early 1920s state representatives from across the country, at the request of Lord Forster, Australia's Governor General, agreed to the convening of an annual event for 21 ft restricted class yachts. Named the "Forster Cup," the event was to be held in January or February of each year. The various states participating were to host the event on a rotating basis. The number of yachts representing each state was limited to a maximum of three. Victoria was scheduled to host the Forster Cup in 1924, Tasmania in 1925, therafter followed by Western Australia, South Australia and New South Wales.

Though enthusiastic to participate in the 1924 Forster Cup, by November 1923 Tasmania still had no boat selected to represent it at the event. Showing his dedication to the interstate competition, Lord Forster offered himself and his boat *Corella* to the Tasmanian contingent if the state could furnish crew members. Accordingly O. R. Tinning, G. S. Crisp, Charles Jones and Angus Cumming travelled from Hobart to Victoria to participate in the 1924 Forster Cup.

Design and Build of *Tassie*

In preparation for the 1925 Forster Cup, Angus Cumming purchased the yacht *Lakatoi* in Melbourne and brought her to Hobart to become the first yacht of the 21 ft restricted class in the state. With less than six months to go before the staging of the event in Hobart, Royal Yacht Club of Tasmania members convened to discuss the possibility of building a second yacht to vie for the cup. It was subsequently agreed that a subscription be opened among members of the club to fund its building.

In October 1924 a model developed by Skipper Batt was selected and soon after his tender to build the yacht was accepted by the Royal Yacht Club of Tasmania's committee. However, owing to the difficulty of sourcing materials, a lack of suitably skilled assistants, and the shortness of the time-frame, with much regret Skipper Batt was forced to withdraw his tender.

Several boat builders were then approached to build the vessel, including E. A. Jack of Launceston and H. Moore of Sydney. All expressed their unavailability. Thankfully Battery Point boat builder Charlie Lucas agreed to build the vessel. Skipper Batt's design, adapted on paper with the assistance of Alfred Blore and John W. Tarleton, remained in place. The resulting yacht, *Tassie,* was hurriedly built of immediately available timber by Lucas and Finnish boat builder Chips Gronfors and launched from Battery Point on 19 January 1925.

The 1925 Forster Cup

The three heats of the 1925 Forster Cup were held on the River Derwent in early to mid-February 1925. Just a few weeks prior to the event's staging, Skipper Batt was honourably selected to be helmsman of the *Tassie* and given free rein to select his own crew from members of any recognised yacht club in Tasmania. His crew, consisting of younger brother Harry, along with Frank Harris, George Makepeace, E. Cohen and Sammy Salter, was named in late January.

With 11 boats competing from around Australia, the *Tassie* was considered untried and unknown, somewhat the Cinderella of the field. However, with Skipper Batt at the helm, remarkably the vessel went on to win all three heats and thus take out the much coveted prize, a significant and historical achievement for Tasmanian yachting.

Crew of *Tassie* that won the 1925 Forster Cup.
Left to Right: George Makepeace, E. Cohen, Harry Batt, Skipper Batt, Sammy Salter and Frank Harris.
Courtesy *Illustrated Tasmanian Mail*, 11 February 1925.

A Busy Period

The months following the 1925 Forster Cup were busy ones for Skipper Batt. In addition to his employment as a cooper, he travelled to Perth, Western Australia, at the request of Sir Waldie Griffiths, owner of the 21 ft restricted class yacht *The Fan*, to provide advice on how to make the vessel more competitive, also taking a set of sails with him made by R. R. Rex and Son. In October 1925 Skipper Batt sent a model and sail plan to W. Howson of Perth for an 18 ft skiff; Howson had sailed *The Fan* in the Forster Cup. Skipper and his brother Harry also converted *Weene* to Marconi rig and installed a new 51 ft mast. In addition, Skipper Batt designed another 21 ft restricted class vessel for a Hobart-based syndicate with the intention of building it the following year. The 12 ft cadet dinghy *Rangare*, built by Skipper Batt at Battery Point to the order of G. A. Robertson for his son Archie, was also launched in late 1925.

The 1926 Forster Cup

Owing to *Tassie*'s success at the 1925 Forster Cup, a public subscription was established to send Skipper Batt and crew to Perth in early 1926 to defend their title. Considering the location, the costs associated with fares, lodging and transportation were substantial, estimated to be around £450, i.e., £150 more than the cost of building and equipping *Tassie* the previous year. Still funds were raised with Skipper Batt and crew, comprising Harry Batt, Sammy Salter, George Makepeace, E. Cohen and new recruit G. Flynn, and their vessel, travelling to Perth in mid-January 1926.

Though not considered the favourite, in a repeat performance *Tassie* won all three heats of the race series in Perth to once again be awarded the Forster Cup. The triumph negated any notion that *Tassie*'s win in Hobart the previous year was based purely on home port advantage. Instead Skipper Batt's supreme helmsmanship and the combined efforts of his crew were duly noted in the press.

Upon immediately arriving back in Hobart, Skipper Batt and crew were transported to the Hobart Town Hall along a route flanked by cheering members of the public. A rousing welcome reception hosted by the Lord Mayor, F. D. Valentine, followed.

Subsequent Forster Cups

The 1927 Forster Cup was held in Adelaide, South Australia. The *Tassie*'s crew remained much the same as in previous years. Skipper Batt, acting as helmsman, was ably assisted by Harry Batt, George Makepeace, Sammy Salter, E. Cohen and newcomer Claude Cooper. Given a tune-up and a new mast *Tassie* continued her phenomenal success at the event, winning the first two heats and thus retaining the Forster Cup for the third consecutive year. Upon arriving back in Hobart, the team was once again greeted by a large crowd of supporters gathered at the Hobart Town Hall.

Considering Tasmania's resounding success at the national event, in preparation for the 1928 Forster Cup, to be held in Sydney, New South Wales, the Royal Yacht Club of Tasmania unanimously agreed that two boats should be sent to represent the state. A new boat designed by Skipper Batt with the assistance of Alfred Blore and John W. Tarleton, and built by Charlie Lucas and Chips Gronfors at Battery Point, was launched on 27 November 1927. Built by public subscription, the new vessel was similar in design to *Tassie* and named *Tassie Too*.

Opting to helm the older *Tassie*, Skipper Batt relinquished helmsmanship of *Tassie Too* to his brother Harry. The crew of *Tassie* comprised Sammy Salter, E. Cohen, George Makepeace, J. Boyes and Claude Cooper. The crew of *Tassie Too* comprised R. Cowle, Frank Harris, C. D. Knight, A. K. Ward and G. Flynn. It was a Batt family trifecta with Harry's son Neall also selected to represent Tasmania in Sydney, competing for the Stonehaven Cup in the cadet dinghy *Gumnut*.

In a series of dramatic races, *Tassie* won the first heat of the 1928 Forster Cup, while *Tassie Too* finished second. The second heat saw the tables turned with *Tassie Too* finishing first, while *Tassie* was forced to retire owing to an issue with the vessel's bowsprit. The third and final heat resulted in *Tassie Too* finishing first and thus being awarded the title. *Tassie* finished second both in the third heat and overall. Success continued for Harry Batt with his son Neall winning the Stonehaven Cup in just two heats at the helm of *Gumnut*. Again a celebratory crowd greeted all three teams upon their arrival back in Hobart with a reception at the Town Hall immediately following.

The 1929 Forster Cup was held in Brisbane, Queensland. The crew of *Tassie* was much the same as with the previous year: Skipper Batt assisted by E. Cohen, Sammy Salter, George Makepeace, J. Boyes and Claude Cooper. *Tassie Too*, helmed by Harry Batt, had somewhat of a new crew comprising H. L. Whitehouse, E. Doolan, A. M. Stuart, G. Flynn and C. D. Knight. The two crews chaperoned three cadet dinghy teams to Brisbane to compete for the Stonehaven Cup: *Gumnut*, helmed by Neall Batt, defending his title; *Aussie*, helmed by J. Taylor; and *Thistle*, helmed by W. Forsyth.

Despite a lacklustre first heat, the second heat of the 1929 Forster Cup saw *Tassie* finish first with *Tassie Too* disqualified. The third and final heat saw *Tassie* again victorious, thereby creating history for Tasmania in claiming its fifth Forster Cup in consecutive years, and the vessel's fourth overall. *Tassie Too* finished a respectable third.

With a need to defend their five year reign against newer, more competitive boats being built by other states, the Royal Yacht Club of Tasmania resolved in October 1929 to commission a new boat in time for the 1930 Forster Cup to be held in Melbourne. Based on a model developed by Skipper Batt and put to paper by P. C. Douglas, *Tassie III* was launched on 21 December 1929, built by Charlie Lucas at Battery Point. Disappointingly, neither *Tassie*, *Tassie Too* or *Tassie III* proved victorious at the 1930 Forster Cup.

Top: *Tassie III* and crew on the Derwent.
Bottom (left): Polishing *Tassie Too*.
Bottom (right): Lifting the centreboard out of *Tassie Too*.
Courtesy *Illustrated Tasmanian Mail*, 5 February 1930.

Left to Right: *Tassie, Tassie III* and *Tassie Too* on the Derwent.
Courtesy *Illustrated Tasmanian Mail*, 5 February 1930.

Between 1931 and 1938 Skipper Batt and his brother Harry continued their participation in the annual Forster Cup with great success. Held in Hobart, the 1931 event resulted in *Tassie III* (helmed by Harry Batt) winning the cup, with *Tassie* (helmed by Skipper Batt) finishing second. Tasmania did not participate in the 1932 Forster Cup owing to the substantial cost associated with sending boats and crews to the host state of Western Australia.

The 1933 Forster Cup was held in Adelaide. The Royal Yacht Club of Tasmania sent one boat, *Tassie III,* helmed by Skipper Batt with a crew of George Makepeace, J. Boyes, H. L. Whitehouse, A. M. Stuart and G. Brown. Under intense competition the team had to settle for a minor place.

Two boats were sent to the 1934 Forster Cup, held in Sydney; *Tassie Too,* helmed by Skipper Batt, and *Tassie III,* helmed by Harry Batt. The former won the event, returning the Forster Cup to Tasmania. *Tassie III* finished equal third.

The 1935 Forster Cup, held in Melbourne, saw the Batt brothers helming the same two boats. The event was won by the Queensland boat *Gwylan*. Yet Skipper Batt at the helm of *Tassie Too* won the 1936 Forster Cup held in Brisbane. Following the race series, he announced his retirement from interstate sailing. His younger brother Harry continued racing in the event, winning the 1937 Forster Cup in Adelaide at the helm of *Tassie Too*.

With the 1938 Forster Cup held in Hobart, Skipper Batt came out of retirement to once again helm *Tassie Too*, with Harry Batt at the helm of *Tassie III*. It was a triumph for the Tasmanian contingent and the Batt family with Harry and crew finishing first and Skipper and crew finishing second. The event proved to be the last Forster Cup both brothers would participate in.

By now Skipper Batt was 57 years of age. Amazingly he had amassed a total of six Forster Cup titles in his 14-year involvement with the event. During the same period his brother Harry had won the event four times. Combined the Batt brothers had sailed into Australian yachting history and were instrumental in advancing Tasmania's sailing reputation at the national level. Their achievements, together with their roles in club administration, culminated in both Skipper and Harry Batt receiving life memberships of the Royal Yacht Club of Tasmania in 1926 and 1938, respectively.

Boat Designs and Builds

Somehow, in addition to his professional responsibilities, his participation in the Forster Cup and sailing activities, Skipper Batt found time to design and/or build several boats throughout the late 1920s and into the early 1930s. Of note is a design for a 20 ft waterline/26 ft overall one-design class yacht with Marconi rig and a bulb fin that was to be considered intermediary to the cadet dinghy and the larger class yachts. Disappointingly, the design proposed by Skipper Batt in March 1927 was not adopted owing to the introduction of E. H. Webster's Derwent class. However, one vessel was built to the design: *Anitra*, built by Charlie Lucas at Battery Point to the order of Rowley Vautin and launched on 2 November 1929.

Above: *Anitra.*
Next Page: Skipper Batt's one-design class plan.
Courtesy Harry Hale.

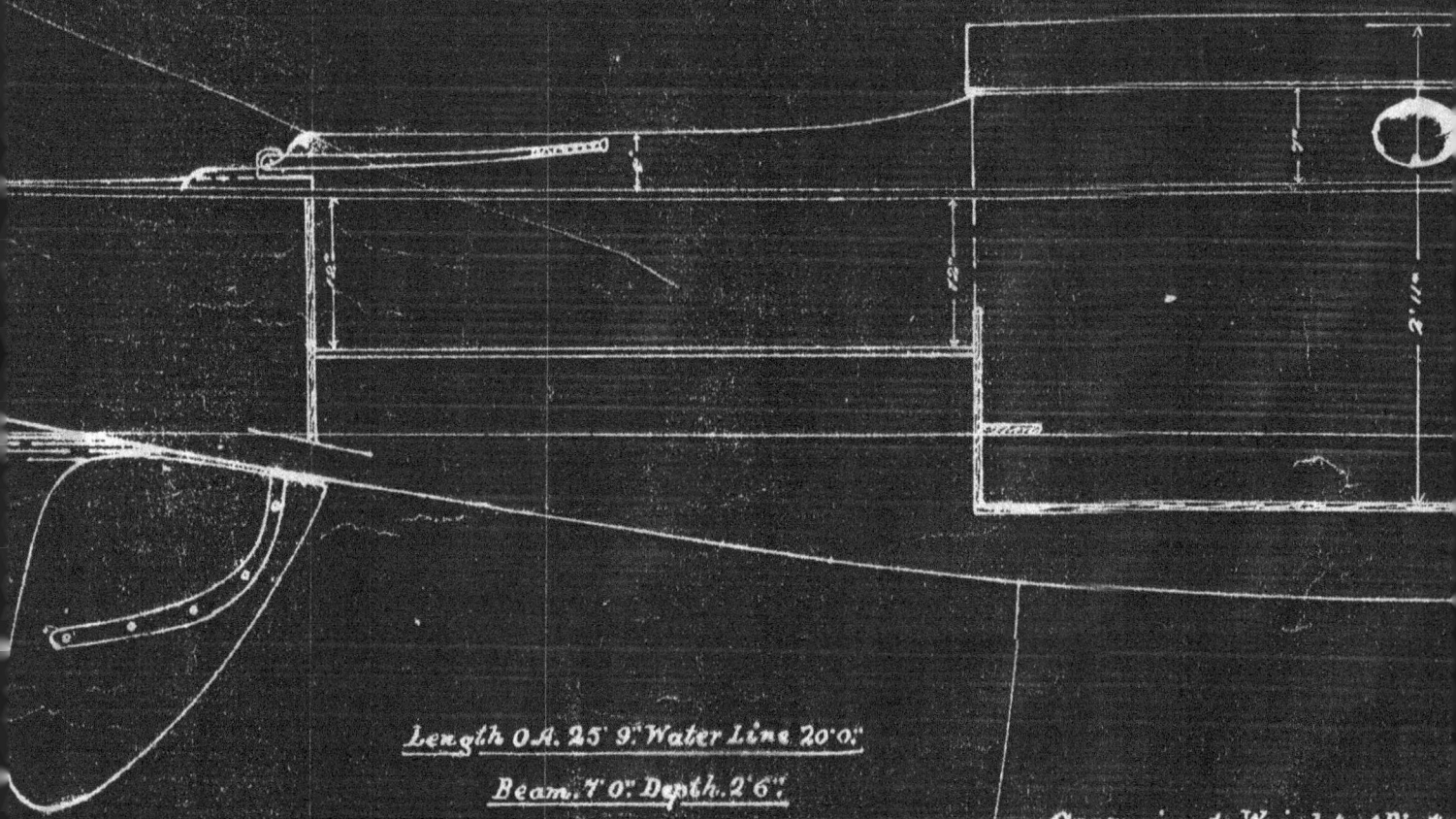

Length O.A. 25' 9". Water Line 20'0".

Beam. 7' 0". Depth. 2' 6".

Draft. 4' 6".

Approximate Weight of Plate

1200 lbs.

Scale 1" = 1 foot.

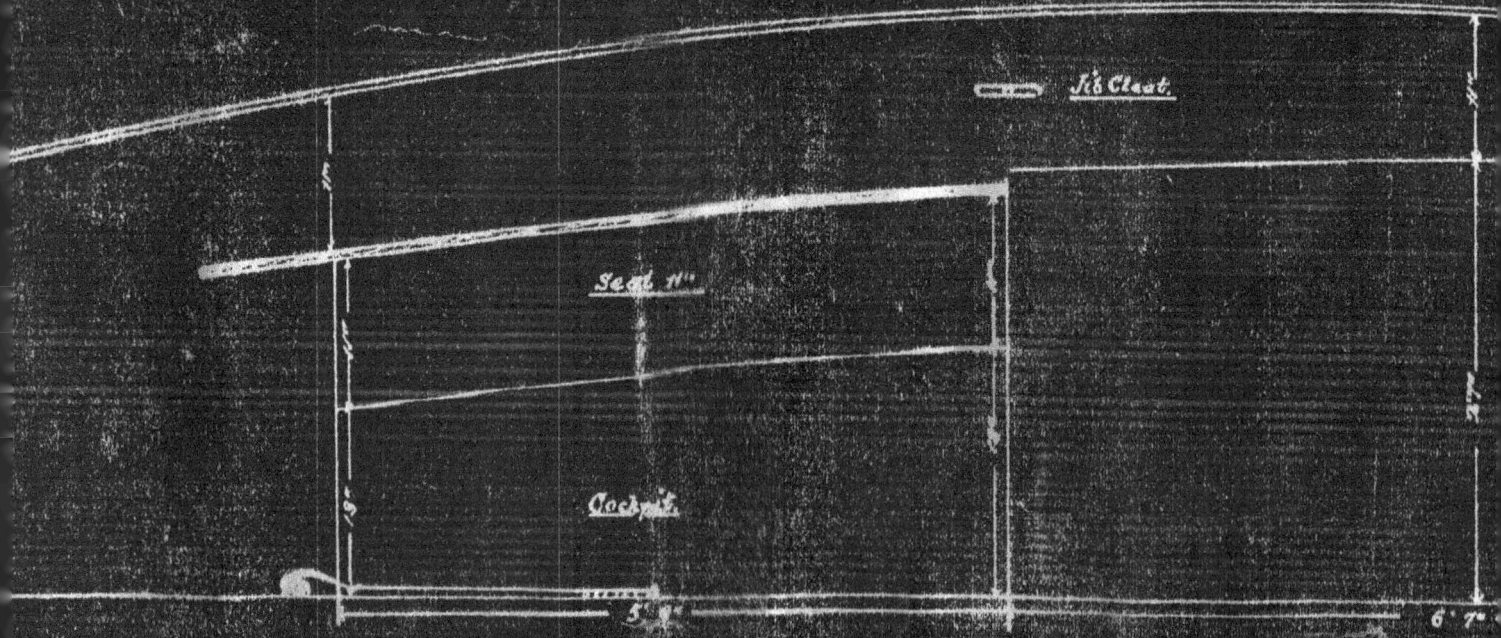

Jib Cleat.

Seat 1"

Cockpit

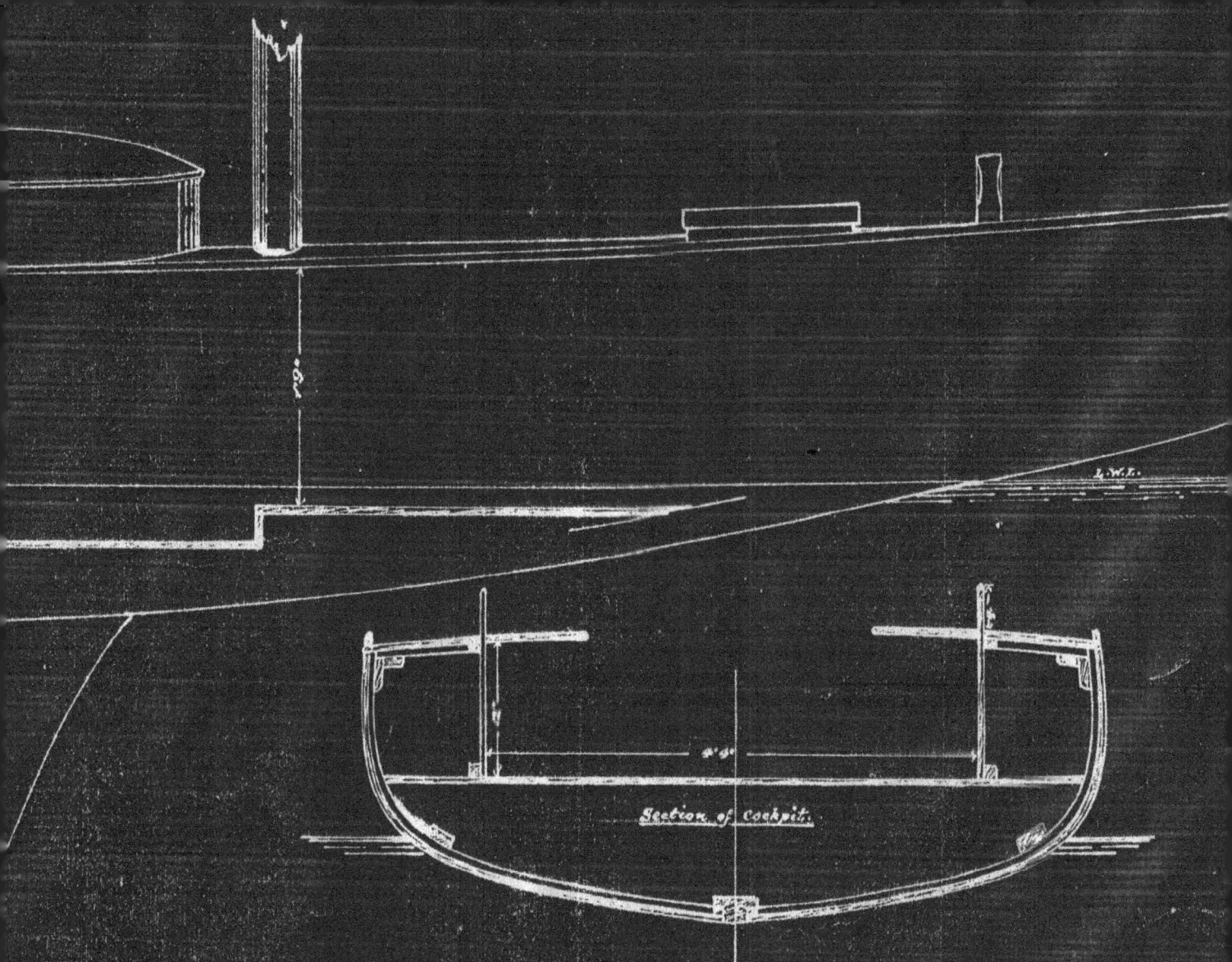

Section of Cockpit.

Outline Plan One D

Designed

—W.P.Ba

—1927

Fore Hatch

16"

L.W.L.

In late 1928 Skipper Batt designed a 16 ft skiff, *The Bat,* to the order of R. E. Senior. The vessel was one of several skiffs to participate in the Cornelian Bay Sailing Squadron's newly-established 16 ft class the following year. Two more 16 ft skiffs were designed by Skipper Batt, the *Meteor* and *Miss Diamond.* Another 16 ft skiff, *Gumnut II,* was designed and built at Battery Point by Skipper Batt for his nephew Neall and launched in late 1930. Skipper also designed and built the 16 ft skiff *Wee Davie.* By this time the 16 ft skiff class was competing with the Derwent Sailing Squadron. Also launched around the same period was *Kittiwake,* a cadet dinghy Skipper Batt built to the order of Ernie Muir for his son Jock at a cost of £40.

The dinghy *Toute Suite* was built by Skipper Batt in 1939 for his daughter Ray. The vessel is now part of the Maritime Museum of Tasmania's collection. Several boats were also built by Jack Hansen during the late 1930s at the Batt family's Battery Point slip, including the 19.6 ft heavyweight sharpie *Noddy,* built to the order of Neall Batt and launched in 1937, and the cadet dinghy *Gumnut III,* built to the order of Ken Batt and first noted in October 1939.

Crew of the 16 ft skiff *Gumnut II* that won the 1931 Ajax Cup.
Right to Left: Neall Batt, Harry Batt, Norman Skeels, Reg Gorringe and G. Cohen.
Courtesy *Illustrated Tasmanian Mail*, 7 January 1931.

Later Years and Legacy

Following his retirement from competitive sailing, Skipper Batt spent his later years continuing to encourage younger generations of his family and others in the sport. His daughter Ray and niece Betty Batt were two of the Derwent's first all-female crew when they sailed the Derwent class yacht *Wendy* during World War II. Skipper's nephews Neall and Ken Batt became distinguished helmsmen in their own right, initially excelling in the cadet dinghy class and later notably competing in the inaugural Sydney to Hobart Yacht Race on board Percy Coverdale's *Winston Churchill* in 1945. Moreover, Neall Batt successfully helmed the 20-year old boat *Tassie Too* to victory in the 1947 Forster Cup, held in Melbourne. Neall also skippered the boat to victory in the 1948, 1949, 1950 and 1952 Forster Cup races. Successive generations of the Batt family continued to enjoy sailing on board the one-design class yacht *Weene* up until it was sold in the 1960s.

Skipper Batt died suddenly of a heart attack on 7 April 1947 while in the process of building a dinghy at his Battery Point home, 54 Napoleon Street. He was 68 years of age. Skipper was survived by his wife Myrtle and daughter Ray. His younger brother Harry died later that year, on 4 December, at his home, 62 Napoleon Street, Battery Point. He was 62 years of age. Harry was survived by his wife Emily and five children: Neall, Ken, Lois, June and Betty.

To this day the Batt brothers' legacy continues, not only in their historic performances in the national Forster Cup events but also in the boats Skipper designed and/or built that are still in existence. These include the yacht *Anitra*, the dinghy *Tout Suite* and the cadet dinghy *Gumnut III*. Several model boats also remain in existence. The Batt brothers' legacy also continues in the generations of sailors they encouraged in the sport.

Weene at Battery Point.
Courtesy *Weekly Courier*, 13 October 1921.

Vessels Built by Skipper Batt and Others at Battery Point (1898 – 1937).

1903. *Trucanini.* **Dinghy.** 15 x 6 ft x 20 in. Designed and built by Skipper Batt for his own use. First noted on the Derwent in November 1903 when competing in Derwent Dinghy Sailing Club events. Remained active in club events for several seasons.

1903. *Kitty.* **Dinghy.** 15 x 6 ft x 20 in. Built by Skipper Batt. First noted on the Derwent in November 1903 when competing in Derwent Dinghy Sailing Club events. Built to the order of A. Bingham, based on a British design that appeared in *Rudder* magazine in August 1902. Active in dinghy sailing events until at least 1905.

1904. *Lallah Rookh.* **Dinghy.** 15 x 6 ft x 20 in. Racing dinghy designed and built by Skipper Batt for his own use. First noted on the Derwent in January 1904. Successfully raced for several seasons. By 1907 sailed by G. Watt and J. Elliott. By 1908 owned by Messrs Blades and Bowman. By 1912 owned by A. Wise. By 1919 owned by Edward Rayner of Rosetta and used as a pleasure boat. Capsized on the Derwent in March 1919 resulting in the death of Albert King.

1904. *Lahloo.* **Dinghy.** 15 x 6 ft x 20 in. First noted in November 1904, built by Skipper Batt for his younger brother Harry. Sailed successfully for several years. By 1912 owned by T. Forsyth. By 1919 owned by A. M. Stuart. By 1922 transferred to the Huon and owned by A. J. Allen, sailing with the Franklin Sailing Club. Advertised for sale in January 1924. Purchased by Angus Cumming of Hobart. For sale again in June 1924 and May 1927. By 1929 owned by Thomas Grubb and competing in C class sailing events. Last noted when advertised for sale in March 1930.

1906. *Lalla Berri.* **Dinghy.** 15 x 6 ft x 20 in. Built by Skipper Batt for his own use and launched in November 1906. Sailed successfully for several years. By 1911 owned by R. S. Mills. Advertised for sale in September 1912, though remained in Mills' hands for several more years. By 1922 transferred to the Huon and owned by R. G. Kellaway, competing with the Franklin Sailing Club. By 1923 owned by R. P. Barnett. By the mid-1930s sailing with the Cairns Bay Yacht Club. Last noted down the Huon in 1937, sailed by D. Jarrett.

1907. *Tasma.* **Dinghy.** 14 ft. Racing dinghy built by Skipper Batt to the order of A. T. Creek of Melbourne, VIC, and completed in October 1907. Actively raced with the St Kilda Dinghy Club in 1908 before being ruled ineligible for the class. After over decade spent as a recreational vessel, used primarily for fishing, returned to competitive racing with the St Kilda Dinghy Club in November 1922, owned by L. Walters.

1925. *Rangare.* **Cadet dinghy.** 12 x 5 ft x 14 in. Built by Skipper Batt to the order of G. A. Robertson. First noted on the Derwent in October 1925, helmed by Archie Robertson. Represented TAS and won the 1927 Stonehaven Cup held in Hobart, helmed by Archie Robertson. For sale in September 1928. By 1931 owned by H. J. Whelan. For sale in July 1932. By 1933 owned by G. D. Gibson and won the 1934 Stonehaven Cup held in Sydney. Between late 1934 and 1937 owned by C. Nicholas. For sale in January 1942. Owned by E. A. Parkes until 1946; between 1947 and 1950 owned by Ian Doolan.

1930. *Wee Davie.* **Skiff.** 16 ft. Designed and built by Skipper Batt to the order of Jack Bennison and launched in early 1930. Sailed successfully on the Derwent for several years. In 1937 transferred to Devonport, TAS, competing with the Mersey Yacht Club, owned by R. H. Hill.

1930. *Kittiwake (Blue Lake)*. Cadet dinghy. 12 x 5 ft x 14 in. Built by Skipper Batt to the order of Ernie Muir and launched in late 1930. Represented TAS at the 1931 Stonehaven Cup held in Hobart, helmed by Jock Muir. Won the 1933 Stonehaven Cup held in Adelaide, helmed by Jock Muir. Represented TAS in the 1934 Stonehaven Cup held in Sydney, helmed by Max Muir. Won the 1935 Stonehaven Cup held in Melbourne, helmed by Max Muir. Sold to Ediss Boyes. Represented TAS in the 1936 Stonehaven Cup held in Brisbane, helmed by Ediss Boyes. Represented TAS in the 1937 Stonehaven Cup held in Adelaide. Won the 1938 Stonehaven Cup held in Hobart, helmed by Ediss Boyes. Represented TAS in the 1939 Stonehaven Cup held in Brisbane, helmed by G. Boyes. For sale in April 1940. By 1943 owned by Ken Johnston. By 1947 owned by L. Turner. Represented TAS in the 1948 Stonehaven Cup held in Hobart, helmed by L. Turner. Represented TAS in the 1949 Stonehaven Cup held in Adelaide. Advertised for sale in March 1949. By 1950 owned by B. Wilson. Possibly sold to the Royal St Kilda Yacht Club, VIC, and renamed *Blue Lake*.

1930. *Gumnut II*. Skiff. 16 ft. Designed and built by Skipper Batt for his nephew Neall and launched in late 1930. Won the 1931 Ajax Cup, held in Hobart. Sailed by Neall Batt for several years. In 1937 transferred to Devonport, TAS, sailing with the Mersey Yacht Club, owned by Will Henry.

1937. *Noddy*. Heavyweight Sharpie. 19.6 ft. Built by Jack Hansen in Skipper Batt's Battery Point shed. Built to the order of Harry Batt for his son Neall. Finished second at the 1938 Australian Sharpie Championship held in Hobart. By 1945 owned by C. Nicholas and returned to local racing after a six year absence. Competed at the 1947 Australian Sharpie Championship held in Melbourne, helmed by C. Nicholas. Advertised for sale in June 1950 and again in October of that year. In January 1951 noted to be a member of the newly-formed Cygnet 12 Square Metre Club, sailed by K. Wilson.

1939. *Toute Suite*. Dinghy. Built by Skipper Batt for his daughter Ray who retained possession until 2007. Still in existence; now part of the Maritime Museum of Tasmania's collection.

1939. *Gumnut III*. Cadet dinghy. 12 x 5 ft x 14 in. Built by Jack Hansen in Skipper Batt's shed with the assistance of Neall Batt and first noted on the Derwent in October 1939. Built to the order of Ken Batt. By 1947 owned by R. P. Iken. Won the 1948 Stonehaven Cup held in Hobart, helmed by R. P. Iken. Represented TAS in the 1950 Stonehaven Cup, helmed by owner D. Gumley. Represented TAS in the 1952 Stonehaven Cup, held in Hobart. Purchased by Max Creese for his son Peter in March 1954. By 1958 owned by D. Palfreyman, by 1962 owned by D. Clark. Still in existence; currently owned by the Knoop family.

1950s. *Temeraire*. Dinghy. International cadet dinghy built by Neall Batt at 62 Napoleon Street, Battery Point, for his daughter Helen.

1965. *Lahloo*. Yacht. 30 ft. Diamond class yacht built by Neall and Rae Batt at 62 Napoleon Street, Battery Point. Represented TAS in several national championships during the 1970s, including winning the 1974 Australian Championship, held in Hobart, skippered by Rae Batt with a crew of Jeff Corkhill, David Makepeace and John Gard.

The Batt family on board *Tassie*.
Courtesy Tasmanian Archive and Heritage Office.

...NTIAL FORSTER CUP winners of the future receive valuable training in the finer points of sailing when they race model yachts off ...y Point during Winter week-ends. The sport calls for a high degree of skill and considerable physical exertion. The picture shows ...up of models, with the "helmsmen" attending their charges from rowing-boats. The picture was taken shortly after the start of the "A" Class race last week-end.

THE MERCURY, THURSDAY, JULY 29, 1937.

MODEL YACHT RACING

Not Child's Play, But a Virile and Strenuous Sport

TO the uninitiated, model yacht racing would appear a childish pastime, unworthy of the attention of skilled, full-grown sailing enthusiasts, but a visit to Battery Point during Winter week-ends would remove any misapprehension of that nature. Competent yachtsmen, several of whom have won their spurs in club, regatta, and inter-State racing, derive a lot of fun and exercise from racing models, and any of them will vouch for the fact that the sport is more strenuous than sailing in real yachts.

No small degree of skill and knowledge is called for in the construction and rigging of the models, which are restricted to an overall measurement of 50in. Actually, the models are not built in proportion to full-size yachts, as if they were they would be much too slow. Thus a model with an overall length of 50in. may have a mast nearly 9ft. high—much higher by proportion than in a racing yacht, and the beam may be as much as 11 or 12 inches—also greater by comparison. The hulls are mostly composite—built of light pine planking or plywood, with a light wooden framework. Varying designs are used, but the most popular section for the hull has a V-bottom with square chines.

The rigging is arranged to give maximum strength with minimum weight, and only the best materials are used. Marconi-type mainsails are popular, and as a rule only one headsail is fitted, with a big spinnaker for running free. An ingenious device is used to prevent the models from "flattening" over too much when a hard puff of wind strikes them. Elastic string is used for the headsail sheets and when a hard puff arrives the sheet stretches, causing the boat to "luff" and spill the wind out of the mainsail.

Two classes are raced regularly at Battery Point during the "off season" for big yachts. There are about 14 models in the two classes, and handicaps are allotted according to the speed of the boats and the capabilities of the "helmsmen." The windward-and-return course is from the starting-point at Coverdale's slipyard, Battery Point, to a buoy off Rocky Point, and back, three times round for "A" Class and twice round for "B" Class. The respective distances covered are two and three miles.

"Helmsmen" follow their charges in rowing-boats, and a good deal of dexterity is required in holding pace with the speedy little craft and keeping their sails trimmed. That there is seldom any confusion at the starting-line and when rounding buoys is evidence of the skill which the model yachtsmen have acquired in their sport. With a fresh breeze blowing and running sail set, the skipper has his work cut out to keep up with his model, and races have been lost through models getting away in this manner. At the end of a hard race competitors are often almost exhausted physically and very glad of a respite.

Good Training Medium

More than one of Hobart's prominent racing helmsmen learned the fundamentals of sailing tactics with the models. "Skipper" Batt and his brother Harry, who have done so much to blazon Tasmania's name on the Australian scroll of yachting fame, regard model yacht racing as a most valuable training medium for young helmsmen, and are always willing to help boys and young men participating in the sport, which is clean, health-promoting and vigorous. The Royal Yacht Club of Tasmania, realising its importance with a view to the evolution of future yachtsmen and the introduction of new blood to the sport, gives the models its official sanction, and presents trophies for competition. Recently a "prize night" for model owners was held at the club rooms, when trophies were distributed and successful helmsmen were congratulated by flag officers of the club.

FLOOD PROTECTION

Launceston City Council Scheme

Cabinet Consideration

Cabinet yesterday discussed the proposal of the Launceston City Council that the main embankment of the flood protection scheme should run through Ogilvie Park at Invermay. The Minister for Lands and Works (Major T. H. Davies) stated it had been decided that the Director of Public Works should confer with the Launceston City Engineer and discuss the position following the conference Cabinet would again consider the proposal.

The Minister added that the Government was pleased that the Launceston City Council had decided to make a move in regard to a flood protection scheme as it was considered a most necessary work.

Hospital Patients

Richard Milsom (24), of Shannon, who was admitted to the Hobart General Hospital on Saturday following an accident at Cambridge when a pea-rifle bullet entered his abdomen, has improved slightly, though his condition late last night was still regarded as serious.

Clyde Proposch (22), of Charles st., Moonah, who was admitted to the hospital last Wednesday with gunshot wounds, has improved, and his condition is satisfactory.

...ealth Scheme ...ocated

...wment was the most ...question in Aus-...tention of Mr. G. W. ..., in an address to ...Denison branch of the ...of the Australian ...the Hobart Trades

...resided.
...raced the history of ...New South Wales, a ...e said, a Labour Go-...ot faced with inter-... He regarded it as ...Commonwealth to ...tter, and he pledged ...i. to assist in evolv-...ble scheme for the ...ian mothers.
...aid child endowment ...portant social ques-...a, and he felt there ...would be more justi-...nd scheme of child ...ghout the Common-...d-being of the nation ...quality of its citizens. ...safety depended on ...virility of the popu-...so, much on arma-...highly essential that ...have a population of ...finest quality, and in ...ould such a popula-...than by increasing ...from their earliest ...e the national spirit. ...Australians prided ...e physique of their ...felt that the lack of ...meant that the child-...ing a fair opportunity ...the struggle of life ...before him the great ...ed by members of ...hose parents were on

...furnished financial ...hat additional taxa-...nvolved and, against ...information how in-...afely bear the re-...hild endowment.

...Cricketers

LONDON, July 28. ...r Surrey, the Austra-...keters scored 120 for ...elmes 55). The Aus-...accorded a civic re-...match created a re-...of interest. It was ...were 5,000 spectators.

...SMISSED

...ton Action

Purdon and Featherstone

Henry Featherstone and his neighbour Tom Purdon established their Battery Point shipbuilding firm in 1903, the former having spent several decades at the site working with his mentor and uncle James Mackey, the latter a second generation master mariner and self-taught boat designer and builder. Between 1905 and Tom Purdon's retirement in 1919 the pair built at least 21 vessels, including eight steamers and eight ketches. Many of these vessels played pivotal roles in local and regional passenger, timber and fishing trades. Continuing to work at the yard under the Purdon and Featherstone name, Henry Featherstone went on to build many more vessels, passing the reins to his sons in the 1930s. Between 1967 and 1991 the business was owned and operated by John Bennetto and John Lucas. Today, as a division of Tasmanian Shipping Supplies, the name of Purdon and Featherstone remains synonymous with Hobart's maritime landscape and was particularly instrumental in Battery Point's ship and boat building history in the 20th century. Overall, between 1905 and 1972, more than 40 vessels were built by Purdon and Featherstone, of which a handful remain in existence.

Henry Featherstone

Henry Inkerman Featherstone was born on 26 July 1871 at Emerald Hill, Victoria, the fourth of six children born to Captain John Frederick and Elizabeth Featherstone (nee Mackey). Both the paternal and maternal sides of his family were involved with Hobart's maritime community. Henry's father was a well-known and much admired master mariner in the late 1860s and early 1870s. His uncles, William, Henry and Lucas Featherstone, were all sea-faring men. Another uncle, Charles Featherstone was for many years honorable secretary of the Hobart Regatta Association and also owned the Battery Point built *SS Enterprise* which he renamed *Silver Queen*.

Henry Featherstone's mother, Elizabeth Mackey, was the second youngest daughter of Battery Point shipwright David Mackey (Sr) and the sister of Battery Point shipbuilders David Mackey and James Mackey. The latter operated a shipyard at Battery Point for over 50 years, building many schooners, ketches, steamers, brigs and barques. Another uncle on the maternal side of Henry Featherstone's family was Captain James Pie who for many years was involved in intercolonial trade. It was only natural that Henry Featherstone would embark on a maritime-related career.

Henry Featherstone spent his infant years in Victoria where his father was master of the brig *Prospero*, and later *SS Edina*. On 9 December 1873 Captain John Featherstone died suddenly and unexpectedly on board the *SS Edina* while the vessel lie at anchor in Portland Bay, Victoria. Pregnant and widowed, Elizabeth Featherstone and her children, including two-year old Henry, returned to Hobart, staying with James Mackey and his family at their Mona Street residence in Battery Point.

With support from a fund established by Captain Featherstone's colleagues and friends, as well as the large Hobart-based Featherstone and Mackey clans, Elizabeth Featherstone and her five surviving sons were able to make ends meet. Henry Featherstone and his brothers attended the nearby Derwent School, noted for its distinctly maritime bias.

In August 1878 Elizabeth Featherstone and her sons returned to Victoria to live leaving seven-year old Henry in the care of his uncle James Mackey. A well-established shipbuilder of Battery Point, James Mackey was to have a profound impact on Henry Featherstone's life, fostering his future in shipbuilding from an early age.

In his early teens Henry Featherstone formally commenced work as his uncle's apprentice. In this role he was involved in the repair, overhaul and slipping of many of Tasmania's staunch and steadfast vessels, including the *SS Warrentinna* which James Mackey had built in 1883.

In the 1890s, with retirement imminent, James Mackey made his nephew Henry Featherstone a partner in the business. In June 1902, following completion of the 98 ft steam scow *Marie Corelli*, James Mackey formally announced his retirement and *The Mercury* advertised the dissolution of the Mackey and Featherstone joint enterprise.

With his uncle's departure from the Battery Point shipyard, Henry Featherstone immediately advertised a new partnership between himself and Patrick Joseph Christie. This joint venture, however, appears to have lasted only a year at most as by mid-1903 Henry had partnered with his neighbour Tom Purdon (both lived at Derwent Lane, Battery Point) to form the now famous Purdon and Featherstone alliance. The pair purchased James Mackey's shipyard located off Napoleon Street, Battery Point. The property had a capital value of £1,000.

TO SHIPOWNERS AND OTHERS.
———
MACKEY AND FEATHERSTONE
Having DISSOLVED PARTNERSHIP,
the Ship-Yard Business will in future
be carried on by
FEATHERSTONE AND CHRISTIE.
H. J. FEATHERSTONE.
P. J. CHRISTIE.

Courtesy *The Mercury*, 23 June 1902.

SS Warrentinna at James Mackey's Battery Point shipyard immediately prior to launch on 20 December 1883. Courtesy Tasmanian Archive and Heritage Office.

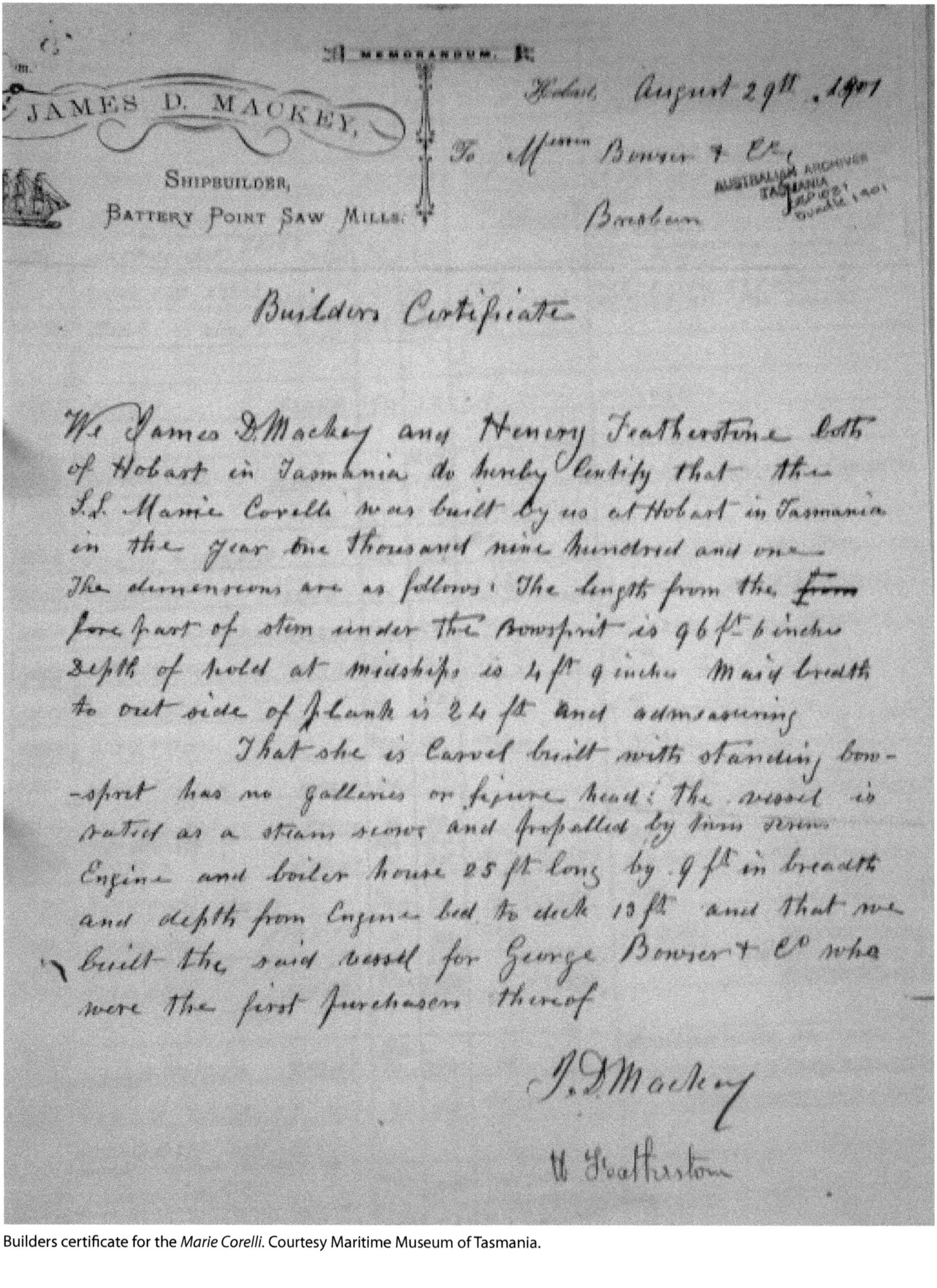

MEMORANDUM

JAMES D. MACKEY,
SHIPBUILDER,
BATTERY POINT SAW MILLS.

Hobart August 29th 1901

To Messrs Bowser & Co

Bristen

Builders Certificate

We James D. Mackey and Henery Featherstone both
of Hobart in Tasmania do hereby Certify that the
S.S. Marie Corelli was built by us at Hobart in Tasmania
in the year one thousand nine hundred and one
The dimensions are as follows: The length from the ~~from~~
fore part of stem under the bowsprit is 96 ft 6 inches
depth of hold at midships is 4 ft 9 inches Main breadth
to out side of plank is 24 ft and admeasuring

That she is carvel built with standing bow-
-sprit has no galleries or figure head; the vessel is
rated as a steam screw and propelled by twin screw
Engine and boiler house 25 ft long by 9 ft in breadth
and depth from Engine bed to deck 13 ft and that we
built the said vessel for George Bowser & Co who
were the first purchasers thereof

J. D. Mackey

H. Featherston

Builders certificate for the *Marie Corelli*. Courtesy Maritime Museum of Tasmania.

Thomas (Tom) Purdon

Over a decade older than Henry Featherstone, Thomas (Tom) Victor Purdon was born at Old Beach, Tasmania, on 19 May 1858, the first of ten children born to Samuel and Eliza Purdon (nee Cloak). Tom's father was a well-established farmer in the rural Old Beach community. Samuel Purdon also had an interest in maritime trade, likely motivated by a need to move hay, firewood and produce to Hobart from his property. Like many of his generation, a lack of formal training was no barrier to the building of vessels, with Samuel Purdon first noted as building the ketch *Eliza* in 1868 to ply in the developing local river trade.

The wreck of the *Eliza* in late April 1874 saw Samuel Purdon immediately build a replacement vessel, a 43 ft ketch, also named *Eliza*, launched in June of that same year. Built under the inquisitive eye of Tom Purdon, the *Eliza's* completion not only allowed Samuel Purdon to continue his involvement in the local river trade, but it also allowed Tom Purdon to continue his apprenticeship on board. Three years later, in 1877, Tom Purdon was noted as master of the *Eliza,* likely the result of Samuel Purdon taking command of the ketch *Phantom* (another vessel he built at Old Beach).

Like many of Hobart's youth with a penchant for maritime employment, Tom Purdon also began competing in local regatta races around this period. He is first mentioned in the local press as competing in a skiff race for youths under 18 years of age at the 1876 Hobart Town Regatta where he finished third in the *Ripple*.

Despite having no formal training, Tom Purdon clearly had natural ability and entrepreneurial determination. In December 1882, after several years spent at the helm of one or more of his father's trading vessels, Tom finished building his own vessel at Old Beach for employment in the local river trade. Built in his spare time over the course of two years, the 42 ft ketch *Mystery* marked Tom's first attempt at building a boat of any sort. Correspondingly, he was highly praised in the local press for his efforts. The positive public sentiment, for both Tom Purdon's workmanship and sailing ability, continued when the *Mystery* won the sailing race at the 1883 Hobart Regatta.

Throughout the mid to late 1880s Tom Purdon continued his success at the helm of *Mystery*, both commercially in the river trade and recreationally in sailing races. During this period Tom also began competing in local yacht races. For example, in January 1888 he won the handicap yacht race at the Hobart Regatta in the *Mayflower*.

The period also saw Tom Purdon tasked by his brother E. H. Purdon with designing a vessel for use in the river trade along the same lines as the *Mystery*. The *E. H. Purdon* was built by Robert Inches at Battery Point and launched on 24 December 1886. Tom would later note that during the vessel's construction he gained a tremendous amount of information from Robert Inches.

Sensing an increase in demand for larger vessels to be employed in the river trade, particularly for the movement of timber to Hobart from outer-lying ports and settlements, the late 1880s saw Tom Purdon begin building a larger ketch to replace the *Mystery*. In March 1888 he advertised the latter for sale and moved himself (and his family) to Old Beach where he could work full-time on construction of the new vessel. Measuring just over 59 ft on the keel, the *Surprise* first arrived in Hobart in August 1889 having taken 14 months to complete; Tom Purdon helped by only one labourer in the building of the vessel.

The *Surprise* was initially placed in the Tasman Peninsula to Hobart route, soon becoming a regular in the trade. As with the *Mystery*, Tom Purdon also raced the vessel in local regattas and sailing events. Her initial success (and the prize money at stake) led Tom to consider sailing the *Surprise* to Melbourne with the goal of competing in more lucrative sailing matches. Instead, however, he appears to have made a reconnaissance trip, sailing the vessel as far as the Bass Strait islands, where she discharged cargo before returning to Hobart via the east coast ports.

It was on the east coast route that Tom Purdon subsequently placed the *Surprise*, using her to convey cargo and passengers between Hobart and Swansea on a regular basis. Beginning in 1894, the *Surprise* also joined the Launceston to Hobart general cargo run. From 1896 Tom Purdon began making occasional trips to Strahan, on one such voyage conveying a cargo of timber and dynamite. Another trip saw him sail the *Surprise* from Macquarie Heads to Esperance in record time. The reputation of Tom Purdon's sailing ability, and his stalwart coastal trading ketch *Surprise*, thus became renowned throughout the many regional ports and settlements of Tasmania.

Though engaged as a master mariner, during the 1890s Tom Purdon was often called upon to design vessels. These include a yacht (28 ft LWL) built by Joseph Clinch at Battery Point in 1892; the ketch *Dart*, built by Marchant Brothers of the Huon and launched in March 1896; the three-masted schooner *Annie McDougall*, built at Recherche Bay by John Wilson of Cygnet to the order of McDougall Brothers; and the trading ketch *Swift*, built by Robert Inches at his Battery Point shipyard to the order of T. and J. Underwood and launched on 30 July 1900.

In April 1903, after more than 13 years sailing the *Surprise* between Hobart and various coastal ports, remarkably without serious incidence, Tom Purdon announced in the local press that he would begin using the vessel as a general store. His intention was to supply residents of the Huon and Channel districts with goods such as flour, bran, oats, peas, groceries, drapery, clothing and footwear and stationery. Operating under the name of "Surprise Trading Company," the business was in partnership with W. A. Johnson and J. T. Johnson.

Tom Purdon's exit from the east coast trade would prove fortuitous. The Dension Canal at Dunalley, completed in 1905, would see the ketch trade superseded by steamers. Though there were hints in the local press that Tom Purdon considered building a steamer to ply the east coast trade, he instead opted for a route change. However, the success of his Huon and Channel aquatic general store venture was short-lived.

Purdon and Featherstone: The Early Years

In August 1903 Tom Purdon sold the *Surprise* and together with his neighbour Henry Featherstone formed the shippbuilding firm of Purdon and Featherstone. Upon establishment of their Battery Point shipyard in mid-1903, Henry Featherstone and Tom Purdon spent the early months of their partnership involved in the repair, overhaul and refit of vessels, including the *SS Huon*, ketch *Good Intent*, steamers *Moonah* and *Ivy*, and schooner *Mariner*. The duo's big break came in July 1904 when they received an order from Whitehouse Brothers for a new steamer to ply between Hobart and New Norfolk. Though work was stalled by a lack of available timber, the 113 ft *Mongana*, designed by Tom Purdon and built at a cost of £6,000, was launched on 1 July 1905.

In the years following the *Mongana*'s launch, Purdon and Featherstone completed their first ketch, the *Myrtle May,* built to the order of G. Sward, as well as their first fishing boat, the *Pacific,* built to the order of Tom Spaulding.

Three more vessels, the ketches *Secret, Pengana* and *Opah*, were launched in 1907. The *Secret* was built for Tom Purdon's own use, while both the *Pengana* and *Opah* were built to the order of Risby Brothers on the scow principle and intended for the local timber trade. 1907 also saw Purdon and Featherstone launch the punt *Nell,* built to the order of Henry Purdon (Tom Purdon's brother) for use in transporting vehicles across the River Derwent at Risdon Ferry (now Lutana).

Mongana shortly after launch. Courtesy Maritime Museum of Tasmania.

Franklin Saw, Planin

Timber Yards: Franklin Wharf, Castr

RISBY

TIMBER M

ESTABLI

We are Ma

Farmyard

Sheep

Bullock Y'

Chu

Mantels, V

Joinery a

Mould

OPAH.

Weatherboard Cottages S

Three More Steamers

In late 1907 Purdon and Featherstone received an order from Whitehouse Brothers for a second steamer. This particular vessel, the *Marana*, was launched on 9 July 1908. Designed by Tom Purdon, the vessel was built to replace the *Mongana* in the New Norfolk passenger trade.

On 2 January 1909, six months following the launch of the *Marana*, Purdon and Featherstone completed the steamer *Rowitta* for Alfred Harrap and Sons of Launceston, and rebuilt the steamer *Taranna* after it had suffered extensive fire damage. Of similar design to the *Marana*, though slightly longer, the *Rowitta* was built for the Tamar River passenger service to replace Alfred Harrap and Sons' steamer *Niree* which had been destroyed by fire in January 1908. The *Rowitta* arrived in Launceston in early April 1909, her delivery voyage skippered by Tom Purdon.

Obviously satisfied customers, Risby Brothers placed an order for a third vessel, a steamer, with Purdon and Featherstone in mid-1908. This particular vessel, the *Wiena,* was launched in August 1909, built to convey cargo and a complement of 280 passengers in the local river and coastal trades.

Launch of the *Marana*. Courtesy *Tasmanian Mail*, 18 July 1908.

Launch of the *Rowitta,* including employees. Courtesy *Weekly Courier*, 14 January 1909.

More Popular Steamers and a Motor Boat

With a well-earned reputation, 1909 saw Purdon and Featherstone receive two more orders for steamers: one from Francis Calvert for use in the South Arm and Lewisham trade (to replace the recently wrecked *Seabird*) and one from the Huon, Channel and Peninsula Steamship Company. The former, named *Reemere*, was launched in October 1909. The latter, named *Awittaka*, was designed by Tom Purdon and launched in June 1910. She was 50 ft larger than the *Reemere* and capable of carrying up to 600 passengers. *Awittaka* was also the largest vessel built in Hobart for many decades.

In a diversion from the building of steam ferries, the *Rose,* a 26 ft motor boat, was built by Purdon and Featherstone and launched in 1910, intended for Tom Purdon's private use. The vessel was sequestered by the Hobart Marine Board in November 1912.

Awittaka at Battery Point. Courtesy Maritime Museum of Tasmania.

Onwards and Upwards

1911 saw Purdon and Featherstone expand and improve their Battery Point shipyard with the installation of a new slipway capable of accommodating vessels up to 130 ft in length, and the rebuilding of their jetty. During this period, and the ensuing years, the yard remained busy with the repair, refit, overhaul and survey of many vessels, particularly steamers.

Towards the end of 1911 Purdon and Featherstone launched the *Lunawanna,* a ketch built to the order of John Sward for employment in the river trade. The following year the pair launched their seventh steamer, the *Cartela*, on 21 September 1912. Designed by Tom Purdon, the vessel was built to the order of the Huon, Channel and Peninsula Company to replace the recently sold *Awittaka*. Still in existence, the *Cartela* has become a doyen of the Derwent, a regular in the local and regional passenger and excursion trade for more than a hundred years.

Launch of the *Cartela* on 21 September 1912. Courtesy Tasmanian Archive and Heritage Office.

Launch of the *Cartela* on 21 September 1912. Courtesy Tasmanian Archive and Heritage Office.

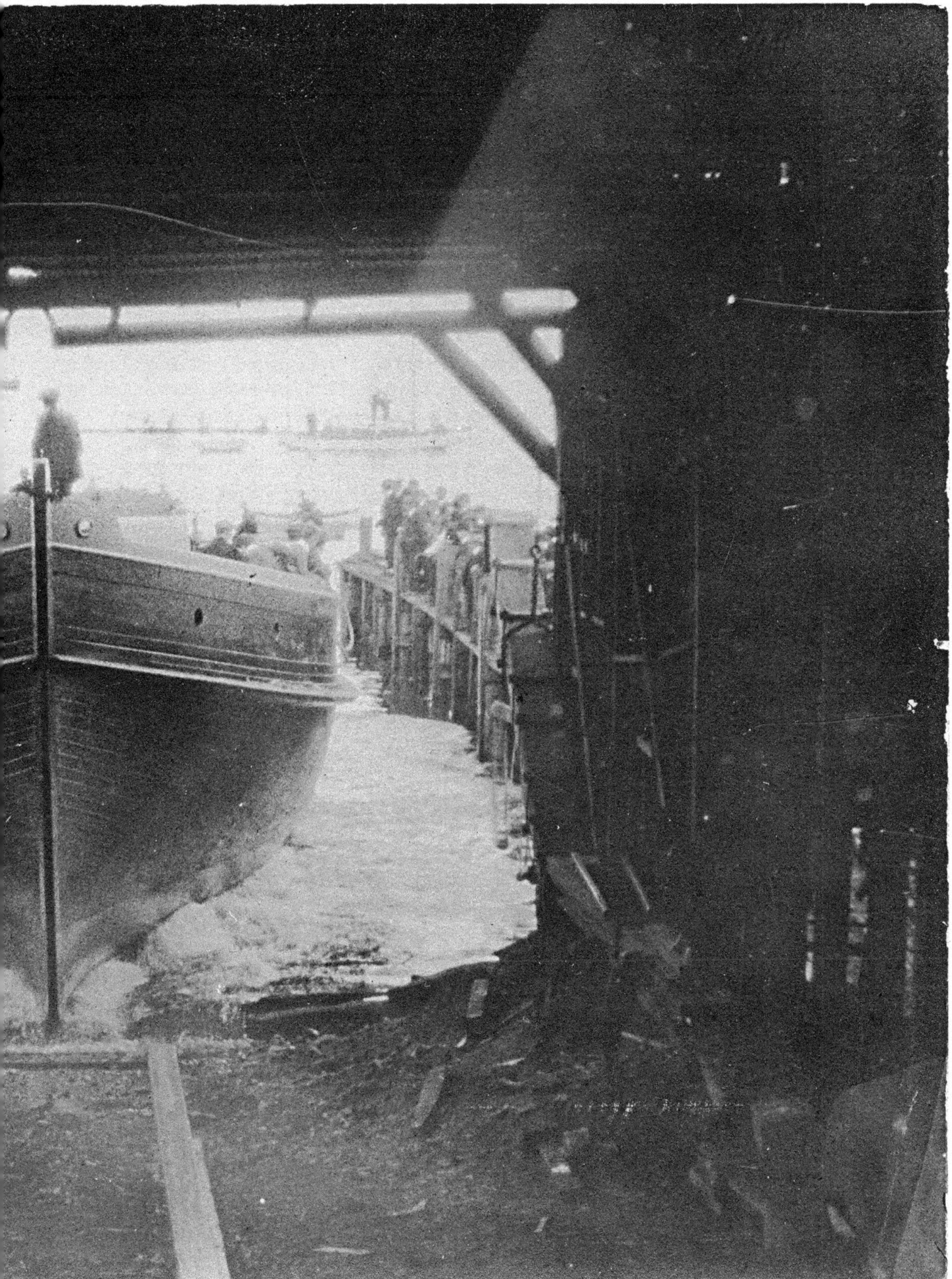

The Last Steamer

On 9 August 1913 Purdon and Featherstone launched the steamer *Maweena*, built to the order of Whitehouse Brothers. The vessel not only marked the eighth steamer they had launched in eight years but she was also significantly the last steamer they built. In addition to the *Maweena*, 1913 saw the launch of the motor boat *Talune*. The vessel was built for J. G. Turner, chairman of the Hobart Regatta Association.

Quiet Years

The years 1914 through to 1917, coinciding with World War I, were generally quiet for Purdon and Featherstone in terms of new builds, with only a few boats constructed, including the motor boat *Tawa* and the ketches *Taynna* and *Myrtle Burgess*. Still, the shipyard was busy with major repair work carried out on the steamer *Huon* following a disastrous accident in the D'Entrecasteaux Channel in 1914, and the steamer *Derwent* following extensive fire damage in 1915. Significant repairs were also made to the ketch *Caroline May* following six months spent underwater off Bruny Island. These projects were augmented by overhaul, maintenance, and survey work.

Launch of the *Maweena*. Courtesy *Tasmanian Mail*, 14 August 1913.

Tawa at the Hobart wharf. Courtesy Tasmanian Archive and Heritage Office.

1. Group of workmen at the shipbuilding yards where the ketch Myrtle Burgess was lau
Myrtle Burgess. 4. Miss Ros

Courtesy *Tasmanian Mail*, 18 October 1917.

ek. 2. Some of the principals. 3. The newly launched de ep-sea fishing ketch
o christened the ketch. "Mail" photo.

Taking a Gamble

Sensing increased demand for new vessels and likely to keep their workers busy, in July 1917 Purdon and Featherstone began building a three-masted schooner on speculation. Part-way through construction, however, the firm was left with little capital to finance its completion. Buoyed by the Tasmanian government's recent support for the local ship building industry, Purdon and Featherstone approached the Premier for a £5,000 governmental loan.

During the many months the government took to respond, a buyer was fortunately found: Rosenfeld and Company of Sydney reportedly paying £12,000 for the vessel, without engines. The 256 ton schooner, named *Valmarie*, was subsequently launched on 4 December 1918 intended for the Australian coastal trade. She was designed by Tom Purdon with plans provided by Alfred Blore.

Launch of the *Valmarie*.
Courtesy Maritime Museum of Tasmania.

Tom Purdon's Semi-Retirement

In 1919, shortly following the launch of the *Valmarie*, Tom Purdon, by now in his early 60s, retired from Purdon and Featherstone, his share in the partnership purchased by Henry Jones and Company. Following, Tom worked in semi-retirement, undertaking survey work, as well as being called on to provide testimony at regular intervals. He also continued his association with Purdon and Featherstone for several more years, designing the schooner *Leprena* and the ketch *Terralinna*, both launched in 1922.

Beginning in 1924 Tom Purdon began advertising the sale of smaller boats from a Battery Point boatyard that he owned and which his oldest son, Tom (Jr), had been operating since 1915. The property had previously been owned by Jacob Chandler. It was here, between 1925 and 1934, that Tom Purdon built several new vessels, including a 16 ft lifeboat and a 10 ft dinghy, both advertised for sale in June 1925.

The 12 ft cadet dinghy *Gumnut* was launched on 20 November 1925, built by Tom Purdon to the order of a Miss Gagin, a lady admirer of the class. Helmed by Neall Batt, the boat won the 1928 Stonehaven Cup (held in Sydney). Another 12 ft cadet dinghy, *Aussie*, was built by Tom Purdon for James Taylor and launched in October 1927.

The following year, on 5 May 1928, the 49 ft yawl-rigged fishing boat *Corona* was launched from the Purdon family's Battery Point yard, built by Tom Purdon with assistance from his son Ernest. Designed by Tom Purdon, the *Corona* was built to the order of Martyn Brothers of Southport and intended for the west coast fishing trade.

Well into his 70s Tom Purdon continued to design vessels. For example, in late 1934 a ketch named *Margaret Twaites* that he designed was launched from Oakwood on the Tasman Peninsula. The 85 ft vessel was built by C. H. McKay to the order of C. Gathercole with the intention of carrying timber from Gathercole's mill to the mainland.

Tom Purdon died at the General Hospital, Hobart, on 16 May 1935, three days shy of his 77th birthday. Tom was survived by his wife Rosina, who died at Hobart on 7 June 1939, and their three sons: Tom (Jr), Ernest and Commodore.

Gumnut.
Courtesy Tasmanian Archive and Heritage Office.

Terralinna. Courtesy Tasmanian Archive and Heritage Office.

Purdon and Featherstone: A Busy Period

Following Tom Purdon's retirement in 1919 Henry Featherstone continued to operate under the Purdon and Featherstone name with the early to mid-1920s marking another busy period for the business. In March 1920 Purdon and Featherstone received an order from Henry Jones and Company for a schooner for employment in the timber trade. This request was likely the result of Tom Purdon's success at designing Henry Jones' schooner *Amelia J* which was built in 1919 by Henry Moore at a neighbouring Battery Point shipyard owned by Robert Kennedy and Sons.

Designed by Tom Purdon, the 115 ft *Leprena* was launched in April 1922. Less than six months later, on 23 September 1922, Purdon and Featherstone launched a ketch, the *Terralinna*, built to the order of John Sward for the local river trade to replace his recently sold *Lunawanna*. Like the *Leprena*, the *Terralinna* was designed by Tom Purdon.

Throughout the 1920s Purdon and Featherstone continued to be involved in the repair, overhaul, maintenance and sale of vessels. Slip work was carried out at their Battery Point yard, and also at the Domain slip which they leased.

Launch of the *Leprena*. Courtesy *Tasmanian Mail*, 13 August 1922.

Speculation

The late 1920s marked a slow period for boat building in general with few new orders received owing to the depressed global economy. Needing to keep their workers busy, Purdon and Featherstone began construction of a ketch in 1927, though it took more than three years for a buyer to be found and the vessel to be completed. The *Helen K.* was finally launched in September 1931, having been purchased by W. Keogh of Kingston with the intention of using her in the local river trade. Uniquely built of steam-bent timbers, the *Helen K.* holds the honour of being the last trading ketch built at Battery Point, the local river trade being made defunct by road transport.

Also launched in 1931 was the 86 ft *Drina,* a motor boat built out of the charred remains of the steamer *Maweena* which had been destroyed by fire in suspicious circumstances while berthed at Bellerive on 14 January 1929. This particular vessel was built to the order of Captain J. A. Thurston, an Australian plantation owner based in New Guinea.

Remains of the *Maweena* at Battery Point.
Courtesy Maritime Museum of Tasmania.

Two Motor Boats

Between 1933 and 1935 two more boats were launched from Purdon and Featherstone's Battery Point yard, both built by employees. These were the cruising yachts *Ronicia*, launched in October 1933, and *Moerangi*, launched in October 1935. The *Ronicia* was built by R. Clark for J. Vallence with the intention of racing her on the Derwent in the cruising class. The vessel measured 30 ft and was built on American lines and fitted with an Oldsmobile six engine. The *Moerangi* was built by Henry Featherstone's son Richard (Dick) Featherstone to the order of G. Neilson. Powered by an Overland motor car engine, she was a regular on the Derwent for many years and was later owned by the Motor Yacht Club of Tasmania.

Purdon and Featherstone Pty. Ltd.

The mid to late 1930s saw Henry Featherstone, by now 65 years of age, easing his involvement with Purdon and Featherstone and also looking to pass the business on to his four surviving sons. In July 1937 Henry formally made his sons joint partners in the firm, and in the process made Purdon and Featherstone a proprietary limited company. With a capital of £7,500, subscribers to and directors of the business were Henry Featherstone and two of his sons (Keith and Dick Featherstone).

Though continuing to focus on slip, overhaul and repair work, in July 1940 Purdon and Featherstone Pty. Ltd. received an order from the Hobart Marine Board to build a motor launch to replace their near 50-year old steam launch *Egeria*. Built under the supervision of Henry Featherstone at a cost of just over £8,000, including engines, the *Egeria* was launched on 20 October 1941.

World War II

The onset of World War II saw Purdon and Featherstone Pty. Ltd. diversify their boat building portfolio with the construction of a new type of vessel: harbour defence patrol launches. Three such launches were built by the firm between 1943 and 1944 specifically for use by the Royal Australian Navy. These were the *HMAS HDML 1321*, commissioned on 11 November 1943; the *HMAS HDML 1322*, commissioned on 17 January 1944; and the *HMAS HDML 1327*, commissioned on 19 May 1944.

On 1 February 1945 Purdon and Featherstone Pty. Ltd. launched the sea ambulance *AH1730 Koorakee*, the first vessel of its kind to be built in Australia. Measuring 80 ft in length, the *AH1730 Koorakee* was capable of carrying a crew of 13, a staff of 10, with room for 33 patients. The vessel was built to the order of the Australian Army Medical Service for use in the Pacific.

The launch of the *AH1730 Koorakee* coincided with the retirement of Henry Featherstone. Having spent more than 60 years working at Battery Point as a shipbuilder, he was forced to retire due to ill health. Henry died on 10 July 1945 at a private hospital in Hobart. His will divided his estate, including administration of Purdon and Featherstone Pty. Ltd., equally among his four surviving sons: Clyde, Keith, Dick and Ralph.

Egeria. Courtesy Maritime Museum of Tasmania.

HMAS HDML 1321.
Courtesy Royal Australian Navy.

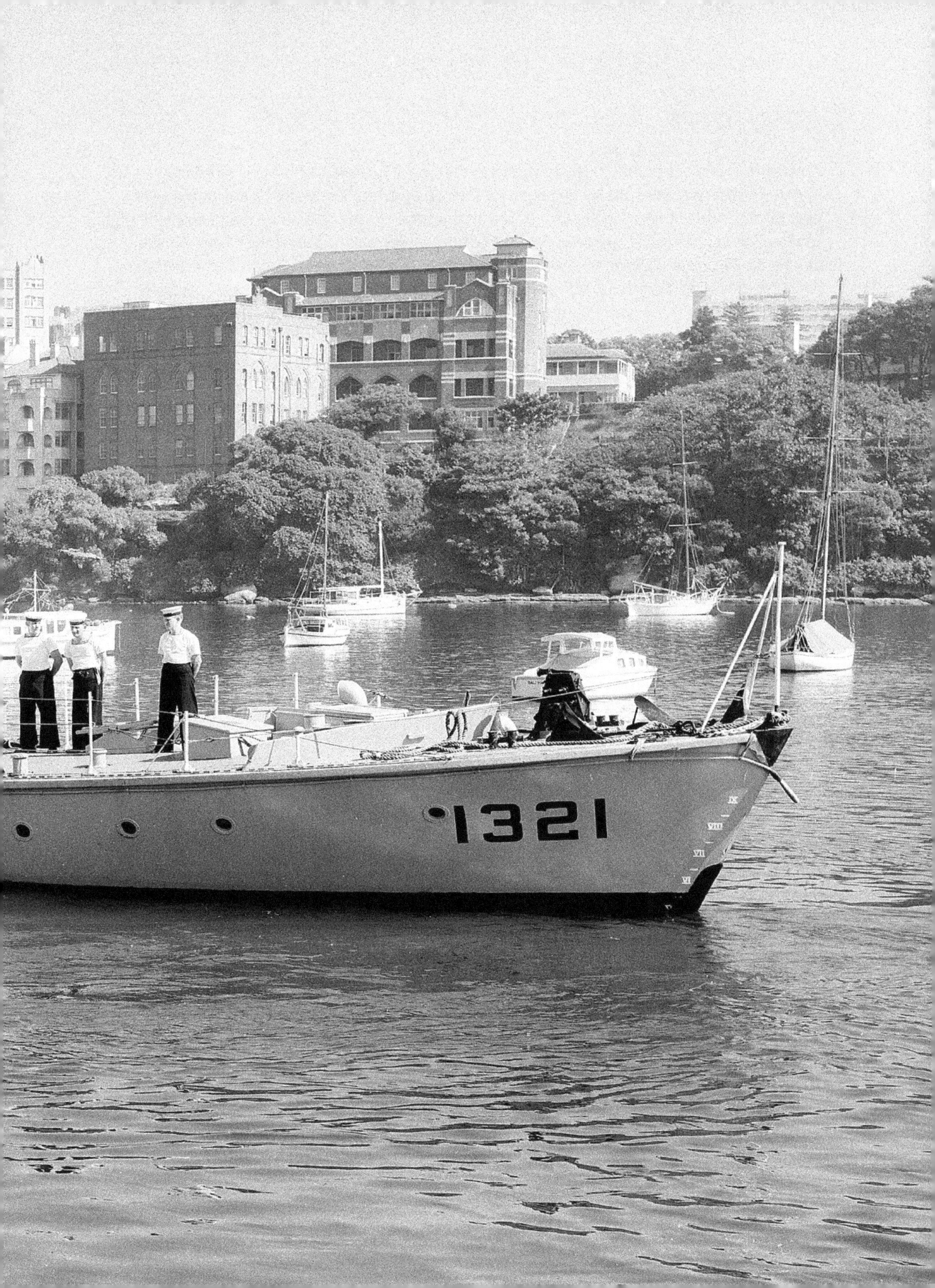
1321

Post World War II

Now owned and operated by Henry Featherstone's sons, the years immediately following the end of World War II were productive ones for Purdon and Featherstone Pty. Ltd. In terms of new builds, in November 1945 a second sea ambulance, the *AH1731 Koroit*, was launched, built to the order of the Royal Australian Army. Just over a year later, in December 1946, Purdon and Featherstone launched the *Waterwitch*, a Marconi cutter-rigged fishing boat intended for use in the local crayfishing industry. The 50 ft vessel was designed by Percy Coverdale (neighbouring boat builder of Battery Point) and built to the order of Neil Campbell of Hobart.

Three More Vessels

In 1947 Purdon and Featherstone Pty. Ltd. completed the 42 ft *Awittaka*, a motor launch built to the order of Clyde Featherstone. The following year the firm launched a gaff-rigged craft named *Yleena*, built to the order of A. N. Ray.

On 8 November 1948 Purdon and Featherstone Pty. Ltd. launched the 47 ft racing sloop *Mistral V*, built to the order of Guy Rex based on a design by the American firm of Sparkman and Stephens. A few weeks later the vessel sailed to Sydney to compete in the 1948 Sydney to Hobart Yacht Race, though was forced to retire off the coast of northern Tasmania owing to a leak. Undeterred, Guy Rex entered *Mistral V* in the 1950 Sydney to Hobart Yacht Race where, helmed by Jock Muir (boat builder of Battery Point), she finished second across the line, 17 minutes behind the winner *Margaret Rintoul*.

Launch of the *Waterwitch* in 1946.
Courtesy Maritime Museum of Tasmania.

Yleena (C17), *Wild Wave* (B4) and *Limelight* (R11) in 1957. Courtesy Tasmanian Archive and Heritage Office.

Then Tamar to Sam

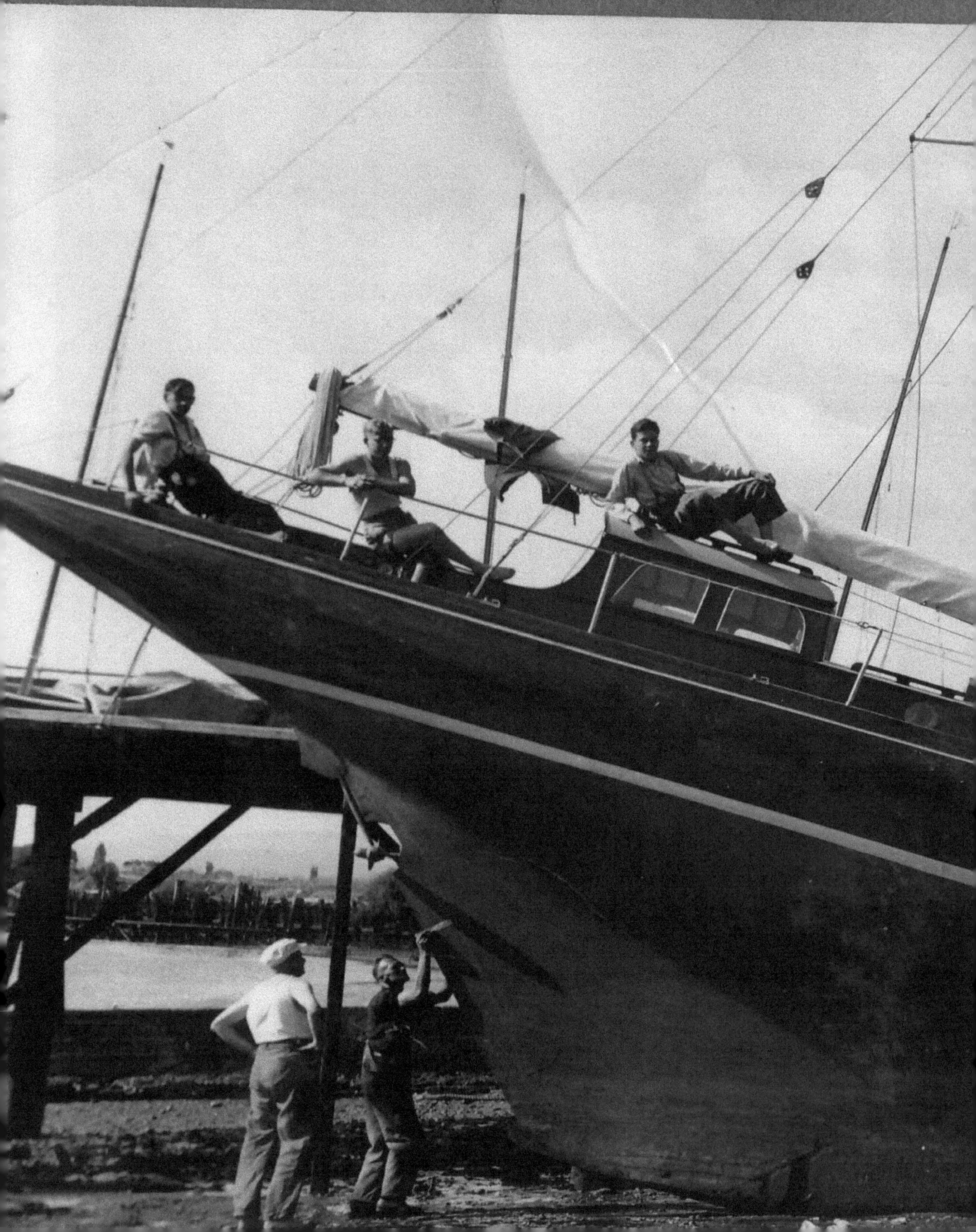

Mistral V under repair at the Tamar Yacht Club following retirement from the 1948 Sydney to Hobart Yacht Race. Courtesy Guy Rex Collection (Suzanne Rex).

The 1950s and 1960s

During the 1950s and 1960s Purdon and Featherstone Pty. Ltd. continued to build boats to order, though as with previous decades the firm's primary workload comprised slip and repair work. One of their new builds was the motor boat *Quest,* built to the order of W. J. Wallis of Melbourne. Launched on 18 April 1950, the 80 ft vessel was constructed from the hull of a sea ambulance Purdon and Featherstone had built in 1945 though was left unused by the conflict ending. Unfortunately the *Quest* was completely wrecked on Gull Island Reef, Bass Strait, on 13 July 1950 while en route to Sydney where hydraulic steering, interior fittings and furnishings were to be installed.

Also built by Purdon and Featherstone Pty. Ltd in the 1950s were the *Jason*, an 18 ft Jubilee class yacht built for Barry Featherstone (Clyde's son), and the 28 ft workboat *James Mackey*.

The Last Vessels

On 1 July 1967 the Featherstone family sold Purdon and Featherstone Pty. Ltd. to John Bennetto and John Lucas with the latter acting as the firm's managing director. In 1969 Purdon and Featherstone Pty. Ltd. completed the steel fishing boat *Vansittart*, built to the order of Nigel King of Lindisfarne to a design by Max Creese (boat builder of Battery Point). The company's work, however, primarily remained the slipping and repair of commercial fishing and recreational vessels, as well as larger vessels over 300 tons at the Domain slipway. These included the Japanese tuna long liners and ships involved in fruit export.

The 82 ft steel motor fishing vessel *Tasmanian Enterprise* has the distinction of being the last vessel built by Purdon and Featherstone at their Battery Point yard. The boat was built to the order of Bern Cuthbertson for use as an abalone mother ship and launched in February 1972.

Quest. Courtesy Maritime Museum of Tasmania.

Following more than 70 years of operation, Purdon and Featherstone Pty. Ltd. sold their Battery Point shipyard in 1973 to a developer. The associated buildings and infrastructure were subsequently demolished. A few years later the site was converted to a public reserve under ownership of the Hobart City Council. A workshop along the foreshore of Battery Point was then established for the purpose of carrying out repair work. The site remained in operation until 1984.

In 1985 Purdon and Featherstone Pty. Ltd. was purchased by a provedoring business. Six years later the business was sold to a syndicate. The new owners were not that interested in ship repair work. Instead, John Lucas, who had been carrying out pre-purchase and insurance surveys, as well as marine loss assessments, took over these projects until 2006 when he retired. Still, to this day Purdon and Featherstone Pty. Ltd. remain in operation, undertaking provedoring and other associated marine enterprises as a division of Tasmanian Shipping Supplies.

Tasmanian Enterprise. Courtesy Maritime Museum of Tasmania.

Trugannini on the Purdon and Featherstone slip (early 1960s).
Courtesy Richard Blundell.

Demolition of the Purdon and Featherstone property in 1977. Courtesy Tasmanian Archive and Heritage Office.

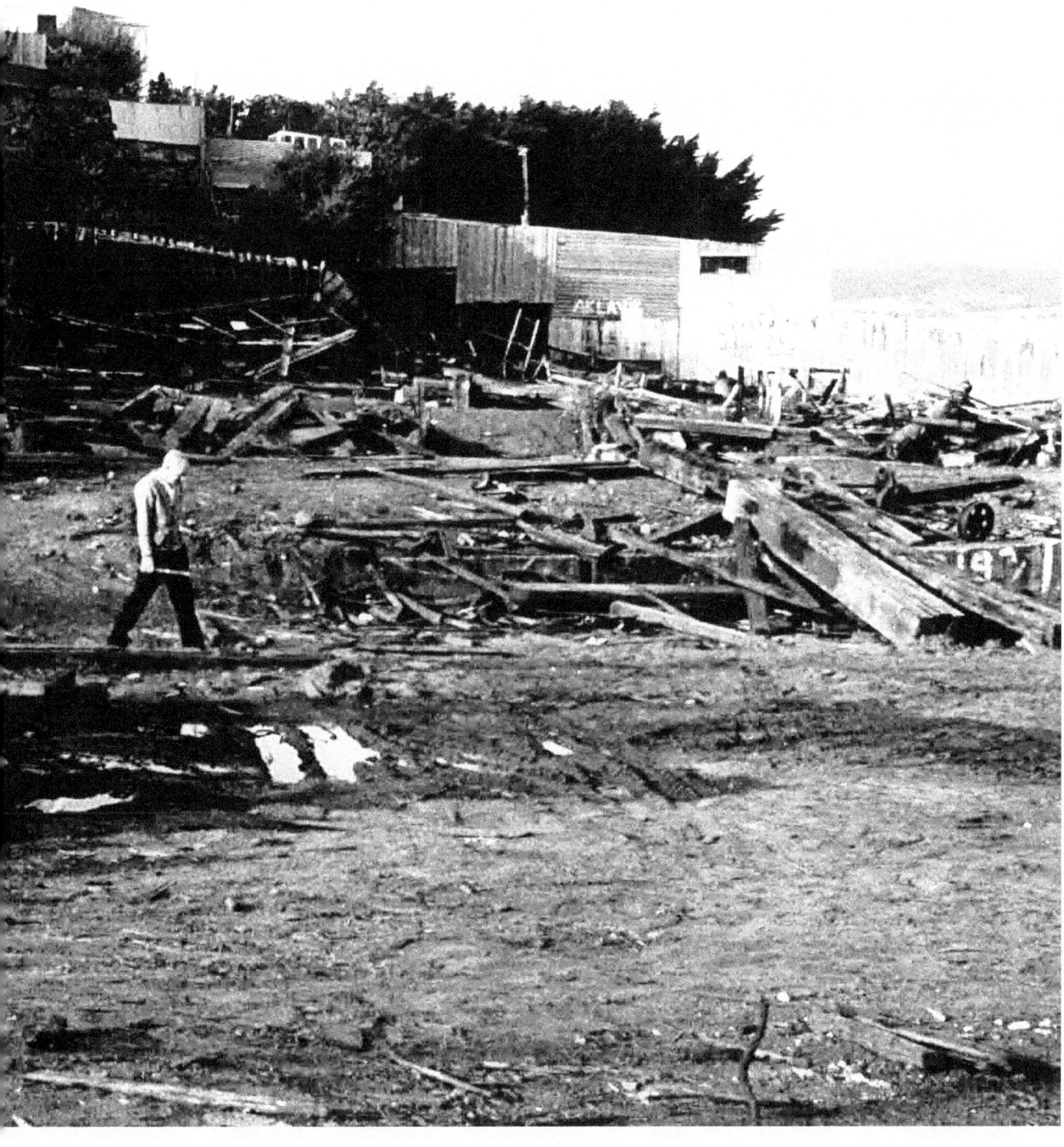

Vessels Built by James Mackey, Tom Purdon, Henry Featherstone, Purdon and Featherstone and Employees at Battery Point (1901 – 1972).

1901. *Marie Corelli*. Steam scow. 98.5 x 23.9 x 5.8 ft. Built by James Mackey and Henry Featherstone to the order of Joseph Graves of Huon Island. Purchased by Bowser and Company of Hobart following Graves' death part-way through construction. Used to transport timber from the Channel for use in building the Alexandra Pier. Chartered in March 1902 to E. A. Bruce for the Huon passenger trade. Subsequently towed to Sydney, NSW, by the *Whangape* in June 1902 and advertised for sale.

1905. *Mongana*. Steam ferry. 113 x 21 x 7.5 ft. Built by Purdon and Featherstone to the order of Whitehouse Brothers for the New Norfolk passenger trade. Designed by Tom Purdon and launched on 1 July 1905. Sold in 1907 to William Holyman and Sons and placed in the east coast trade. Purchased by a local syndicate for the Huon and Channel trade in 1912. By the late 1920s employed in the Hobart to Bellerive ferry service under charter to O'May Brothers. Requisitioned by the Commonwealth in 1942 seeing service in the Pacific, eventually falling under charter to the U.S. Army Auxiliary Transport Service. In June 1945 advertised for sale in Sydney, NSW, as part of the Australian Navy's vessel surplus program. Subsequently converted to a fishing vessel. Disappears from the records after having blown ashore during a gale at Point Piper in Sydney Harbour in May 1949.

1906. *Myrtle May*. Ketch. 52 x 14.7 x 5.2 ft. Built by Purdon and Featherstone to the order of G. Sward. Intended for the river trade, where she spent over a decade employed. Advertised for sale in June 1921. Converted to a fishing boat by the mid-1920s and owned by the Burgess family of VIC. Sprang a leak and foundered in Bass Strait, near Cape Paterson, on 8 April 1929; all hands saved.

1906. *Pacific*. Fishing boat. 50 x 13 x 5.2 ft. Built by Purdon and Featherstone to the order of Tom Spaulding for deep-sea fishing off the TAS coast. Possibly renamed *Eleanor Nicholls* in the early 1920s, and involved in the Bass Strait fishing trade for several decades under ownership of Jim Sward and later Vere Petterson.

1907. *Secret*. Ketch. 48.6 x 15.5 x 4.9 ft. Built by Purdon and Featherstone for Tom Purdon's own use. Employed in the river and then coastal trade. Abandoned at Triabunna, TAS, in the 1950s.

1907. *Pengana*. Ketch. 60.4 x 19.5 x 5 ft. Built by Purdon and Featherstone to the order of Risby Brothers and launched on 10 May 1907. Intended for the local timber trade. Advertised for sale in October 1909. Sold to buyers from Adelaide, SA, and involved in the St Vincent Gulf trade up until 1940 when advertised for sale by tender. Purchased by Hartley Arthur of Hobart for £4,000 and forced ashore at Tyrendarra near Portland, VIC, while en route to Hobart on 17 May 1940; all hands saved. Successfully refloated, rejoined the TAS timber trading fleet more than 30 years after her launch.

1907. *Opah*. Ketch. 70 x 18 x 5 ft. Built by Purdon and Featherstone to the order of Risby Brothers as a sister ship to the *Pengana*. Involved in the timber and then coastal trade for many years. Destroyed by fire off Passage Island in Bass Strait on 24 January 1923; all hands saved.

1907. *Nell*. Punt. Built by Purdon and Featherstone for Risdon Ferry operator Henry Purdon, brother of Tom Purdon, for use in transporting vehicles across the River Derwent at Risdon Ferry. Operated for several years. Condemned by the Hobart Marine Board in December 1914.

1908. *Marana.* **Steam ferry.** 104 x 20.6 x 8 ft. Built by Purdon and Featherstone to the order of Whitehouse Brothers expressly for the New Norfolk passenger trade and launched on 9 July 1908. Designed by Tom Purdon. In operation on the Derwent up until the late 1960s under various owners. Broken up in VIC in the early 1970s.

1909. *Rowitta (Sorrento, Tarkarri).* **Steam ferry.** 110 x 20.5 x 8 ft. Built by Purdon and Featherstone to the order of Alfred Harrap and Sons of Launceston and launched on 2 January 1909. Intended for the Tamar River passenger and cargo trade where she spent three decades employed. Requisitioned for service during WWII, thereafter seeing a number of uses in various locations, including in TAS, VIC and NSW, under different names. In 1951 returned to Hobart from NSW having been purchased by the Richards family. By 1968 owned by Bern Cuthbertson and used as an abalone mother ship. From 1975 located at the Flagstaff Hill Maritime Museum in Warrnambool, VIC; displayed under her original name of *Rowitta* and exhibited as she would have been in the 1930s. Demolished in April 2015 in a state of disrepair.

1909. *Wiena.* **Steam ferry.** 90 x 17.5 x 7.5 ft. Built by Purdon and Featherstone to the order of Risby Brothers and launched in August 1909. Intended to convey cargo and a complement of 280 passengers in the local river and coastal trades. Wrecked on 15 September 1919 on a reef near Maria Island, TAS, after loading coal at Piccaninny Point. At the time of loss, under charter to the Dalmayne Colliery Company from William Casey who had only purchased the vessel the year prior.

1909. *Reemere.* **Steam ferry.** 83 x 17.3 x 7 ft. Built by Purdon and Featherstone to the order of Francis Calvert for the Hobart-South Arm-Lewisham passenger trade and launched on 21 October 1909. Remained on the Derwent for more than a decade, transferred to Launceston in late 1920 for employment in the Tamar River passenger and cargo trade. Returned to the Derwent five years later, operating between Lindisfarne and Hobart where she remained for 30 years. Following, spent several decades employed as a fishing vessel off the TAS and VIC coasts before being transferred to Vanuatu. Noted to still be in active service, conveying passengers, goods and livestock in 2012, though since believed to have sunk.

1910. *Awittaka (HMS Belama).* **Steam ferry.** 133 x 22 x 8 ft. Built by Purdon and Featherstone for the Huon, Channel and Peninsula Steamship Company Ltd. and launched in June 1910. Capable of carrying up to 600 passengers. Commenced service in the Tasman Peninsula passenger trade in November 1910. Soon found too expensive to run and too big to operate. Particularly unsuited to the loading and unloading of passengers and goods at smaller regional jetties. Sold to the British Government for use as a patrol vessel in the Solomon Islands in August 1911. Given the name of *HMS Belama*. Wrecked on a reef off Santa Isabel Island in 1921.

1910. *Rose.* **Motor boat.** 26 x 8 x 3.5 ft. Built by Purdon and Featherstone for Tom Purdon's private use. Sequestered by the Hobart Marine Board in late 1912 for use in association with various harbour projects. Subsequently advertised for sale in Hobart in April 1915 and sold for £120. LIkely renamed.

1911. *Lunawanna.* **Ketch.** 50 x 17 x 4.8 ft. Built by Purdon and Featherstone to the order of John Sward for the local river trade. Traded between Hobart and Bruny Island. A popular entrant in local regatta races for many years. Sold in February 1921 to trade in Vanuatu.

Vessels Built by James Mackey, Tom Purdon, Henry Featherstone, Purdon and Featherstone and Employees at Battery Point (1901 – 1972).

1912. *Cartela.* **Steam ferry.** 123 x 24.5 x 8.5 ft. Built by Purdon and Featherstone to the order of the Huon, Channel and Peninsula Company Ltd. and launched on 21 September 1912. Designed by Tom Purdon. A regular in the local and regional passenger and excursion trade for 100 years. Significantly saw service in WW1 and, in her early years, raced against many of the local steamers, being awarded "Cock of the River" several times over. Since 1951 owned and operated by Roche Brothers, cruise and ferry boat operators of Hobart. Still in existence. In 2012 gifted by Roche Brothers to a not-for-profit organisation specifically established to coordinate her restoration. Located at Franklin on the Huon River.

1913. *Maweena.* **Steam ferry.** 96 x 20.3 x 7 ft. Built by Purdon and Featherstone to the order of Whitehouse Brothers for their New Norfolk passenger service and launched on 9 August 1913. Maintained a regular service for 13 years, also making several trips to Sydney and Melbourne to transport fruit and general cargo between 1917 and 1919. By the late 1920s owned by O'May Brothers and operating between Hobart and Bellerive. Destroyed by fire under suspicious circumstances while berthed at Bellerive on 14 January 1929. Remains subsequently towed to Purdon and Featherstone's Battery Point shipyard and used in the construction of the motor yacht *Drina*.

1913. *Talune.* **Motor boat.** 35 x 8 x 3.5 ft. Built by Purdon and Featherstone to the order of J. G. Turner. Remained in Turner's possession until January 1924 when purchased by the National Portland Cement Ltd. to run a daily service between Maria Island and Triabunna. Destroyed by fire while moored at Darlington, Maria Island, TAS, on 7 July 1929.

1914. *Tawa.* **Motor boat.** 30 x 7.5 ft. Built by Purdon and Feathstone for Henry Featherstone's own use. By 1924 owned by C. Thompson. Advertised for sale in 1927 and 1931. Still active in the late 1930s.

1914. *Taynna.* **Ketch.** Built by Purdon and Featherstone. First noted on the Derwent in February 1915. By 1919 owned by S. Purdon. By 1930 owned by W. Price. Sold to buyers from New Guinea in 1952. Sank off Kar Kar Island near Madang in the 1960s.

1917. *Myrtle Burgess.* **Fishing ketch.** 70 x 15 x 7.5 ft. Built by Purdon and Featherstone to the order of Bernard Burgess of VIC and launched on 10 October 1917. Following the tragic death of Burgess in November 1920, advertised for sale. Sold to F. W. Diergarten of VIC, and a few years later sold to John Alfred Rae of Ulverstone, TAS. Temporarily acquired by the Commonwealth on 18 June 1943, and permanently in November of that year, for use as a merchant navy vessel in WWII. Traversed various ports, including Port Moresby and Milne Bay, Papua New Guinea, and Labuan, Malaysia. Last noted as being a vessel of the British Borneo Civil Affairs Unit in January 1946.

1918. *Valmarie (Mapu).* **Schooner.** 141 x 30 x 12 ft. Built by Purdon and Featherstone on speculation though purchased by Rosenfeld and Company of Sydney, NSW, just prior to completion. Launched on 4 December 1918. Designed by Tom Purdon with plans provided by Alfred Blore. Initially transported timber between Melbourne, Sydney, and New Zealand. Ran aground in thick fog at Ninety Mile Beach, VIC, while en route to Melbourne from New Zealand on 30 September 1919. Refloated and pulled by tug to Melbourne for repairs. Went ashore near Farewell Cape, NZ, on 17 February 1922. Reported to be a total loss with salvage operations abandoned. Sold for the diminutive sum of £215 to E. Tasker of Nelson, NZ. Resurrected and renamed *Mapu*. In 1929 converted to a coal hulk at Nelson, NZ.

1922. *Leprena*. Schooner. 115 x 28 x 11 ft. Built by Purdon and Featherstone to the order of Henry Jones and Company and launched in April 1922. Designed by Tom Purdon. Employed in the interstate timber trade. Wrecked on 27 February 1925 near Eddystone Point, TAS, en route to Adelaide, SA; all hands saved.

1922. *Terralinna*. Ketch. 65 x 16.5 x 5 ft. Built by Purdon and Featherstone to the order of John Sward for the Channel timber trade and launched on 23 September 1922. Designed by Tom Purdon. A regular in the river trade and a popular participant in local regatta races for many years. Later converted to a fishing vessel. By the late 1990s moored at Prince of Wales Bay, TAS. Demolished, owing to her condition, in May 2012.

1925. Lifeboat. 16 ft. Built by Tom Purdon of Huon pine. Advertised for sale in June 1925.

1925. Dinghy. 10.8 ft. Built by Tom Purdon of Huon pine. Advertised for sale in June 1925.

1925. *Gumnut*. Cadet dinghy. 12 x 5 ft x 14 in. Built by Tom Purdon to the order of a Miss Gagin and launched on 20 November 1925. Won the 1928 Stonehaven Cup held in Sydney, helmed by Neall Batt. Presented as a gift to Neall Batt upon his return to Hobart. Represented TAS at the 1929 Stonehaven Cup held in Brisbane, helmed by Neall Batt. Won the 1930 Stonehaven Cup held in Melbourne, helmed by Neall Batt. By 1936 transferred to Launceston and owned by Syd Manchester. Owned by W. Tyson between 1939 and 1949 and subsequently purchased by the Tamar Yacht Club. Believed to be still in existence into the 1960s.

1927. *Aussie*. Cadet dinghy. 12 x 5 ft x 14 in. Built by Tom Purdon to the order of James Taylor and launched in October 1927. Represented TAS at the 1929 Stonehaven Cup held in Brisbane, helmed by James Taylor. Represented TAS at the 1931 Stonehaven Cup held in Hobart, helmed by James Taylor. Advertised for sale in September 1933. By 1935 owned by Ron O'May, by 1937 owned by M. D. O'May, by 1939 owned by W. E. Reeve, and by 1950 owned by J. R. Nettlefold. Advertised for sale in March 1950.

1928. *Corona (Corona Astron)*. Fishing boat. 48.6 x 13.7 x 6 ft. Built and designed by Tom Purdon (and his son Ernest Purdon) to the order of Martyn Brothers, Southport, TAS, and launched on 5 May 1928. Wrecked off Kangaroo Island, SA, on 3 March 1976; all hands saved.

1931. *Drina*. Motor boat. 96 x 20.3 x 7 ft. Built by Purdon and Featherstone from the charred remains of the *Maweena*. Built to the order of Captain J. A. Thurston, an Australian plantation owner of New Guinea. Left Hobart for New Guinea on 23 June 1931. Wrecked in July 1933 off Cape Cunningham, New Guinea.

1931. *Helen K. (Ethel)*. Ketch. 50 x 12 x 5 ft. Built by Purdon and Featherstone on speculation. Launched in September 1931 having been purchased by W. Keogh of Kingston with the intention of using her in the river trade. By July 1933 converted to a fishing boat and renamed *Ethel*. For sale in Hobart in February 1934, and subsequently in Melbourne, VIC, in October 1936 (at the time owned by George Cheverton of Hobart). Possibly chartered by CSIRO for TAS fisheries survey work in 1938 under the name of *Peter R*.

1933. *Ronicia*. Yacht. 30 x 9 x 2.5 ft. Built by R. Clark for J. Vallence with the intention of racing her on the Derwent in the cruising class. Launched in October 1933. A regular on the Derwent for many years, successfully competing in races for power cruisers. By 1946 owned by D. Pearsall.

Vessels Built by James Mackey, Tom Purdon, Henry Featherstone, Purdon and Featherstone and Employees at Battery Point (1901 – 1972).

1935. *Moerangi*. Yacht. Built by Dick Featherstone to the order of G. Neilson. Powered by an Overland motor car engine. A regular on the Derwent for many years, successfully competing in races for power cruisers. By the early 1950s owned by the Motor Yacht Club.

1941. *Egeria*. Motor launch. 60 x 13 x 5 ft. Built by Purdon and Featherstone to the order of the Hobart Marine Board based on plans drafted by J. I. Thornycraft and Co. Ltd of England and launched on 20 October 1941. Still in existence; has spent the last 70+ years employed on the Derwent. Currently managed by the Motor Yacht Club of Tasmania and available for private charter and cruises.

1941. *Plimsoll*. Yacht. 27 x 8 x 5 ft. Likely built by Purdon and Featherstone to the order of Ralph Featherstone. Launched in early 1941. Advertised for sale in May 1946, though remained in Featherstone's hands. Advertised for sale again in February 1948. Disappears from the records thereafter, though very likely renamed *Hermione V* by October of 1948, owned by T. L. Roberts. Remained in Roberts' hands well in the 1950s.

1943. *HMAS HDML 1321 (Rushcutter)*. Harbour defence launch. 80 ft. Built by Purdon and Featherstone to the order of the Royal Australian Navy and commissioned on 11 November 1943. Deployed to New Guinea and other areas of the Pacific. Remained in service until 1971. Subsequently converted to a charter vessel operating out of Darwin, NT, by the name of *MV Rushcutter*. For sale in September 2016 though sank (later recovered) in Darwin Harbour the following month. An association has since been formed to save/restore the vessel.

1944. *HMAS HDML 1322*. Harbour defence launch. 80 ft. Built by Purdon and Featherstone to the order of the Royal Australian Navy and commissioned on 17 January 1944. Based out of Darwin, NT, during WWII, deployed in and around Timor, Thursday island and Dutch New Guinea. Post-War transferred to Sydney. In 1958 sold to the Philippines Navy.

1944. *HMAS HDML 1327*. Harbour defence launch. 80 ft. Built by Purdon and Featherstone to the order of the Royal Australian Navy and commissioned on 19 May 1944. Employed in and around the Pacific. Post-War, attached as a tender to *HMAS Tarangua* at Manus Island. In 1958 sold to the Philippines Navy.

1945. *AH1730 Koorakee*. Sea ambulance. 80 x 15.5 x 5 ft. Built by Purdon and Featherstone to the order of Australian Army Medical Service and intended for service in the Pacific. Launched on 1 February 1945. Capable of carrying a crew of 13, a staff of 10, with room for 33 patients.

1945. *AH1731 Koroit*. Sea ambulance. 80 x 15.5 x 5 ft. Built by Purdon and Featherstone to the order of Australian Army Medical Service and intended for service in the Pacific. Launched in November 1945. Capable of carrying a crew of 13, a staff of 10, with room for 33 patients.

1946. *Waterwitch (Moorina)*. Fishing boat. 52 ft. Marconi cutter-rigged fishing boat built by Purdon and Featherstone to the order of Neil Campbell. Launched in December 1946. Designed by Percy Coverdale. Intended for use in the crayfishing industry. Purchased by R. Woodward, of Invercargill, NZ, in 1953 and renamed *Moorina*. Left TAS for NZ in July 1953. Sadly lost with all hands at the entrance to Kaipara Harbour, NZ, on 5 May 1974.

1947. *Awittaka*. Motor launch. 42 x 10. x 3.5 ft. Built by Purdon and Featherstone to the order of Frederick Featherstone. Sold to the Jones family in 1969 and remained in their possession until 2017. Located in southern TAS and now owned by Braye Sutherland.

1948. *Yleena*. Yacht. 31.6 x 10 x 5.2 ft. Built by Purdon and Featherstone to the order of A. N. Ray who retained ownership for many years. Still in existence; located in southern TAS and owned by Brent McKay.

1948. *Mistral V (Orionis II)*. Yacht. 47 x 10 x 7.5 ft. Built by Purdon and Featherstone to the order of Guy Rex. Designed by Sparkman and Stephens. Launched on 1 November 1948. Competed in the 1948 Sydney to Hobart Yacht Race though forced to retire off northern TAS owing to a leak. Competed in the 1950 Sydney to Hobart Yacht Race, helmed by Jock Muir, finishing second across the line. Sold in April 1953 to Adam Gray Dalziel, a wealthy businessman based in Hong Kong. Renamed *Orionis II*. In the late 1950s transferred to Kirkeudbrightshire, Scotland, Dalziel's native place. Possibly still in existence.

1950. *Quest*. Motor launch. 80 x 15.5 x 5 ft. Built by Purdon and Featherstone to the order of W. J. Wallis of Melbourne, VIC. Launched on 18 April 1950. Wrecked on Gull Island Reef, Bass Strait, on 13 July 1950 while en route to NSW where hydraulic steering, interior fittings and furnishings were to be installed; all hands saved.

1951. *Jason*. Yacht. 18 x 6.7 x 4 ft. Jubilee design. Built by Purdon and Featherstone for Barry Featherstone. Still in existence, currently located in QLD.

1958. *James Mackey*. Workboat. 28 ft. Built by Purdon and Featherstone. Launched in 1958. Later sold to the Royal Yacht Club of Tasmania and is still in their possession.

1969. *Vansittart*. Fishing boat. 47 x 14.8 x 6.4 ft. Steel fishing boat built by Purdon and Featherstone to the order of Nigel King of Lindisfarne and intended for the abalone industry. Designed by Max Creese. Transferred to Cairns, QLD, in 1975. Possibly still in existence.

1972. *Tasmanian Enterprise*. Fishing boat. 82 x 18 x 11.2 ft. Built by Purdon and Featherstone to the order of Bern Cuthbertson for use as an abalone mother ship and launched in February 1972. Later owned by Wayne and Ellen Baker. Capsized off South Cape, TAS, on 13 April 1995; all hands saved.

View of Battery Point and surrounds (circa 1979) following demolition of the Purdon and Featherstone property. Courtesy Tasmanian Archive and Heritage Office.

Rowitta at the Flagstaff Hill Maritime Museum in 2012.
The vessel was demolished in 2015.
Courtesy author's private collection.

William Lucas

William Lucas was a determined and well-respected carpenter and boat builder of both Strahan and Hobart. The son of Battery Point shipwright John Lucas, it was unfortunate that the lean years of the 1880s meant that William was unable to take over his father's shipyard. Instead he persevered and moved to the west coast where he successfully undertook contract and tender work for many years, building some of Strahan's more well-known hotels and structures. Yet, William Lucas' life goal appears to have been to operate his own shipyard at Battery Point. His hard work and determination eventually paid off when, in 1904, he took over the yard operated by the late Robert Inches. By this time, however, William Lucas was 49 years of age. Still, between 1904 and 1914, he built a handful of vessels, most notably the ketch *Fleet* and the police patrol boat *Lallaby*.

William Joseph Lucas was born on 19 July 1855 in Hobart, the third of nine children born to John and Sophia Lucas (nee Strang). William's father, John Lucas, was a highly respected shipwright of Battery Point, operating his own yard between 1856 and 1884. Growing up, William and his family lived at Mona Street, Battery Point, a stone's throw from the boat and ship yards. William attended school in nearby Macquarie Street.

As a teenager William Lucas developed a love of all things aquatic, a passion that would last his life time. In 1869 he competed in the youth's race for lads and apprentices under 18 years at the Hobart Regatta where he finished third in the whaleboat *Velocipes*. In the early 1870s William Lucas began competing in paired-oared races. By 1878 he had progressed to yachting, having purchased the 8 ton yacht *Neva* (built by Lark Macquarie at Battery Point). He successfully raced the vessel in Derwent Yacht Club events for several years.

Apprenticeship

The oldest surviving son of John Lucas' children, it was only fitting that William followed in his father's professional footsteps. Having undertaken his apprenticeship at his dad's Battery Point shipyard, it was likely the two men continued to work alongside one another for many years. Unfortunately a downturn in the economy during the early 1880s meant that John Lucas sold his Battery Point yard in September 1884, thereby negating the opportunity for William Lucas to continue its operation following his father's retirement.

View of Battery Point from Dunkley's Point, Sandy Bay (circa 1880s).
Courtesy Tasmanian Archive and Heritage Office.

Contracts and Tenders on the West Coast

Persevering, William Lucas and his young family moved to Strahan on Tasmania's west coast where they lived for nearly two decades with William carrying on building and contract work. During this period he most notably built the Shamrock and Terminus hotels. He also built warehouses for Cascade Cordials, as well as several residential cottages.

While in Strahan William Lucas remained professionally active in the maritime realm. In 1902 he was appointed by the Strahan Marine Board to superintend the building of a barge to aid with local dredging activities. The 87 ft vessel, named *Macquarie*, was built by William Lucas at Risby Brothers' timber yard and launched on 26 March 1902.

The dredge *Maquarie* prior to launch at Strahan in 1902.
Courtesy *Weekly Courier*, 5 April 1902.

A Return to Hobart

In late 1902 William Lucas and his wife Amy returned to Hobart, likely to be closer to family. Continuing to undertake contract work, in October 1903 he successfully tendered the Hobart Marine Board to extend the Alexandra Pier shed, estimating the work to cost £460 and take six weeks to complete. The following year William Lucas was awarded the contract to undertake repair work of the Dunn Street Pier.

Back to Battery Point

In July 1904, at the age of 49, William Lucas returned to his shipwright roots, succeeding the late Robert Inches at his Battery Point shipyard. The first vessel noted as being on William Lucas' slip was the ketch *Brothers* which underwent repair in October of that year. A short time later William was noted as building a 45 ft yawl-rigged fishing boat, as well as a 62 ft ketch. The former, *Inez*, was launched in early 1905 and built to the order of George Bridge of Nubeena, who likely named the vessel after his young daughter. The latter, *Fleet*, was launched in late 1905 and built to the order of John Underwood of North West Bay for employment in the local timber trade. The vessel was modelled by Tom Purdon.

Fleet.
Courtesy Graeme Broxam.

Slip Work and a Few New Vessels

Like his father, the building of new vessels seems to have been supplementary to slip work operations for William Lucas. During his yard's 13 years of operation the majority of William's time seems to have been spent slipping, repairing, overhauling and altering vessels. William also received income from the lay-up of vessels, particularly yachts over winter. In mid-1907, for example, the yachts *Thelma, Gladys, Maysie, Volant, Nordica, Defiance, Lark, Clara, Viga* and *Hermione* were all noted as being laid up on his slip. That same year William Lucas was tasked with repairing the *SS Papua*, cleaning and painting the fishing boats *Holly* and *Ripple*, as well as installing an engine in a motor boat.

Still, in addition to the *Inez* and *Fleet* there were a few vessels built at William Lucas' Battery Point yard. In June 1907 he was noted as having secured the Marine Board of Hobart contract for the building of a punt to house a dredge that was recently imported from England. By September of that year the new dredge was complete and ready for use, to be employed initially at the Hobart wharves.

In September 1908 William Lucas received an order for a motor launch to furnish the Strahan tourist trade. Built to the order of Louis Sadewasser, proprietor of Strahan's Bay View Hotel, the 36 ft *Bay View* was launched in December of that year and immediately shipped to the west coast on board the *SS Mahinapua*.

In September 1910 William launched a 29 ft motor boat built to the order of F. H. Chesterman of Port Esperance. Named *Kooyong* and fitted with a 12 hp Sterling engine, this particular vessel was raced by Chesterman at local regattas for many years.

A party on board the *Kooyong*. Courtesy *Tasmanian Mail,* 10 January 1924.

A Possible Move to the Domain

Sensing opportunity, in April 1911 William Lucas partnered with his brother-in-law Alfred Willing to lease the Domain shipyard and slipway from the Tasmanian government. The pair immediately set about repairing the slipway such that it could accommodate vessels up to 500 tons. While repairs were underway William Lucas continued to work at his Battery Point yard. In August 1911, for example, he was noted as having various vessels under repair, as well as having in the course of construction a motor boat for the Tasmanian Police Department to be used as a patrol boat.

By October 1911 repairs to the Domain slipyard were complete. However, William Lucas appears to have had a change of mind, withdrawing his arrangement with Alfred Willing who thus became the site's sole operator.

Police Boats and Motor Boats

Remaining put at his Battery Point yard, in June 1912 William launched the police patrol boat, the 32 ft yawl-rigged cutter *Lallaby*. Designed by Alfred Blore, the vessel was intended for work in Bass Strait by officers stationed at Whitemark on Flinders Island.

In winter 1912 William Lucas was noted as making progress on a 25 ft motor launch for H. Cramp of Cramp Brothers. Likely named *Vanda* and launched a month or two later, little is known about this vessel, except that she was made of Huon pine and her engines were imported from England.

The police boat *Lallaby*.
Courtesy *Tasmanian Mail,* 7 June 1934.

The Final Years

Despite many local businesses suffering from a downturn during World War I, William Lucas remained working at his Battery Point yard up until 1914 when he sold the property to Percy Coverdale.

William Lucas died on 8 October 1917 at Highbury Hospital, Hobart, aged 62, and was buried at Cornelian Bay Cemetery, New Town. William was survived by his wife Amy (nee Willing) and their son Cecil.

Vessels Built by William Lucas and Employees at Battery Point (1905 – 1912).

1905. *Inez*. Fishing boat. 45 x 10.5 x 4.8 ft. Built to the order of George Bridge, fisherman. Remained in Bridge's possession until the early 1950s. Later owned by the Spaulding family and subsequently W. E. Murphy. Ran aground on 28 February 1983 off Waterhouse Island, TAS; all hands saved.

1905. *Fleet (Corwa)*. Ketch. 65.4 x 17.5 x 5.5 ft. Coastal trading ketch built to the order of John Underwood. Modelled by Tom Purdon. Sold to S. J. Staughton of Melbourne, VIC, in May 1913 and converted to a cruising yacht. Renamed *Corwa* in 1917. Sold in 1929 and placed in the NSW to QLD coastal trade. Sold again and placed back in the TAS coastal trade. Later involved in the SA tuna industry. In 1945, sold to the Dutch East Indies Government.

1907. Punt. Built by contract to the Hobart Marine Board. Intended to house a dredge for use around the Hobart wharves that was imported from England.

1908. *Bay View*. Motor launch. 36 x 8 x 3 ft. Built to the order of Louis Sadewasser of the Bay View Hotel, Strahan, for his private use, as well as for use in the local tourist trade. Shipped to the west coast on board the *SS Mahinapua*. Equipped with a 15 hp San Francisco engine. Remained in Sadewasser's possession until at least November 1914 when he left Strahan for the north west coast of TAS.

1910. *Kooyong*. Motor boat. 29 x 7.6 x 3.8 ft. Built to the order of F. H. Chesterman of Port Esperance. Fitted with a 12 hp Sterling engine. Competed in local and regional motor boat races up until 1915. Advertised for sale as part of Chesterman's estate in 1927 though remained on the Huon. Advertised for sale at Wattle Grove in March 1940.

1912. *Lallaby*. Patrol boat. 32 x 9.5 x 3.8 ft. Built to the order of the Tasmanian Police Department. Designed by Alfred Blore. Intended for work around the Bass Strait islands by officers stationed at Whitemark, Flinders Island. Remained in service up until 1938. Sold in 1941 and purchased by Toby Cheverton of Hobart. Sold to Max Parker of Triabunna in 1957. Later sold to Frank Peddler.

1912. *Vanda*. Motor launch. 25 x 7.6 x 4 ft. Built to the order of H. Cramp of Cramp Brothers. Constructed of Huon pine with engines imported from England.

Battery Point boat yards (circa 1920s). Percy Coverdale's yard is to the left; Charlie Lucas' yard is to the right. Courtesy Maritime Museum of Tasmania.

Percival (Percy) Coverdale

One of Australia's more well-known 20th century boat builders, Percy Coverdale first embarked on a career in boat building as a teenager in the late 1890s when apprenticed to the celebrated Battery Point shipbuilder Robert Inches. In 1914 Percy established his own yard at Battery Point which remained in operation for nearly 50 years. Here Percy Coverdale successfully merged the old and modern day landscape of boat building, particularly in terms of cruising yachts. Of the more than 35 vessels Percy is known to have built up until his retirement in 1961, at least 16 are still in existence. More than a boat builder, Percy Coverdale was also a highly respected, charismatic and competitive sportsman, successfully competing in the Sydney to Hobart Yacht Race three times, including the inaugural race in 1945, and winning many of the Royal Yacht Club of Tasmania's coveted prizes.

Percival (Percy) George Coverdale was born at Holebrook Place, Davey Street, Hobart, on 20 March 1882, the second of four children born to Norrison John and Mary Elizabeth Coverdale (nee Hinsby). As a child Percy and his family lived at several residences in Hobart, including Holebrook Place; 184 Goulburn Street, West Hobart; and later, "Bertrams," 30 Byron Street, Sandy Bay, where Percy spent his teenage years.

Growing up, Percy and his brothers (Harry, Fred and Eric) attended the Macquarie Street State School and were actively involved in sports with a leaning towards those of an aquatic nature. Unlike many of his peers, it was likely location, opportunity and interest rather than family heritage that steered Percy's interest in this realm. His father was a clerk, and later a theatre manager of Hobart, while Percy's grandfather was Dr John Coverdale, a prominent colonial medical practitioner.

In 1897, at the age of 15, Percy Coverdale and his younger brother Fred were apprenticed to Robert Inches at Inches' Battery Point shipyard. Working alongside Charlie Lucas, the two brothers were likely involved in the construction of several distinguished racing yachts built to William Fife (Jr) designs, including the *Fairlie II* and *Fairlie III*. Other boats built at Robert Inches' yard during this period were the trading ketches *Swift* and *Olive*, the oil launch *Oceana* and the cutter *Dauntless*.

Sadly, the untimely death of Robert Inches in May 1904, just as Percy and Fred Coverdale were completing their apprenticeships, would have resulted in the loss of employment. It is likely they found work at one of the nearby yards, possibly with William Lucas, where Percy Coverdale is known to have completed a short four racing boat, built in September 1906 to the order of the Hobart Rowing Club, and the 46 ft yacht *Florence May* completed in late 1906/early 1907.

A Sporting Family

Supplementary to his work activities, as a young adult Percy Coverdale continued his involvement with aquatic sports. In the early 1900s and up until the 1920s, Percy and his three brothers dominated the Tasmanian rowing landscape. Individually and collectively all four Coverdale boys successfully competed in local, state and interstate races and regattas, often teaming up with fellow Battery Point boat builders Ernest and Esker Bayes. Highlights of the Coverdale family's achievements include the Southern Tasmanian Amateur Sculling Championship which Percy won in 1904 and Fred won between 1906 and 1912. Fred also won the Australian Single Sculls Championship in 1913, finished second at this event in 1909, and was Tasmanian Sculling Champion in 1909, 1910, 1912 and 1913. During this period Percy and his family were instrumental in the establishment of the Sandy Bay Rowing Club.

Sailing was also on the agenda. Beginning in 1901 Percy Coverdale competed in Derwent Yacht Club events in the 16.5 ft *Nancy*, and in Derwent Dinghy Sailing Club events in the *Zoe*. Percy's father presented the perpetual Coverdale Championship Shield to the Derwent Dinghy Sailing Club in 1904.

Percy Coverdale's sporting commitments also extended to club administration. In 1902 he was elected to the committee of the Hobart Rowing Club. 1905 saw him elected to the committee of the Southern Tasmanian Rowing Association.

An all-round athlete, in 1906 Percy Coverdale developed an interest in cycling and for the next decade successfully competed in local and state road races, including the 100 mile road race between Launceston and Hobart. He also served on the committee of the Suburban Cycling Club.

Sandy Bay Rowing Club (circa 1914).
Courtesy Tasmanian Archive and Heritage Office.

Boatyard Proprietor

In 1914, at the age of 32, Percy Coverdale purchased the Battery Point boatyard owned and operated by William Lucas and previously in the possession of his mentor Robert Inches. The outbreak of World War I, however, resulted in low demand for new builds. Instead, like his peers, the primary work initially undertaken at the yard appears to have been the slipping of existing vessels and the on-sale of smaller boats, boat parts and motors. Still, at least two vessels were built in 1914 by Percy, including the 30 ft yawl *Naomi* (later *Telopea*), designed and built for Percy's own use, and the 54 ft fishing boat *Volito*.

Two more boats were built by Percy Coverdale in 1915. These were the 22.5 ft motor boat *Tuna*, built to the order of W. J. Mangan, a fellow member of the Sandy Bay Rowing Club, and the 14.5 ft motor boat *Gray* which Percy Coverdale built for himself. Likely built in tandem, both boats were fitted with Gray marine engines: the *Tuna* was fitted with a 4.5 hp model and the *Gray* with a 6 hp model, the latter earning a reputation as the fastest motor launch in Tasmania.

Tuna. Courtesy *Tasmanian Mail,* 2 September 1925.

The 1920s

The early 1920s saw Percy Coverdale continue to solidify operations at his Battery Point boatyard, particularly through the building of commercial fishing vessels. Of particular note were the 50 ft *Alida R.*, launched in 1920 and built to the order of R. Spaulding, and the 40 ft *Valma*.

Next off the stocks was the ketch *Eveline May*, built to the order of Arthur Sward of Bruny Island and launched in November 1923. Intended to carry timber to Hobart from the Huon, the 44 ft vessel was only one of a handful of vessels built in southern Tasmania that year.

On 21 July 1925 Percy Coverdale launched the 52 ft fishing boat *Storm Bay*, built to the order of George Bridge of Nubeena and intended for the local barracouta trade. This particular vessel was designed by Alfred Blore.

Eveline May.
Courtesy Tasmanian Archive and Heritage Office.

Launch of the *Storm Bay*. Courtesy *Tasmanian Mail*, 29 July 1925.

A Motor Boat for the Mainland

In a diversion from the commercial fishing boats and ketches Percy Coverdale had primarily built up to this point, in late 1926 an order was received from Reginald Prevost, a prominent architect of Sydney, for a 45 ft motor boat. Designed by Alfred Blore, the luxurious *Tanda* was launched from Percy Coverdale's yard in early August 1927 and stated to be one of the smartest motor boats yet launched on the Derwent. Also deemed one of the best and most elaborately fitted motor cruisers ever to leave the Derwent, the *Tanda* was sailed to Sydney by Prevost and crew immediately following her launch.

Tanda. Courtesy *Tasmanian Mail,* 10 August 1927.

Derwent Class Yachts

The stalwart of Hobart yachting, E. H. Webster, was Percy Coverdale's next customer with a request to build a new "one-design" class of yacht with the intention of advancing a class intermediary to the cadet dinghies and larger A class yachts. The resulting vessel, *Imp*, was designed by A. C. Barber of Sydney in conjunction with P. C. Douglas of Hobart and launched on 7 December 1927. Orders for several more "Derwent class" yachts were duly placed with local boat builders, supporting E. H. Webster's intention that six yachts of the class be racing by the start of the 1928 yachting season. Copies of plans for Derwent class yachts were also made available from the Royal Yacht Club of Tasmania at a cost of £1, in an effort to encourage amateurs to build the vessels.

Imp. Courtesy Guy Rex Collection (Suzanne Rex). Note bowsprit added later and became standard on future Derwent class yachts.

In May 1928 a Derwent class yacht under construction at Percy Coverdale's yard was purchased by Arthur Coole of Cygnet. Named *Pixie*, the vessel was launched in September of that year. A third yacht of the class, *Gnome*, was built by Walter Taylor and Eric McCreary and launched from Percy Coverdale's boatyard on 16 October 1928. She was shortly thereafter joined by the *Clytie* and *Nymph*, both built by local amateurs. Another Derwent class yacht, *Sprite*, was launched later that year from Charlie Lucas' Battery Point yard, making a total of six yachts in the class.

For more than five decades the Derwent class proved a popular and competitive addition to local and regional racing fixtures, helped in part by the low cost of the vessels, the addition of more boats to the class and the evenness of the competition.

Derwent class yachts on the River Derwent.
D8 - *Sylph*, D17 - *Geni*, D12 - *Janus*, D10 - *Titania*, D1 - *Imp*, D18 - *Merlin*, D2 - *Gnome*, D15 - *Goblin*.
Courtesy Tasmanian Archive and Heritage Office.

Three More Fishing Boats

Between 1928 and 1930 Percy Coverdale launched at least three fishing boats, two of which were built for Victorian customers. These were the *Rachel Irene*, *Rowena* and *Amy Johnson*. The 42 ft *Rachel Irene* was built to the order of C. and E. Fredericks of Portland, Victoria, and launched in late 1928. The 55 ft *Rowena* was built to the order of McKay Brothers of Hobart and launched in 1929. The 45 ft *Amy Johnson* was built to the order of George Darley of Port Fairy, Victoria, and launched on 25 June 1930.

A Return to Yacht Racing

Concurrent with the building of fishing boats, during the late 1920s Percy Coverdale renewed his interest in yacht racing, often competing in the A class yacht *Ozone*. He also received several orders for yachts, including for the 43.6 ft staysail-rigged schooner *Windward* (later *Windward II*) which was launched on 18 December 1929. Sparing no expense in her construction, despite a bleak global economy, the luxurious vessel was built to the order of E. H. Webster to a design by Norman Dallimore of England.

Windward II (in 2011)
Courtesy Steb Fisher.

The next yacht built by Percy Coverdale was one for his own use. In the early 1930s Percy continued to compete in local and regional yacht races and regattas, often in vessels loaned to him by associates. Opting to sail his own yacht Percy Coverdale built the 42 ft *Ninie* with the intention of racing her in the local A class. Based on an American R type design and named for his wife, the *Ninie* was launched on 8 January 1931 and stated to represent the most modern ideas in the design of racing craft. The vessel's 51 ft hollow mast was also noted to be the first of its type installed in a Tasmanian vessel.

Ninth months following the launch of *Ninie*, Percy Coverdale was noted as building an auxiliary launch to the order of Eric McCreary who had previously part-owned the Derwent class yacht *Gnome*. Stated in the press to be similar in design to Jack Forsyth's cruiser *Margaret* (recently built by Charlie Lucas at Battery Point), unfortunately few details about this vessel are known. However, it is possible that the sale fell through and instead Percy Coverdale shipped the vessel's hull to Sydney having sold it to J. D. Borrowman, a local hairdresser. Fitted out at Halvorsen's at Neutral Bay, the 30 ft yacht *Adina* was launched in early 1933.

Adina
Courtesy Andrew Tait.

More Innovative Designs

The unwavering E. H. Webster was Percy Coverdale's next customer with an order for another luxurious A class yacht. The 43.5 ft Bermuda-rigged *Wanderer* was designed by Percy and launched on 27 October 1932. It was considered to be at the forefront of modern technology, design and innovation. However, consistent with Webster's previous commissions, she spent little time on the Derwent, making her way to Sydney in June 1933 after being purchased by Dr Rupert Furber who renamed the vessel *Thetis*.

Continuing his association with Sydney Harbour, in October 1934 Percy Coverdale launched the 6 metre yacht *Sjo-Ro*, built to the order of Sir Claude Plowman, a notable Tasmanian yachtsman who at the time was living in Sydney. Based on a design developed by William Fife (Jr) for a new class proving popular overseas, the vessel was notably selected as the New South Wales representative for the 1935 Northcote Cup. *Sjo-Ro* disappointly experienced mixed success in her early years, including at this event and on Sydney Harbour where she often raced against the more successful Coverdale-builds *Windward II* and *Thetis*.

Soon after completing the *Sjo-Ro*, Percy Coverdale received an order from Guy Rex and Charles Davies for a 44 ft yawl similar to the *Dorade*, the vessel that had won the trans-Atlantic race between the United States and England in 1930. Intended as a cruising yacht, plans for the vessel were provided by Olin Stephens of Sparkman and Stephens, an up-and-coming American yacht designer. The resulting yacht, *Landfall*, was launched on 10 October 1935.

In August 1936 Percy Coverdale was noted as building a 36 ft auxiliary cruiser for his own use. This particular vessel, *Chloe,* took several years to complete and was launched just in time for the 1938/39 yachting season. Though she won the coveted Bruny Island race in her first season, *Chloe*'s time on the Derwent was short with Percy sailing the vessel to Sydney in March 1939 where *Chloe* was sold to W. H. Walton for £925. In her place, Percy Coverdale began building a 52 ft cruiser though it would be several years before this particular vessel took to the water.

It is likely that the building of *Chloe* was stalled by the commissioning of another yacht to an innovative design. This was the 30 square metre yacht *Lewan* which Percy Coverdale began building in November 1937. Designed by Knud Reimers of Sweden and of a design not previously seen in Tasmania, the vessel was built to the order of Neil Campbell and launched in September 1938. Yet a year later she too made her way to Sydney, racing under the ownership of G. E. Bryant for several decades.

Rounding out the decade, Percy Coverdale launched a 225 ci inboard speedboat in 1939, built to the order of his nephew Saxe Coverdale. Considered one of the fastest speedboats in the state, the *Mercury* was a regular and successful competitor at local regattas and Motor Yacht Club of Tasmania events for many years.

Opposite (Top and Bottom): *Landfall* under construction.
Courtesy Guy Rex Collection (Suzanne Rex).

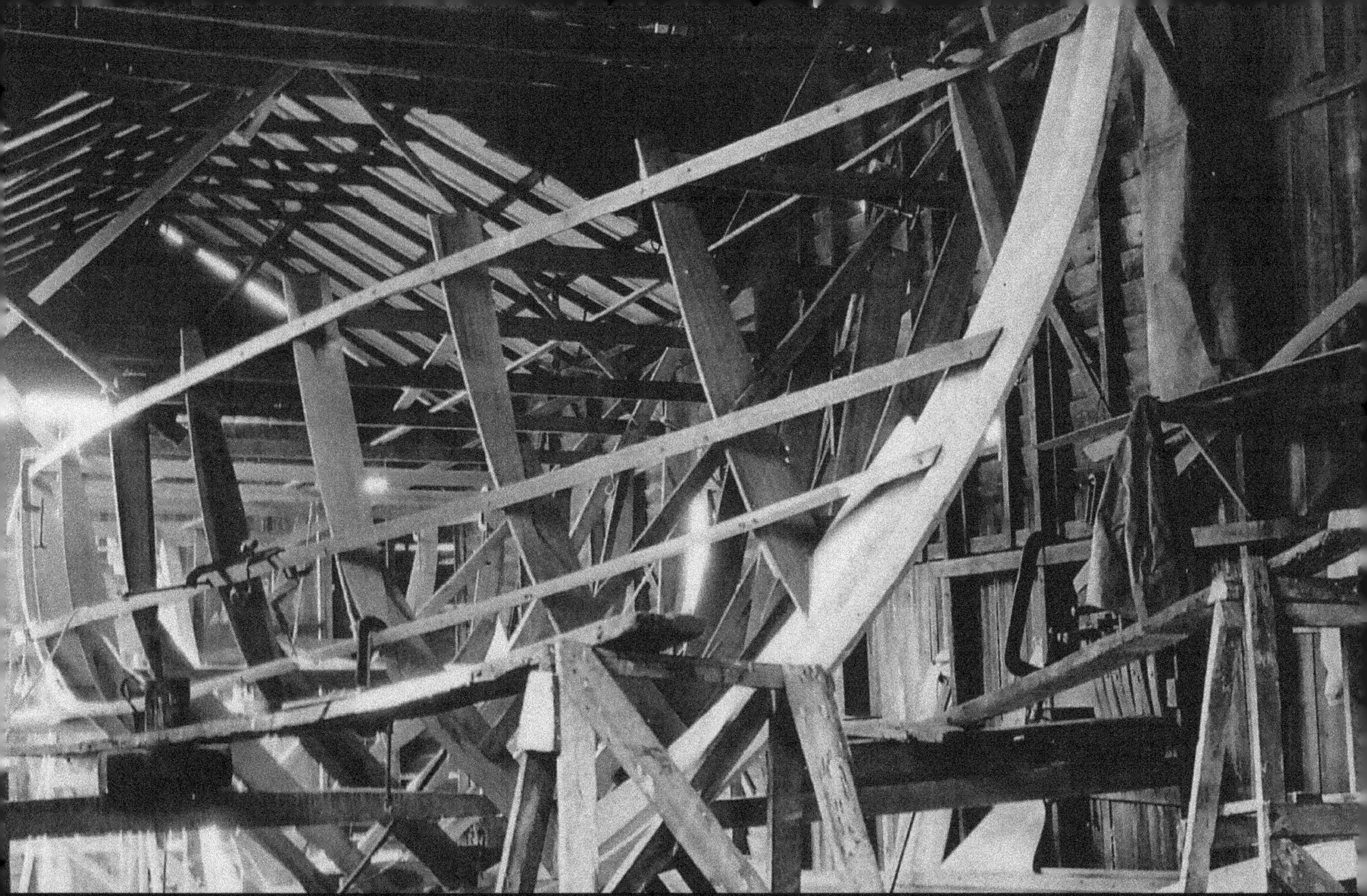

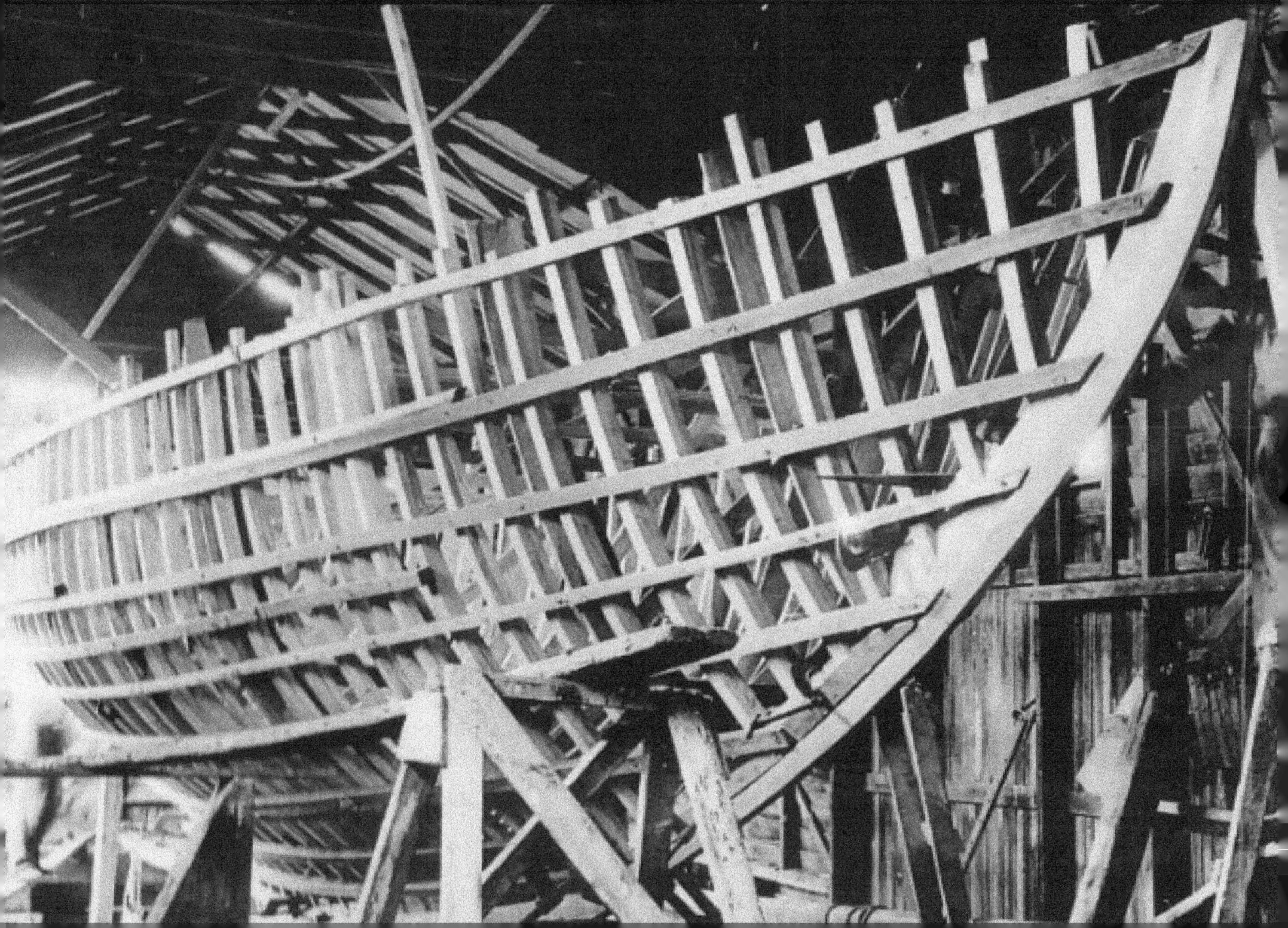

Left and Right Pages: ***Landfall*** **under construction.**
Courtesy Guy Rex Collection (Suzanne Rex).

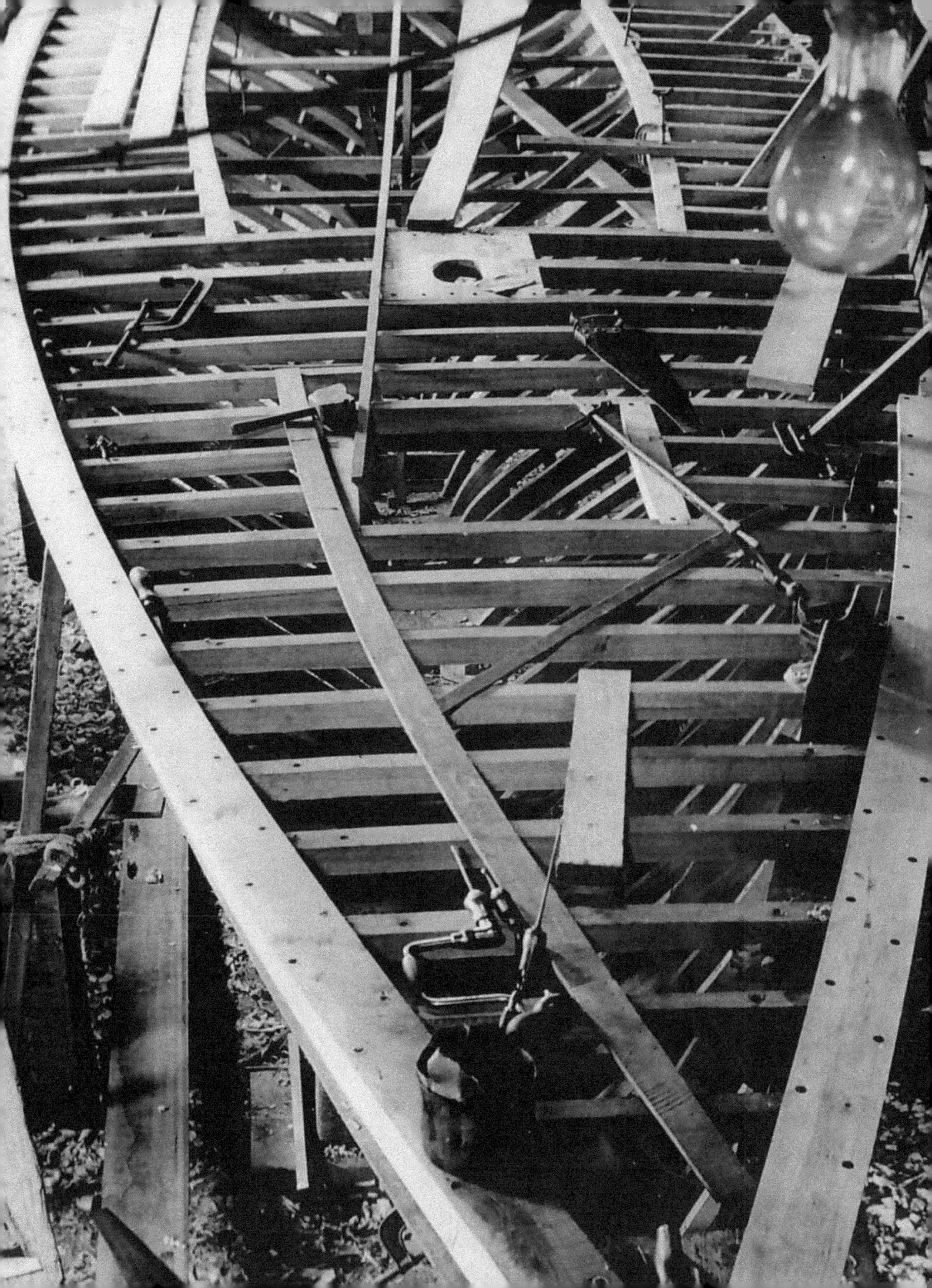

Left and Right Pages: *Landfall* under construction.
Courtesy Guy Rex Collection (Suzanne Rex).

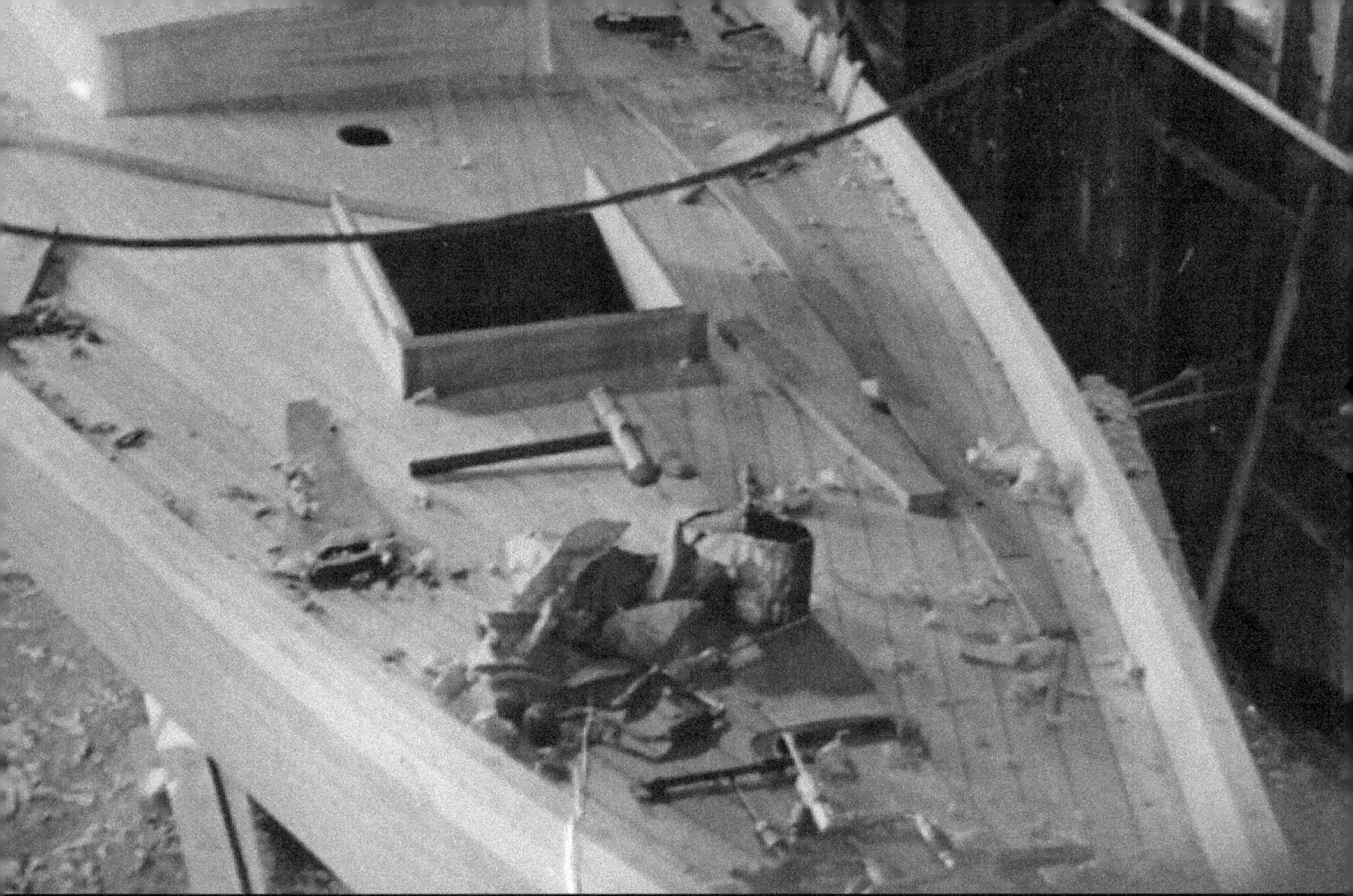

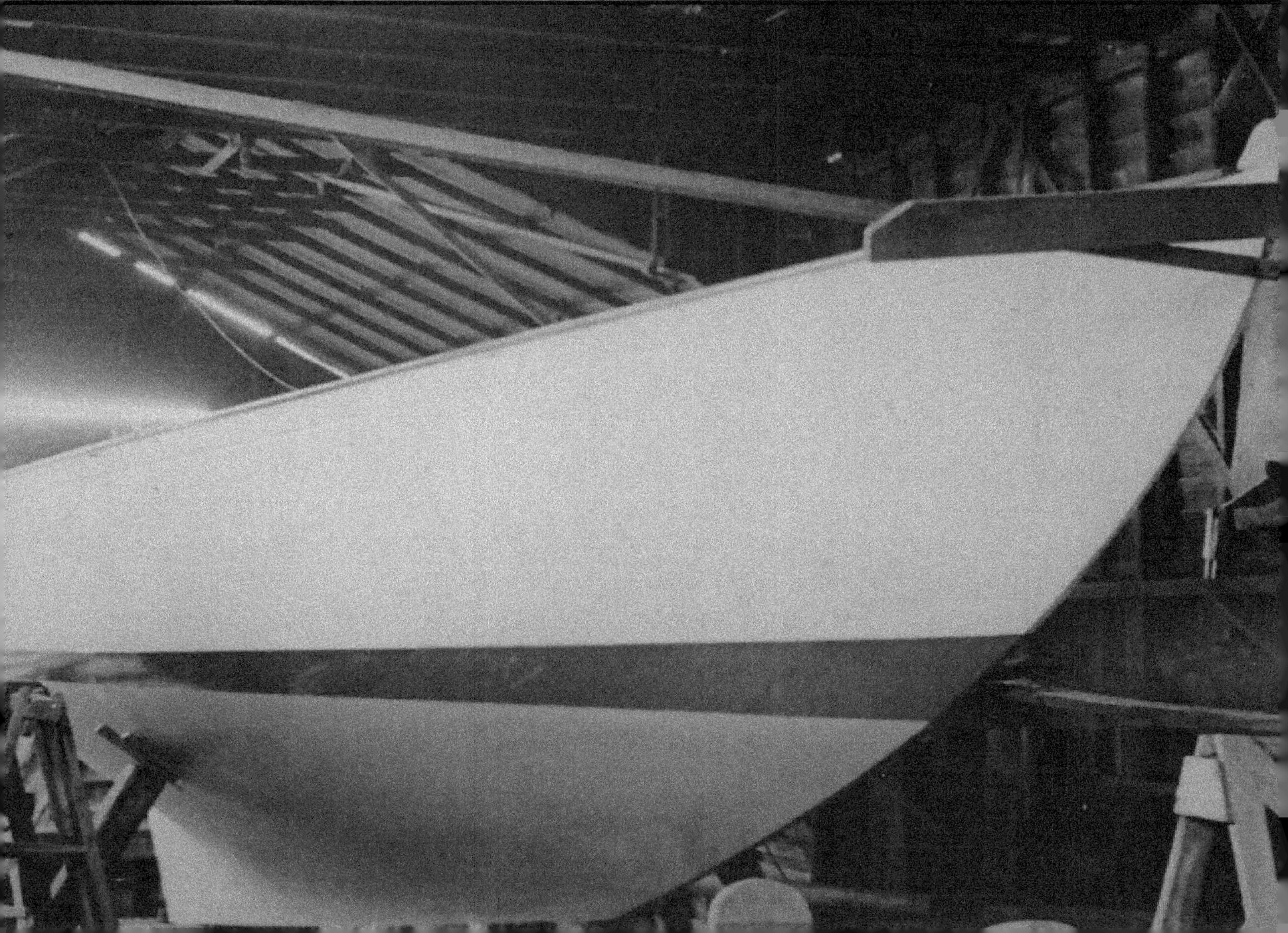

World War II

Though World War II hindered the work load at many of Tasmania's boatyards, Percy Coverdale's 52 ft cruiser, built to replace the *Chloe*, was one of a handful of recreational vessels launched during this period. Dubbed the "largest and finest auxiliary cruising yacht turned out of a Hobart slipyard," the Bermuda-rigged *Winston Churchill* was launched on 29 October 1941.

Immediately following the *Winston Churchill's* launch, Percy Coverdale laid the keel of a cruiser to the order of Audie Palfreyman. This particular vessel, *Matthew Flinders*, also took a few years to complete and was launched in mid-1945. Under Palfreyman's tutelage, she went on to compete in several of the early Sydney to Hobart yacht races, often racing against Percy Coverdale in *Winston Churchill*.

Another vessel built during this period was the Bermuda-rigged 32 ft yacht *Prelude*. Though not noted in the Tasmanian press, she was advertised for sale in Sydney in the mid-1940s.

Matthew Flinders. Courtesy Maritime Museum of Tasmania.

The Late 1940s

Post World War II, the 52 ft fishing boat *Waterwitch*, designed by Percy Coverdale, was built by Purdon and Featherstone to the order of Neil Campbell and launched in December 1946. Percy also began construction of a Marconi-rigged ocean racing sloop adapted from an American design by Colin Philp of Hobart and built to the order of Justice Hutchins. Named *White Cloud*, the vessel took over two years to complete, Percy assisted by Norm Taylor in the latter stages of construction. Unfortunately due to ill health, Justice Hutchins sold the *White Cloud* to A. E. Herbert of New South Wales just prior to launch, which took place on 23 December 1948.

In March 1949 Percy Coverdale completed the speedboat *Miss Pam*, the second such boat built for his nephew Saxe Coverdale. Later that year Percy completed a 36 ft cruising ketch to a design by William Garden of Seattle, USA, and built to the order of Jack West Lau, a yachtsman of Launceston. The vessel included a 4 ton cast iron keel produced by a Launceston foundry which at the time was considered the largest casting ever made in Tasmania for a private vessel. Though initially called *Frayja,* the vessel's name was later changed to *Sailmaker*.

White Cloud.
Courtesy Tasmanian Archive and Heritage Office.

The Last Vessels

The 1950s saw Percy Coverdale slowing down, both at his boatyard and in terms of his sailing activities. In March 1955, at the age of 73, he sold his large cruiser *Winston Churchill*. Instead he opted to use a 23 ft open boat, *Chloe II*, as his own boat. The last big boat Percy is noted as building was the yacht *Secheron*, launched in 1958.

Sydney to Hobart Yacht Races

In addition to his boat building activities, Percy Coverdale was a passionate competitor and ardent supporter of the 640 nautical mile Sydney to Hobart Yacht Race, most notably competing in the inaugural race held in 1945. Up until this point Australia's longest ocean race was the Royal Yacht Club of Tasmania's Bruny Island Race.

One of nine competitors, and the only Tasmanian entrant to participate in the first Sydney to Hobart Yacht Race, Percy Coverdale's cruiser *Winston Churchill* was scheduled to leave Hobart for Sydney on 13 December 1945. However, owing to Percy breaking his wrist while launching the vessel two days prior, the boat's departure was delayed. Determined to compete and stating in the press that his injury would not be "much" of a hindrance, Percy sailed the *Winston Churchill* to Sydney on 15 December, her crew comprising Max Creese (boat builder of Battery Point), brothers Neall and Ken Batt, Keith Wilson and F. Chamberlain.

Expected to perform well in the race, the *Winston Churchill* enjoyed a substantial lead until becoming becalmed off Tasmania's east coast. Still, she managed to cross the line second behind *Rani* and was greeted by hundreds of spectators at the Hobart wharf.

Obviously enticed by his experience Percy Coverdale signed on to compete in the 1946 Sydney to Hobart Yacht Race. This time the *Winston Churchill* was one of five Tasmanian yachts to compete and one of 21 in total. With an entirely new crew (comprising E. R. Taylor, E. Edwards, G. Peacock, D. Williams and A. Watchorn) and with Percy again at the helm, the boat suffered a mishap while sailing down Tasmania's east coast and was forced to retire owing to her mast snapping while 30 miles off Scamander. *Winston Churchill* was in a race-winning position at the time.

Remaining a fervent competitor, Percy Coverdale registered for the 1947 Sydney to Hobart Yacht Race. By now in his mid 60s, he was noted in the press as having reduced his participation in minor yacht races, opting instead to focus his efforts on the larger races, including the Maria Island Ocean Race. *Winston Churchill* was one of eight Tasmanian yachts to compete in the 1947 Sydney to Hobart Race and one of 30 yachts overall. Along with Percy Coverdale, her crew comprised D. Williams, E. R. Taylor, A. Watchorn, Ernest Parker and W. Aylisse. A fisherman from Triabunna, Ernest Parker, had come to Percy Coverdale's assistance when *Winston Churchill* lost her mast during the 1946 race. In return Percy invited him to partake in the 1947 race. After an uneventful journey from Sydney, the consistently competitive *Winston Churchill* finished sixth across the line.

Right: Crew of the *Winston Churchill* just before the start of the 1945 Sydney to Hobart Yacht Race. From left: Keith Wilson, Ken Batt, Max Creese, Neall Batt, and F. Chamberlain. In front: Percy Coverdale, the skipper, with his arm in a sling. He broke a wrist shortly before leaving Hobart. Courtesy: *The Mercury,* 28 December 1945.

Below: Percy and Minnie Coverdale following completion of the 1945 Sydney to Hobart Yacht Race.
Courtesy: *Australian Women's Weekly,* 19 January 1946.

HOBART CREW IN OCEAN RACE

EETING for Percy Coverdale, skipper of the Winston Churchill, from his wife.

Stoical husband

THE Winston Churchill, after seeming to have the race won, came in second, 17 hours after the Rani, but this chilling disappointment did not lessen the schoolgirl-like welcome her gaunt, 65-year-old skipper, Percy Coverdale, received from his wife.

Mrs. Coverdale is 67—a bright, charming woman with dark hair turning a steely gray.

She hugged and kissed her stoical husband, who sailed from Hobart to Sydney and then returned as a race competitor with his badly fractured right arm in plaster.

It was the fifth Sydney-Hobart voyage he has made since he married, 33 years ago.

The Coverdales, like the Livesays, have loved sailing-boats as long as they can remember, and have sailed together all round Tasmania.

Before Mr. Coverdale broke his arm, Mrs. Coverdale was signed on to sail in the Winston Churchill to Sydney and return in her as a member of the crew.

"But when my husband broke his arm he talked me into staying behind," said Mrs. Coverdale. "He said he couldn't look after me with one arm as well as he could with two.

"I am sorry now I didn't go, because at least I could have fed him during the worst parts of the trip."

The Coverdales live in a neat little cottage built behind Mr. Coverdale's slipway.

The walls and mantelpiece of their living-room are covered with a striking collection of sailing trophies and pictures of sailing-boats, gathered together over thirty years.

Pride of place is held by an enlargement of Mr. Winston Churchill, who, after Mr. Coverdale, is Mrs. Coverdale's greatest hero.

"He's my favorite," Mrs. Coverdale said. "That's why our boat is named after him.

"My husband wanted to call her Southern Light, but I held out for Winston Churchill.

"I think Mr. Churchill is a Christian man, and a one-woman man. Altogether I like his ideals.

"We didn't win, but one has to rise above disappointments like that.

"All that matters is I am proud of my husband and his boat."

Mrs. Illingworth, wife of the winning skipper, is proud of her husband's success in the race, but frankly admits she wouldn't have liked to have been on the trip.

"My yachting has been confined to Sydney Harbor up till now, and I don't think that's any apprenticeship for an ocean race," she said.

Formerly Philippa Vaughan, of Sydney, she met her husband some years ago in Bombay, where he was with the R.N. and she was attached to the Ministry of War Transport. Before that she lived in Holland.

When Capt. Illingworth was transferred to Australia she came out to Sydney, and they were married just a year ago.

She is hoping her husband will be home in time to celebrate their first wedding anniversary, on January 13.

"Perce could tell good yarns. I can still picture him - sucking on an old pipe out the side of his mouth - telling how, in a fog, he dropped the anchor, went to sleep, and when he got up in the morning found he was in Constitution Dock. And coming up the river, finding a rock he had never seen before and landing on it to boil the billy, only to find it was a whale. As an apprentice, he saw a practical joke misfire. A plank over the water toilet on the slipyard was partly cut through underneath with a saw. The boss (Lucas I think) came down to use the toilet, the plank broke, and the boss ended up in the water - the wrong person! The cut was made for someone else."

Noel D. Barrett
(*Maritime Times of Tasmania,*
 Autumn 2015)

Percy Coverdale did not enter *Winston Churchill* in the 1948 Sydney to Hobart Yacht Race, likely owing to his time taken up in getting the *White Cloud* launched. And though he did not compete in any further races, many of the vessels he built have and continue do so. For example, at 81 years of age, *Landfall*, helmed by owner Mike Strong, most notably participated in the 2016 Sydney to Hobart Yacht Race.

Deliveries

As well as being involved in the building of vessels, Percy Coverdale's yard was actively involved in the slipping, repair, maintenance and overhaul of vessels. In the 1930s, another component of his business emerged, the delivery of vessels to and from the mainland.

In April 1937 Percy Coverdale sailed E. H. Webster's yawl *Spindrift* to Sydney, with a crew comprising Neall Batt, Jack Hansen and Jerry Chamberlain. In January of the following year Percy sailed the auxiliary yawl *Utiekah III* from Hobart to Melbourne owing to illness of the vessel's owner, Mr. I. Giles. A few months later, Percy was back in Melbourne to sail the yacht *Acrospire III* (renamed *Acushla*) to Hobart on behalf of A. J. Drysdale who had recently purchased the vessel. In March 1939 Percy Coverdale sailed his own yacht *Chloe* to Sydney following the vessel's sale. Combined, these journeys allowed Percy Coverdale to fulfil his love of sailing while supplementing his income. They also made him one of the country's most experienced deep-water helmsmen.

Retirement and Death

Percy Coverdale contined working at his boatyard until his retirement in 1961 at the age of 79. He died at New Town on 29 March 1963, aged 81. Percy was cremated with his ashes deposited at Cornelian Bay Cemetery. His beloved wife, Minnie (nee Rodgers), predeceased him by four years.

With no children, Percy Coverdale bequeathed his estate, including his Battery Point boatyard, to his only surviving brother Eric. The yard was subsequently leased to Bill Foster for a number of years before being sold and converted to a private residence.

Winston Churchill (circa 1960).
Courtesy Tasmanian Archive and Heritage Office.

Vessels Built by Percy Coverdale and Employees at Battery Point (1906 – 1958).

1906. Rowing boat. Short four racing boat built to the order of the Hobart Rowing Club.

1906. *Florence May*. Yacht. 46 x 10.5 x 4.2 ft. Attributed to Percy Coverdale and likely built at a Battery Point boatyard owned by another builder. Originally built as a yacht to the order of George Cheverton. In May 1907 noted as being fitted with an oil engine at Charlie Lucas' yard. Advertised for sale in February 1913, fitted with a 12 hp Union engine. Later owned by the Sward family for several decades. By 1954 owned by Alfred and Don Haigh. Later transferred to Gippsland Lakes, VIC. In 2017 returned to southern TAS, located at Kermandie.

1914. *Volito*. Fishing boat. 54 x 12 x 5.5 ft. Huon pine ketch. Built to the order of John Rae of Hobart and launched in late 1914. Leased to Henry Parker of the Tasman Peninsula. Seized by the water police in July 1917 for use of illegal craypots, though returned to Rae after payment of a fine. By 1927 owned by Walter and Leslie Marks of San Remo, VIC; the pair sadly drowned off Babel Island in the vessel's dinghy in September 1928. Advertised for sale by tender in October 1929. By 1935 owned by James Rattenbury of St Helens. Noted to be still in existence into the 1950s.

1914. *Naomi (Telopea)*. Yacht. 29.8 x 8.2 x 3.8 ft. Yawl designed and built by Percy Coverdale for his own use and first noted on the Derwent in early 1914. By 1918 in use as a fishing boat though still owned by Coverdale. Advertised for sale in July 1923. Relaunched by July 1924 as the auxiliary cruiser *Telopea* owned by Clive Lord, curator of the Tasmanian Museum and Art Gallery. Named after Lord's home at 5 Quorn Street, Sandy Bay. Advertised for sale in January 1931. Purchased by Norman Pearce. Post WWII, converted to a fishing boat and advertised for sale. By 1950 owned by Ray Etchell of Stanley. Wrecked on 25 October 1952 off Robbins Island on TAS north east coast with the unfortunate loss of three lives, including Ray Etchell and his young son.

1915. *Tuna*. Motor boat. 22.5 ft. First noted on the River Derwent in November 1915. Built to the order of W. J. Mangan. Fitted with a 4.5 hp Gray engine. By 1924 owned by V. Horlock. Advertised for sale in October 1926. By 1927 owned by C. Smith. By the late 1930s and well into the 1950s owned by R. E. Smith. Still in existence, more recently owned by Andrew Nichols. Advertised for sale in late 2015.

1915. *Gray*. Motor boat. 14 ft. First noted on the River Derwent in November 1915. Built by Percy Coverdale for his own use. Fitted with a 6 hp Gray engine. Successfully raced for several seasons. Disappears from the records after 1919.

1920. *Alida R*. Fishing boat. 50.6 x 15.5 ft. Built to the order of R. Spaulding and launched in late 1920. By June 1926 owned by John Rae (Jr) of Hobart and seized by the Tasmanian Inspector of Fisheries for illegally crayfishing in Bass Strait. Seized again in February 1929, this time for fishing without a licence. Advertised for sale in October 1929. In August 1936 noted to be owned by A. Lockwood of Crib Point, VIC, and employed in Bass Strait. Remained operating in Bass Strait until at least 1945. Disappears from the records thereafter.

1920. *Valma*. Fishing boat. 40 x 11 x 6.5 ft. Likely built during the early 1920s and known by a different name. First shows up in the records in 1941 when competing at the Shipwrights Point Regatta, owned by F. W. Marks of Dover. A regular at local regattas and sailing events throughout the 1940s, remaining in the Marks family's hands for several decades. Wrecked on 10 November 1990 at Conical Rocks on TAS west coast; all hands saved.

1923. *Eveline May (Premier)*. Ketch. 44 x 14 x 4.7 ft. Built to the order of Arthur Sward of Bruny Island and launched in November 1923. Intended to carry timber to Hobart from the Huon. Remained in Sward's possession until July 1938 when sold to the Tasmanian government for use as a training ship for unemployed youths. Renamed *Premier* and subsequently converted to a motor ketch. Used as a patrol and police boat. Still in existence, privately owned since 1983 and based in Launceston, TAS. Recently transferred to Hobart and advertised for sale in 2017.

1925. *Storm Bay*. Fishing boat. 52 x 13 x 6.5 ft. Built to the order of George Bridge of Nubeena and launched on 21 July 1925. Designed by Alfred Blore, possibly in conjunction with Percy Coverdale. Spent more than 50 years employed in the local fishing industry. Sold by the Bridge family in 1963 and transferred to St Helens for use as a crayboat. Still in existence, restored back to her original condition by owner Tim Phillips of The Wooden Boatshop, Sorrento, VIC.

1927. *Tanda (Esmeralda, Ralda, Lady Margaret)*. Motor cruiser. 45.6 x 12 x 6.3 ft. Built to the order of Reginald Prevost of Sydney, NSW, to an Alfred Blore design. Sold in October 1935 to Claude Carter, and renamed *Esmeralda*. Requisitioned by the Navy during WWII and said to have been used as an "Air Force Rescue Boat". Sold in June 1946 as war surplus and acquired by L. Coleman of Mackay, QLD, and used as a tourist vessel to cruise the Whitsunday Islands. By the late 1950s and into the 1960s owned by the Markwell family of Bulimba, QLD. Later moved to far north QLD and renamed *Ralda*. Still in existence. Now named *Lady Margaret* and located at Gippsland Lakes, VIC. Advertised for sale in 2017.

1927. *Imp*. Yacht. 24.5 x 6.7 x 4 ft. The first Derwent Class yacht. Built to the order of E. H. Webster based on a design by A. C. Barber and P. C. Douglas. Launched on 7 December 1927. Purchased by Guy Rex in late 1929. Advertised for sale in May 1934 and subsequently purchased by Brian Gibson. Shortly thereafterpurchased by T. Roberts. In 1938 sold to K. R. Gourlay. Several owners during WWII, including C. M. Elliott, owing to Gourlay being called up for active duty. Advertised for sale in April 1948, and regularly between December 1951 and December 1954. Owned by Tom Pilkington of Battery Point during the mid-1950s.

1928. *Pixie*. Yacht. 24.5 x 6.7 x 4 ft. Derwent class yacht built to the order of E. H. Webster but purchased part-way through construction by Arthur Coole of Cygnet. Designed by A. C. Barber and P. C. Douglas. Launched in mid to late 1928. Based out of Cygnet though regularly joined in with D class races on the Derwent. Transferred to G. Coole following the death of Arthur Coole in October 1933. By the mid to late 1930s, owned by E. R. Taylor, and later R. H. Taylor. Advertised for sale in September 1951. Subsequently sold and converted to a cruiser. Between 1985 and 1988 owned by Jonothan Davis; in 1994 owned by D. McCulloch. Still in existence, located at Wynyard, TAS.

1928. *Gnome*. Yacht. 24.5 x 6.7 x 4 ft. Derwent class yacht built by Walter Taylor and Eric McCreary and designed by A. C. Barber and P. C. Douglas. Launched from Percy Coverdale's slip on 16 October 1928. Helmed by owner Walter Taylor for several decades, and in the 1950s by Dave Barrett. Subsequent owners included B. C. Butler, A. G. Kemp, P. C. Makepeace, D. Gumley, A. D. Fahey, Mick Cusick and Derek Adams. Still in existence, and currently under restoration.

1928. *Rachel Irene (Karen Ann)*. Fishing boat. 42.6 x 13 ft. Built to the order of C. and E. Fredericks of Portland, VIC, and launched by November 1928. Employed in the crayfishing and fishing industries off the VIC and SA coasts. Sold in 1950 to W. H. Peters of Millicent, SA, and renamed *Karen Ann*. After several more changes of ownership, wrecked on 28 December 1980 off the coast of Robe, SA.

Vessels Built by Percy Coverdale and Employees at Battery Point (1906 – 1958).

1929. *Rowena (Mary Norling).* Fishing boat. 55.3 x 15.3 x 6.2 ft. Built to the order of McKay Brothers of Hobart and launched in 1929. Employed in the coastal fishing industry. Sold to J. Norling of Phillip Island, VIC, in March 1939 and renamed *Mary Norling*. Wrecked at the entrance to Georges Bay, TAS, on 21 July 1979; all hands saved. At the time owned by Raymond and Marion Brearly of Point Lonsdale, VIC.

1929. *Windward (Windward II).* Yacht. 43.5 x 10.3 x 6.5 ft. Built to the order of E. H. Webster and launched on 18 December 1929. Designed by Norman Dallimore of England. Transferred to Sydney, NSW, in late 1930 having been purchased by James March Hardie, rear commodore of the Royal Prince Alfred Yacht Club. Successfully competed in Sydney Harbour racing events and regattas for many decades, re-rigged as a cutter in 1938 and consequently renamed *Windward II* owing to a vessel of the same name already being present in Sydney. Sold to K. S. Hansen two years prior to Hardie's death in 1979. After several more changes of ownership and locations, transferred to Melbourne, VIC, in 2000. Still in existence. Has been extensively restored and currently races with the Royal Melbourne Yacht Squadron and the Classic Yacht Association of Australia in VIC, owned by James Woods.

1930. *Amy Johnson (Whyalla).* Fishing boat. 45 x 14 x 5.5 ft. Built to the order of George Darley of Port Fairy, VIC, and launched on 25 June 1930. Initially employed in the crayfishing industry. Purchased by the SA government in June 1936 for use by the Fisheries and Game Department as a research and patrol vessel. Following alterations, including to her rig, and installation of a diesel engine at Port Adelaide, relaunched in April 1937 under the name of *Whyalla*. Possibly sequestered by the RAAF for use in WWII.

1931. *Ninie.* Yacht. 42 x 8 x 6.2 ft. A class yacht built for Percy Coverdale's own use based on an American R type 8 metre design. Launched on 8 January 1931. Raced successfully over many seasons, including winning a number of Royal Yacht Club of Tasmania and Derwent Sailing Squadron pennants, as well as the Betsey Island and Bruny Island races. Sold in 1938 to Don and Doug McKean who retained possession until recently. Still in existence, currently under restoration down the Huon, TAS, by Dave Golding.

1932. *Adina (Seawind, Maskee).* Yacht. 30 x 9.2 x 4.5 ft. King Billy. Shipped to Sydney, NSW, as a hull and fitted out at Halvorson's in Neutral Bay by owner J. D. Borrowman. First noted as a "comparative newcomer" in December 1933. Used by the RAAF during WWII to train pilots on water navigation. By 1953 owned by Norm Brooker and renamed *Seawind*. By 1959 owned by H. B. Vaughan and T. M. Taylor. By the early 1960s owned by S. Berg and renamed *Maskee*. Reverted back to *Adina* in the 1980s when purchased by Lindsay Buckmaster. Still in existence, owned by the Tait family since 2000 and currently under restoration in Perth, WA.

1932. *Wanderer (Thetis).* Yacht. 43.5 x 8.5 x 7 ft. Bermuda-rigged cutter. Built to the order of E. H. Webster based on Percy Coverdale's own design and launched on 27 October 1932. Purchased by Dr Rupert Furber of Sydney in June 1933 and renamed *Thetis*. A successful Division 1 racing yacht for several decades. Advertised for sale in late 1949 and purchased by L. Vickery who retained ownership for many years. By 1960 owned by Ray Hutcherson and noted to be aground at Ettalong, NSW, though recovered with only minor damage. For sale in Sydney in April 1962. More recently advertised for sale in Sydney in August 1987 and again in July 1992.

1933. Dinghy. Donated to the Derwent Sailing Squadron.

1934. Dinghy. Cedar. Donated to the Derwent Sailing Squadron.

1934. *Sjo-Ro*. Yacht. 29.4 x 6.8 x 7.1 ft. Built to the order of Sir Claude Plowman of Sydney, NSW, and launched in October 1934. Designed by William Fife (Jr). Represented NSW in the 1935 Northcote Cup. Advertised for sale in September 1940. By 1945 owned by F. H. Walker. By 1947 owned by W. Fesq. Advertised for sale in May 1948, in March 1950 and again in May 1956. By 1957 owned by J. Dempster, by 1959 owned by C. Halliday, by 1964 owned by A. Darvell, by 1967 owned by P. Harvey. Advertised for sale in June 1973. Still in existence, recently restored in Sydney by owner Jeremy Arnott.

1935. *Landfall*. Yacht. 44 x 9.8 x 6.5 ft. Built to the order of Guy Rex and Charles Davies and launched on 9 October 1935. Intended as a cruising yacht, plans provided by Olin Stephens of Sparkman and Stephens, New York. Sold to J. Linacre, commodore of the Royal Brighton Yacht Club, VIC, in April 1938. Subsequently sold to Don Richardson of Melbourne. Competed in the 1952 Sydney to Hobart Yacht Race, finishing third across the line. Competed in the 1954 Sydney to Hobart Yacht Race though was forced to retire. Competed in the 1976 Sydney to Hobart Yacht Race, skippered by owner Ken Elliott of Geelong, VIC. Purchased by Jamie Saunders of Hobart in November 1978. Purchased by Mike Strong in April 1992 and transferred to Sydney, NSW. Still in existence; owned by Mike Strong and most recently competed in the 2015 and 2016 Sydney to Hobart yacht races, retiring in the 2015 race and finishing 81st in the 2016 race.

1938. *Lewan*. Yacht. 43 x 7.8 x 4.5 ft. 30 square metre yacht built to the order of Neil Campbell based on a design by Knud Reimers of Sweden and launched in September 1938. Transferred to Sydney, NSW, in mid-1939, racing under the ownership of G. E. Bryant for several decades. By 1960 owned by A. Oakes. Advertised for sale in February 1965. By 1967 owned by P. Geddes, by 1977 and into the early 1980s owned by J. Crawford, by 1986 owned by J. Taylor. Still in existence, currently located in Wangaratta, VIC, and advertised for sale in 2016.

1938. *Chloe*. Yacht. 36 ft. Designed and built by Percy Coverdale for his own use. Took several years to complete and launched by October 1938. Won the 100 mile Bruny Island Race in her first season. Sailed to Sydney in March 1939 and sold to W. H. Walton for £925. Still in existence, owned by Sean Langman of Port Huon, TAS, and undergoing restoration.

1939. *Mercury*. Speedboat. 225 ci inboard speedboat built to the order of Percy Coverdale's nephew Saxe Coverdale and launched by September 1939. A successful competitor in local regattas and Motor Yacht Club of Tasmania events for many years. Sold to L. Stewart in 1949. Advertised for sale in July 1950. Likely purchased by Don Elliott.

1941. *Winston Churchill*. Yacht. 52 x 12.5 ft. Designed and built by Percy Coverdale for his own use and launched on 29 October 1941. Competed in the first Sydney to Hobart Yacht Race in 1945, finishing second. Also competed in the 1946 and 1947 races. Transferred to Melbourne in March 1955 when purchased by Sir Arthur Warner. Competed in the 1955, 1956, 1957, 1958, 1959, 1960, 1961, 1962, 1963, 1969, 1971, and 1977 Sydney to Hobart yacht races, helmed by the Warner family. Later transferred to Sydney where she was advertised for sale in the early 1990s. Competed in the 1994 Sydney to Hobart Yacht Race. Purchased by Richard Winning in 1995. Competed in the 1997 Sydney to Hobart Yacht Race. Sank off the south coast of NSW on 28 December 1998 while competing in the 1998 Sydney to Hobart Yacht Race with the sad loss of three lives.

Vessels Built by Percy Coverdale and Employees at Battery Point (1906 – 1958).

1941. *Prelude.* **Yacht.** 32 x 10 x 5.5 ft. Advertised for sale in Sydney in July 1945.

1945. *Matthew Flinders.* **Ketch.** 58 ft. Built to the order of Audie Palfreyman. Construction began in 1941, though not completed until October 1945. Competed in the 1946 and 1947 Sydney to Hobart yacht races. Embarked on a 4,500 mile cruise of northern Australia in May 1951, returning to Hobart by February 1952. Possibly transferred to QLD in the 1960s.

1946. *Novar.* **Boat.** 14 ft. Clinker built rowboat. Transferred to VIC and used for many years to swim racehorses on the Mornington Peninsula. Still in existence; owned by Peter Harvey.

1948. *White Cloud.* **Yacht.** 49 x 11.5 x 7 ft. Built to the order of Justice Hutchins with the assistance of Norm Taylor. Based on an American design adapted by Colin Philp of Hobart. Sold to A. E. Herbert of Sydney, NSW, just prior to launch (on 23 December 1948). By December 1952 owned by George Brenac and competed in that year's Sydney to Hobart Yacht Race finishing fourth. In September 1953 left Sydney for a 1,180 mile ocean race to Noumea, finishing first across the line and second on handicap. Also competed in the 1954 Sydney to Hobart Yacht Race, finishing sixth. Later sold to Kees Huyer, a member of the New York Yacht Club. Still in existence, based in Florida, USA.

1949. *Miss Pam.* **Speedboat.** Built to the order of Percy Coverdale's nephew Saxe Coverdale. A successful competitor in many local regattas and Motor Yacht Club of Tasmania events. Sold to a mainland buyer in October 1951.

1953. *Frayja (Sailmaker).* **Ketch.** 36.7 x 10.1 x 5.4 ft. Built to the order of Jack West Lau of Launceston based on a design by William Garden of Seattle, USA. Initially named *Frayja*, though later changed to *Sailmaker*. Transferred to Melbourne, VIC, in 1953. Competed in the 1958 Sydney to Hobart Yacht Race, owned by A. Raisback. Advertised for sale in Melbourne, VIC, in March 1962. Later owned by Dr Richard Ham of Melbourne and cruised extensively around TAS and QLD. Still in existence; owned by Michael Couch since 1999 and based in Sydney, NSW.

1950s. *Chloe II.* **Open boat.** 23 ft. Likely built by Percy Coverdale for his own use. Still in existence; located in southern TAS and owned by Ethan O'neal.

1958. *Secheron.* **Yacht.** 26 ft. Built by Percy Coverdale for his own use. Later owned by Roy Scott. Last noted to be at Franklin, TAS, in 2014 in a deteriorated state.

Ninie (in 1985). Courtesy Ed Glover.

Ernest Bayes

The son of a shipwright and nephew of two of Battery Point's renowned 19th century boat builders, Ernest Bayes continued the family tradition, building boats at Battery Point between 1907 and the mid-1920s. He later moved to the north west coast where he built a punt for use on the Arthur River. Following, Ernest Bayes took on public works projects, including building the Hastings swimming pool. Still, at least a handful of boats were built by Ernest Bayes at Battery Point, many in conjunction with his brother Esker, of which the motor boats *Brooke* and *Latura* are still in existence.

Ernest Franklin Bayes was born at Battery Point on 18 November 1880, the sixth of eight children born to Thomas and Isabella Bayes (nee Parker). The Bayes family were well-known in Hobart's boat building sphere. Ernest Bayes' father was a shipwright of Battery Point. Two uncles (William Bayes and William Whitehouse) were accomplished boat builders of Battery Point, between them building several steam ferries that furnished regional passenger trades, and many smaller vessels. Ernest Bayes' cousin Tucker Abel also owned and operated a boatyard at Battery Point. Given location, circumstance and family connections there was likely little opportunity for Ernest Bayes to not consider a maritime-related career.

In addition to boat building, several generations of the Bayes family were prominent in local rowing fixtures. Continuing this tradition, Ernest Bayes and his three brothers (Thomas, Esker and Charles) successfully competed in local, regional and state rowing races and regattas beginning in the early 1900s. Most notably, between 1902 and 1905 the foursome earned the title of the Champion Fours of Tasmania.

Thomas Bayes and his four sons. Left to Right: Charles, Thomas, Ernest and Esker.
Cox: Clyde Chancellor. Courtesy *Weekly Courier*, 19 April 1902.

Bayes Brothers of Battery Point

After undertaking a boat building apprenticeship, and following several years spent gaining further experience, Ernest Bayes and his brother Esker established a boatyard at Battery Point some time around 1907, operating out of a shed on the Purdon and Featherstone property. During their time at Battery Point the Bayes brothers were primarily involved in repair work, particularly of rowing boats, as well as the on-sale of existing boats. However, a handful of vessels were built. These include the motor launch *Brooke* (built in 1912) and the motor boat *Natoma* (built around 1915). It is also possible that Bayes Brothers built several more motor boats during this period, including the *Eagle, Osprey* and *Wayaree*. Numerous rowing boats and dinghies were additionally built by the pair. The fishing boat *D.J.V.* (built in 1915) is often credited as being built by Ernest Bayes, though was more than likely built by original owner H. G. Spaulding.

Around 1916 Bayes Brothers appear to have relinquished work at Battery Point. Ernest instead opted to operate out of a yard in Collins Street, Hobart, where the C class yacht *Wavie* (later converted to a fishing boat and named *Mavis*) was likely built. However, the pair returned to Battery Point several years later. For example, the motor boat *Latura* was built by Ernest Bayes to the order of Henry Featherstone in 1924. The cruiser *Tahume*, built to the order of George Evans, though destroyed by fire the day after her launch in October 1926, was also built by Bayes Brothers. This particular vessel was modelled off the lines of the motor boat *Wayaree* though was somewhat larger. A replacement vessel, the *Nordecia*, was built by Neave Brothers out of Bayes Brothers' Battery Point shed the following year.

Additional Projects

Independent of his professional boat building work at Battery Point, Ernest Bayes is noted as having assisted F. L. Staples with construction of the Alfred Blore designed speedboat *Henry Ford,* which was launched in 1924, likely at Sandy Bay. Another vessel designed and built by this trio, the motor boat *Lady Madge*, was launched at Sandy Bay in January 1926. Ernest Bayes is additionally noted as undertaking repair work, including of an eight rowing scull at Franklin in 1927.

Following his time at Battery Point, Ernest Bayes and his son Randolph were noted as building a punt for use on the Arthur River over a period of 10 weeks in 1935. Ernest later worked for the Public Works Department and, in 1938, was involved with construction of the Hastings Cave swimming pool.

Death

Ernest Bayes died in Hobart in February 1963 at the age of 82 and was buried at Cornelian Bay Cemetery, New Town. He was survived by his wife Amy (nee Allwood), and their only son Randolph.

Vessels Built by Ernest Bayes and his brother Esker at Battery Point (1907 – 1926).

1907. Rowing boat. Built to the order of the Derwent Rowing Club.

1912. *Brooke*. Motor launch. 25.6 x 7.1 x 2.6 ft. Built by Esker Bayes for his own use. Competed in local motor boat races and regattas. In the 1920s owned by George Evans, and subsequently D. H. Harvey. Several more changes of ownership in the succeeding decades. Still in existence, located in southern TAS. Advertised for sale in 2015.

1913. Motor boats. Numerous motor boats and hulls advertised for sale with and without engines.

1914. Dinghy. 12 ft. Built for the fishing boat *Clytie*.

1915. *Natoma*. Motor boat. 30 x 9.5 x 3.5 ft. First noted on the River
Derwent in March 1915. By 1916 owned by R. J. Chipman. In the 1920s owned by F. T. and C. Thompson. Advertised for sale in 1943, 1947 and 1953. Later owned by T. F. Pulfer. In the 1990s purchased by Henry and Kay Jacobs and extensively restored. Advertised for sale in 1995 in southern TAS. Later transferred to NSW.

1916. Cabin launch. 26 ft. Advertised for sale in June 1916.

1916. Dinghy. 10 ft. Advertised for sale in June 1916.

1921. Dinghy. 11 ft. Advertised for sale in December 1921.

1921. Dinghy. 12 ft. Advertised for sale in December 1921.

1924. *Latura*. Motor boat. Built to the order of Henry Featherstone and first noted on the River Derwent in March 1924. By the 1940s owned by A. Davis. Several decades later, extensively restored by owner Dr Lewis Garnham and relaunched in 2003. Since sold but still located in Hobart. A participant in the 2017 Australian Wooden Boat Festival.

1926. *Tahume*. Motor launch. 38 ft. Built to the order of George Evans, modelled off the motor boat *Wayaree,* though was somewhat larger. Destroyed by fire at Sandy Bay on 21 September 1926, one day following her launch.

A regatta at Prince of Wales Bay showing many motor boats (circa 1920s).
Courtesy Tasmanian Archive and Heritage Office.

Thomas Neave

A local lad and the son of a mariner, Thomas Neave undertook his shipwright apprenticeship at Battery Point with Purdon and Featherstone. In the years that followed he periodically operated out of Bayes Brothers' shed on the Purdon and Featherstone property where, between 1925 and 1933, Thomas Neave built at least seven vessels. Of these the *Grayling* and the *Aralla* are still in existence. One of Battery Point's lesser-known boat builders, Thomas Neave later successfully tendered for public works projects and also undertook residential building projects. For many years he was active in the Master Builders Association.

Thomas George William Neave was born on 9 September 1896 in Hobart, the eldest child of four boys born to William Thomas and Ida Sarah Elizabeth Neave (nee Groombridge). His father was a mariner and the Neave family lived at 2 South Street, Battery Point, close to the boat and ship yards.

Thomas Neave and his younger brothers were educated at the Central State School in Murray Street, Hobart. Upon leaving school Thomas secured work as a shipwright, undertaking an apprenticeship with Purdon and Featherstone at Battery Point where he was involved in building several vessels, including the steamer *Reemere*.

Grayling

Beginning in January 1917 Thomas and his younger brothers began competing in local regattas and races in the yacht *Yaralla*. Looking to replace the vessel with something bigger and faster, in August 1921 the Neave brothers began building a 37 ft A class yacht in the backyard of their parents' home in South Street, Battery Point. Designed by Alfred Blore, the *Grayling* was launched at Constitution Dock in Hobart on 9 September 1922, coinciding with Thomas Neave's 26th birthday. Showing his commitment to yachting, that same year Thomas was elected to the committee of the Derwent Sailing Squadron. He would remain active on the committee for more than a decade.

Grayling (circa 1929). Courtesy Harry Hale.

Boats and Public Works Projects

Beginning in the mid-1920s Thomas Neave began supplementing his boat building income by tendering for public works projects. Thomas' success in this field would see him cease boat building within a decade.

Between the years 1925 and 1933, however, several vessels were built by Thomas Neave (and his brothers) at Battery Point. For example, in March 1925 Thomas Neave completed the 12 ft cadet dinghy *Miss Joan*, built to the order of Harry Oliphant. In October 1926 Neave Brothers began building a motor yacht to the order of George Evans to replace his recently destroyed *Tahume*. Designed by Alfred Blore, the 40 ft *Nordecia* was built at Bayes Brothers' shed on the Purdon and Featherstone property and launched on 3 March 1927.

In June 1927 Neave Brothers were awarded the tender to build a fisheries patrol boat for the Sea Fisheries Board at a cost of £570. The contract marked the third vessel they had built to a design by Alfred Blore. William Gates was also noted to be involved with the design of this particular vessel, and Blore was notably involved with its build. The *Allara* was launched from Battery Point on 2 March 1928.

In mid-1928 Thomas Neave and his brothers began building a 58 ft fishing ketch intended for their own employment in the crayfishing industry. Named for their mother, the *Ida N.* was launched from Purdon and Featherstone's yard on 22 May 1929 and was the fourth vessel they had built to an Alfred Blore design.

In February 1929 Thomas Neave advertised a 10 ft Huon pine dinghy for sale. This particular boat was likely built at his residence, 11 McGregor Street, Battery Point. Just over three years later, in mid-1932, Thomas Neave and his brothers began building a fishing boat to replace the wrecked *Ida N.* Designed by Thomas Neave, the *Advance* was built behind 2 South Street and trucked to Constitution Dock in Hobart where she was launched on 28 September 1933. *Advance* is the last vessel known to have been built by Thomas Neave.

Boat Builder Turned Residential Builder

The late 1920s through to the 1950s saw Thomas Neave continue to successfully tender for public works projects and also undertake residential building projects. Of the latter, he is noted as the builder of 18 Clarke Avenue, Battery Point, a flat-roofed architecturally-designed house built to the order of A. J. White in 1938.

Continuing his public service activities, for many years Thomas Neave was a prominent member of the Master Builders Association of Tasmania. In 1940 he was elected to the association's committee, in 1941 he was elected secretary, and in 1942 he was elected treasurer. During 1943 and 1944 Thomas served as president. He retained a position on the committee throughout the late 1940s and 1950s.

Thomas Neave died in Hobart in October 1960 and was buried at Cornelian Bay Cemetery, New Town. He was survived by his wife Beatrice (nee Partridge) and two sons.

Above: *Miss Joan.* Courtesy Tasmanian Archive and Heritage Office.
Below: *Nordecia.* Courtesy Tasmanian Archive and Heritage Office.

Vessels Built by Thomas Neave and his brothers at Battery Point (1922 – 1933).

1922. *Grayling*. Yacht. 37 x 9.5 ft. Built by Neave Brothers at their residence in South Street, Battery Point, and launched in September 1922. Designed by Alfred Blore. Remained in Thomas Neave's hands until his death in 1960. Subsequently sold to A. B. Richard and later owned by B. Dickson. Still in existence. In April 2017 purchased by Craig Purdon of Hobart and undergoing extensive restoration.

1925. *Miss Joan (Firecrest)*. Cadet dinghy. 12 x 5 ft x 14 in. Built to the order of Harry Oliphant and launched in March 1925. Made her debut at the 1925 Sandy Bay Regatta, incorrectly referred to as *Little Joan* in the press. Represented TAS in the 1928 Stonehaven Cup held in Sydney, helmed by A. Smith. Advertised for sale in July 1928. In 1929 owned by A. E. Snow, by 1932 owned by F. H. Johnstone, by 1935 owned by P. Johnson. By 1936 renamed *Firecrest*. Advertised for sale in August 1939. By October 1945 owned by L. M. Turner. In 1948 owned by R. Kemp. Sold in November 1952 for use as a lifeboat.

1927. *Nordecia*. Motor cruiser. 40 x 10 x 6.4 ft. Built to the order of George Evans to a design by Alfred Blore and launched on 3 March 1927. Sold to Len Nettlefold in 1932. In 1963 sold to buyers from Sydney, NSW.

1928. *Allara (Aralla)*. Patrol boat. 48.5 x 12 x 5.8 ft. Fisheries patrol boat built to the order of the Sea Fisheries Board at a cost of £570. Designed by Alfred Blore (in conjunction with William Gates); Blore also supervised the build. Launched on 2 March 1928. Renamed *Aralla* in 1942 when first registered.Sold in 1972 after four decades of service. Still in existence, located in QLD and owned by Guy Reuter.

1929. Dinghy. 10 ft. Huon pine. Advertised for sale in February 1929. Likely built at 11 McGregor Street, Battery Point.

1929. *Ida N.* Fishing boat. 58 x 14.4 x 6.5. ft. Built by Neave Brothers for their own use to an Alfred Blore design. Intended for Albert and Herbert Neave's employment in the crayfishing industry. Launched from Purdon and Featherstone's Battery Point shipyard on 22 May 1929. Swept onto the rocks in wild seas on 18 January 1930 at Erith Island in Bass Strait; her marooned crew lucky to escape.

1933. *Advance*. Fishing boat. 50 x 12.5 x 6.2. ft. Built for Neave Brothers' own employment in the Bass Strait fishing industry. Designed by Thomas Neave. Built at Battery Point and trucked to Constitution Dock in Hobart where she was launched on 28 September 1933. Possibly transferred to the mainland.

Opposite: A series of photos showing construction and transport of the *Advance*.
Courtesy *Tasmanian Mail*, 5 October 1933.

A photograph of the boat in the middle stage of construction in its "back yard slipyard."

A narrow Battery Point thoroughfore presents its transport difficulties as the ketch is slewed from slipyard to roadway.

Under careful control the Advance advances through city streets towards Constitution Dock.

Norman (Norm) Taylor

Norm Taylor and his younger brother Athol established their Battery Point boatyard in 1936, the former a builder, the latter after undertaking a boat building apprenticeship with Charlie Lucas. The pair's first vessel, the 42 ft schooner *Brilliant,* was launched in September 1936. Five heavyweight sharpies were launched in early 1937. Unfortunately this period coincided with the tragic drowning of Athol Taylor. Opting to continue operation of Taylor Brothers, Norm went on to build several small and large vessels at Battery Point, including the 44 ft yawl *Sirocco*. Up until 1946 he was assisted by Charlie Lucas. In the decades that followed Norm's son Geoff increasingly took the helm of Taylor Brothers, fostering its diversification into local engineering and construction projects. Geoff's death in 1995 saw his wife Jan Taylor become chief executive officer, overseeing a move to a new site at Derwent Park and leading the company's continued success well into the new millenium. With more than 80 years of operation under its belt, Taylor Brothers remains a stalwart of Tasmania's maritime industry, since 2012 lead by Geoff and Jan's two sons, Greg and Phillip.

Norman (Norm) Henry Taylor was born on 28 July 1903 at Macquarie Street, Hobart, the third of six children born to William Ralph and Mary Josephine Taylor (nee Hanlon). After serving his apprenticeship with Francis Rowntree, an engineer, Norm's father William spent several years employed on board the *SS Banks Peninsula, SS Glenelg* and *SS Australia*, plying between Hobart and Strahan and Hobart and Launceston. By the early 1900s he was working as an engineer for the Hobart City Council's Tramways Department, a role in which William remained for nearly 50 years, ultimately becoming superindendent of the department's rolling stock. Norm Taylor's grandfather (Robert Taylor) and great-grandfather (William Taylor) were both associated with Hobart's maritime industries, Robert as a shipwright at Hobart's Domain slip, and William, an ex-convict, who set up a sail loft in Hunter Street.

Born in Hobart in 1849, Norm Taylor's grandfather Robert Taylor spent five decades working as a shipwright at Hobart's Domain slip, beginning work as an apprentice to John McGregor on 1 January 1860 at the age of 10. Here, in addition to slip, overhaul and repair work, Robert was involved in the building of the schooner *Petrel* (launched in 1865), the schooner *Hally Bayley* (launched in 1869), the infamous barque *Harriet McGregor* (launched in 1870), and the barque *Loongana* (launched in 1878), among other vessels. By the mid-1880s, Robert Taylor had become the yard's foreman and was living with his family in a cottage on the property. Like many of his peers, Robert was also prominent in local yachting circles.

Following John McGregor's retirement in 1888, Robert Taylor partnered with John Dalgleish to continue operation of the Domain shipyard. Though their work continued to involve slipping, repair, refit and alteration of existing vessels, several vessels were built by the pair, including the steam launches *Lancer* and *Sir Lancelot* and the three-masted schooner *Lourah*.

In 1903, the same year that Norm Taylor was born, Robert Taylor and John Dalgleish dissolved their partnership by mutual consent, Robert Taylor opting to continue as sole lessee of the Domain shipyard. He would remain living and working at the yard until shortly before his death in 1910.

Four Brothers

Growing up, Norm Taylor and his two older brothers, Walter (born 1900) and Cecil (born 1901), would have regularly visited their grandfather at his Domain shipyard. Together with their younger brother Athol (born 1910), the four siblings were also active and successful participants in local sports, including football, shooting, rowing and yachting.

With a leaning towards aquatic activities, helped in part by the family's move to Battery Point in 1916, Norm Taylor became involved in the Derwent Model Yacht Club, often serving as timekeeper in the early 1920s. Later that decade his older brother Walter, together with Eric McCreary, built the Derwent class yacht *Gnome* which was launched from Percy Coverdale's Battery Point boatyard on 16 October 1928. The following year Norm's younger brother Athol was noted as building his own Derwent class yacht. This particular vessel, *Elfin*, made a triumphant debut at the Woodbridge Regatta in October 1930. Athol continued to have great success at the helm of *Elfin* in the years that followed.

Not to be outdone, Norm Taylor also proved a steadfast sailor, often taking the helm of the A class yacht *Elf*. Moreover, in January 1930, Norm was selected to crew on board *Tassie Too* in that year's Forster Cup, the vessel helmed by N. Winzenberg. The 1930 Forster Cup was held in Melbourne. Despite three Tasmanian vessels entered, the New South Wales teams reigned supreme with *Tassie* finishing equal third and *Tassie III* fourth. *Tassie Too* did not place.

The 1931 Forster Cup was held in Hobart. Once again Norm Taylor was named in the *Tassie Too* team. Though the event was won by *Tassie III* (helmed by Harry Batt) with the original *Tassie* (helmed by Skipper Batt) finishing second, the crew of *Tassie Too* did well, improving on their performance from the previous year to finish third.

It was also during this period that Norm Taylor was elected to the committee of the Derwent Sailing Squadron. He would remain active in the club's administration for many years.

Tassie Too crew. Left to Right: Norm Taylor, L. Burt, W. T. Gibson, E. Doolan, J. Hood and N. Winzenberg. Courtesy *Illustrated Tasmanian Mail*, 11 February 1931.

A Career Change

Into the early 1930s Norm Taylor was professionally employed as a builder, having served an apprenticeship with Claude Cooper of Hobart. Norm's younger brother Athol was an up-and-coming boat builder, underaking his apprenticeship with Charlie Lucas at Battery Point. With a keen interest in boat building, Norm spent much of his spare time at the Battery Point slipyards working alongside his brother.

Though only in his early 20s, by the mid-1930s Athol Taylor was developing a reputation as a boat builder in his own right. The 12 ft cadet dinghy *Apex*, for example, built to the order of Ken Gourlay and launched by October 1935, is credited as being constructed by Athol.

Bigger orders were to come. On 5 December 1935 Athol Taylor received an order from Neil Campbell of Hobart for a flush-decked 42 ft schooner modelled on the lines of the Sparkman and Stephens designed yacht *Brilliant* which, on her maiden voyage in 1933, had crossed the Atlantic Ocean in just over 15 days, 1 hour and 23 minutes; a record for a sailing yacht of its size. In January 1936 Norm Taylor gave up the building trade to join his brother working on the vessel's construction. The pair operated out of Charlie Lucas' Battery Point boatyard. At the time Charlie was working on his last vessel prior to retirement, the 40 ft cruiser *Saona*, built to the order of Morton Weston of Austins Ferry and launched in early 1936.

Taylor Brothers

With Neil Campbell's vessel well underway, on 27 July 1936 Norm and Athol Taylor negotiated the purchase of Charlie Lucas' Battery Point yard. The contract was completed with full payment on 7 August. The pair paid £100 each for a half share in the business. Operating as Taylor Brothers, Neil Campbell's 42 ft schooner (named *Brilliant* after her predecessor) was launched seven weeks later, on 24 September, built at a cost approaching £1,000. The following month saw the launch of the 12 ft cadet dinghy *Aero*, built to the order of N. Johnston.

Launch of *Brilliant*. Courtesy Jan Taylor.

Brilliant. Courtesy Maritime Museum of Tasmania.

Heavyweight Sharpies

Business opportunites continued to grow. In the months before *Brilliant*'s launch, Taylor Brothers received an order for four 19.6 ft heavyweight sharpies, a class of vessel recently introduced to Tasmania. The first heavyweight sharpie in Australia, *Comet,* had began racing in Adelaide in late 1934. By March 1936 there were more than 30 sharpies competing in South Australia. With an interest in establishing the class in Tasmania, the Royal Yacht Club of Tasmania obtained a set of plans from Adelaide, and George Peacock purchased and imported one of the South Australian built boats, *Gull.* The vessel arrived in Hobart in June 1936. That same month Taylor Brothers received orders for four sharpies to be built at their newly-established Battery Point yard at a cost of £40 each.

Built simultaneously and launched on 23 January 1937, the vessels were *Seamew* (built to the order of F. Peacock), *Albatross* (built to the order of B. G. Jones), *Petrel* (built to the order of P. A. Canning) and *Grebe* (built to the order of J. T. Joyce). Meanwhile a sharpie, *Gannett,* built by A. T. O'May at Bellerive, was launched a few days later. The following month saw the launch of *Sealark,* a fifth sharpie built by Taylor Brothers. At the same time, Jack Hansen was building the sharpie *Noddy* at Skipper Batt's Battery Point shed. Collectively, these early boats were instrumental in establishing the international 12 square metre, i.e., sharpie, class in Tasmania.

Tragedy

With seven vessels already under their belt and Taylor Brothers proving a faithful operation, in autumn 1937 Athol Taylor opted to join Neil Campbell on board *Brilliant* for a month-long cruise. Fred Rodway and Dennis Page were also on board when the vessel left the Derwent for Sydney on 18 April, in step with E. H. Webster's *Spindrift,* helmed by Percy Coverdale, which was also sailing to Sydney.

After five days of sailing *Spindrift* reached Sydney on 23 April. No word was heard of *Brilliant* until 28 April. The news was grim. At 2 am on 23 April, 15 miles off Gabo Island, the yacht was struck by a fierce sea resulting in its near capsize, the mast nearly touching the water. At watch alone, while his crew mates were asleep below, was Athol Taylor, aged 26. With water pouring down the hatch the crew were rapidly awoken and attempted to salvage the vessel. A sudden list resulted in Athol, who was last sighted at the tiller, being washed overboard. No trace of his body was found. Dismayed by the outcome of their intended pleasure trip, the remaining crew made *ad hoc* repairs and limped into Sydney where *Brilliant* was later sold.

Heavyweight sharpies under construction in 1936 at Taylor Brothers.
Courtesy Maritime Museum of Tasmania.

A Helping Hand

With the tragic loss of his younger brother, Norm Taylor had two options: continue operation of the boatyard or sell the business altogether. He chose the former. Fortunately help was immediately at hand. Battery Point's boat building patriarch, Charlie Lucas, by now 73 years of age, had had enough of retirement and wanted to get back on the tools. It proved a symbiotic relationship. In fact two years later, in October 1939, an article published in the Melbourne press, which referred to Charlie Lucas as "Old Redgum," though he was better known as "Bluegum Charlie" or "Hardwood Joe," eloquently relayed Charlie's inability to retire:

"Down on the waterfront I was elated to find him working as usual in his dissipated bowler hat. Actually, he had retired, but only officially. An 'interferring doctor' had compelled him to sell the yard and lay up. Not that Old Redgum hadn't the means to retire - he had, and he could put his name to five figures. But you must remember he wasn't a capitalist or a unionist, or even a husband - he was a boat builder.

So every morning in retirement, as usual, Old Redgum wandered down into the yard at 7 and began work. He designed boats, brought business and attended to everthing, so that the new owners automatically placed him on wages. Old Redgum was happy again. He didn't, of course, want the money, but being on the pay roll simply gave him a right to live again, the long day through in his Valhalia - that colourful, old fashioned boat builders yard.

Source: *The Age*, Saturday 14 October 1939. Pg. 10.

Resolute to keep Taylor Brothers' boatyard in operation, Norm Taylor and Charlie Lucas returned to the building of smaller vessels. The heavyweight sharpie *Osprey*, built to the order of Ken Gourlay, was launched by October 1937. The hull of another heavyweight sharpie, *Sea Gull*, was transported to Devonport, built to the order of H. E. Baily of the Mersey Yacht Club. Also sent to Devonport were the keel and frames of a heavyweight sharpie built to the order of R. Masterman, commodore of the Mersey Yacht Club. Named *Vagbond*, this particular vessel was completed by Hugh Millbourne of Devonport and launched in November 1938.

During this period a 35 ft auxiliary cruiser, *Kareela,* was also completed, built to the order of Gahey Brown, rear commodore of the Royal Yacht Club of Tasmania. A great deal of time and effort was additionally spent transforming the coastal trading ketch *Eveline May* into the motor ketch *Premier* for the Tasmanian government. Taylor Brothers also began work on a yawl of modern design, built to the order of Charles Davies. This particular vessel measured 44 ft and was designed by Sparkman and Stephens. *Sirocco* was launched on 5 October 1939.

Series of photos showing the launch of *Sirocco*.
Courtesy Guy Rex Collection (Suzanne Rex).

World War II

The early years of World War II saw Norm Taylor and Charlie Lucas continue operation of Taylor Brothers' Battery Point yard, primarily undertaking repair and overhaul work. They also made significant alterations to the cruiser *Falcon* for the Tasmanian government. However, as the global conflict intensified many of Hobart's boat builders were classified as essential services personnel and engaged to build vessels for Australia's armed services. Norm Taylor was duly made a foreman at Purdon and Featherstone's Battery Point shipyard where he supervised the building of three harbour defence patrol launches (the *HMAS HDML 1321*, commissioned on 11 November 1943; the *HMAS HDML 1322*, commissioned on 17 January 1944; and the *HMAS HDML 1327*, commissioned on 19 May 1944) and an 80 ft sea ambulance (*AH1730 Koorakee*, launched on 1 February 1945). Also undertaken was repair work on liberty ships arriving in the Port of Hobart.

Post War

The end of World War II saw Taylor Brothers complete a 57 ft fishing trawler, *Ben Boyd*, built to the order of James Alderton of Cremorne, New South Wales. Alderton had sailed to Hobart in the 1945 Sydney to Hobart Yacht Race as skipper of the *Ambermerle*. In January 1946 he sailed the newly-built vessel back to the mainland, though it returned to local waters later that year having been purchased by the Rattenbury family and renamed *Ronnell*.

The 42 ft motor launch *Silver Cloud II*, built to a Max Creese design, was the next vessel completed by Taylor Brothers at Battery Point. Launched on 30 November 1946, *Silver Cloud II* was built to the order of H. A. Nichols, commodore of the Motor Yacht Club of Tasmania. Sadly the building of this particular vessel coincided with the passing of Charlie Lucas, who died on 24 August 1946 at the age of 82. He had worked for Taylor Brothers up until his final days.

In the years that followed, Norm Taylor continued operation of Taylor Brothers' boatyard, though the number of new vessels built was significantly reduced. The first class cruising yacht *Marauder* (launched in 1947) was one of only a handful of vessels built in the late 1940s. This particular vessel was built for Geoff Cripps and owned by H. C. Butler for many years.

1948 saw Norm Taylor assisting neighbouring boat builder Percy Coverdale with the construction of a Marconi-rigged ocean racing sloop. Named *White Cloud*, the vessel took over two years to complete and was launched on 23 December 1948. Around the same time Taylor Brothers completed the heavyweight sharpie *Fulmar*, built to the order of Peter Donovan, and the the Kiwi class yacht *Te Lua*, built to the order of David Glover.

The Next Generation

In October 1949 Norm Taylor renewed the lease on Taylor Brothers' Napoleon Street property with the Hobart Marine Board. Though no large vessels were built, work continued to be brisk with alterations, overhaul, slip and repair work taking place, including major repairs to the auxiliary ketch-rigged yacht *Ariki*. Norm Taylor also fostered the next generation in the craft of boat building and sailing, including his apprentice Sam Purdon. In December 1950 Norm established a fund to raise money to send Sam to Brisbane to defend his national title at the 12 Square Metre Sharpie Championship.

On 19 March 1959 Norm Taylor's son Geoff joined Taylor Brothers following completion of his carpentry apprenticeship with Crisp and Gunn. During this period, and into the next decade, Taylor Brothers primarily undertook slip, survey and maintenance work at their Battery Point yard, along with installation of engines and rudders.

The 1970s

In 1970 Geoff Taylor was made a partner in Taylor Brothers and increasingly took on more responsibility of running the business. With Norm Taylor now in his 70s, on 1 May 1973 Taylor Brothers became a group of limited companies. Norm spent his retirement years attending horse and greyhound races and travelling, including to America to witness the Kentucky Derby, a life-long dream

Under Geoff Taylor's management Taylor Brothers began diversifying into local engineering and construction projects. In 1974, for example, a wharf was pre-fabricated, transported and erected at Partridge Island in the D'Entrecasteaux Channel for Dr Richard Ham. That same year a 27 ft steel barge, the *Bill Leitch*, was designed and built at Battery Point to the order of IXL Timber for use in the salvage of Huon pine on Lake Gordon. Other projects undertaken by Taylor Brothers during this period include the demolition of the old Hobart floating bridge, and work on the salvage and then reconstruction of the Tasman Bridge following its ill-fated collapse.

The late 1970s saw another generation of the Taylor family enter the business with Geoff's oldest son Greg joining the firm as an apprentice fitter and turner, and Geoff's youngest son Phillip as an apprentice shipwright. Combined these skill sets added to the flexibility and future development of the company. For Norm Taylor and his son Geoff, this was a dream come true as the name of Taylor Brothers was once again truly represented. Geoff's wife Jan also became involved, initially working as the firm's payroll officer, then becoming its accountant.

Top: Demoliition of the Hobart Floating Bridge.
Bottom: *Bill Leitch* at Taylor Brothers, Battery Point.
Courtesy Jan Taylor.

End of an Era

Norm Taylor died on 4 September 1983 at the age of 80 follwing a six month battle with cancer. In addition to his son Geoff, Norm was survived by two daughters (Fay and Lesley). Norm's wife Thelma (nee Shrimplin) had died several years earlier, on 5 September 1978. Norm remarried the following year (on 16 June 1979) to Nita Graves McCreary.

Another Tragedy

Following the death of his father, Geoff Taylor further shepherded Taylor Brothers into new areas. Projects included the supply of deck equipment and building and installation of winches and fairleads for a barge used in constuction of the Bowen Bridge, installation and operation of cement and mud pumping equipment for Baroid on Macquarie Wharf, building of rig anchors and drilling equipment for Diamond Offshore Exploration, and foundation work on the Convention Centre island at Wrest Point Hotel and Casino. Many projects were also undertaken in association with the Australian Antarctic Division.

However, another tragedy struck the Taylor family when, on 23 May 1995, Geoff Taylor died in an industrial accident. He was 56 years of age. Persevering Jan Taylor went on to become chief executive officer of the slipway and engineering company, overseeing a move to a new site at Derwent Park. This location has since supported greater opportunities for the company to move forward. Since 2012 Geoff and Jan's two sons, Greg and Phillip, have taken over the firm, leading Taylor Brothers well into the new 21st century.

The Legacy Continues

In 2016 Taylor Brothers celebrated its 80th birthday, a monumental achievement for any business. From humble beginnings at Battery Point, Taylor Brothers has grown and diversified during this period and today is involved with offshore support services, rig maintenance and equipment installation, accommodation units, defence contracts, Antarctic projects, and shipping refit and repairs. The company operates out of a large workshop at Prince of Wales Bay, near Hobart. Significantly, Taylor Brothers' Napoleon Street slipyard also remains in active use with some slipping and repair work conducted at this auspicious location; the site where the company was initiated by two brothers in 1936.

Vessels Built by Taylor Brothers and Employees at Battery Point (1930 – 1974).

1930. *Elfin*. Yacht. 24.5 x 6.7 x 4 ft. Derwent class yacht built by Athol Taylor for his own use and launched in late 1930. Sailed by R. Taylor following Athol Taylor's death in 1937. Advertised for sale by the Taylor family in December 1944. By 1946 owned by D. A. Griggs and L. J. Durkin; in 1948 by D. A. Griggs. Advertised for sale in Hobart in September 1953. By 1955 owned by M. A. Connor and later by Robert Clifford. Still in existence. Located in Hobart and advertised for sale in April 2017.

1935. *Apex*. Cadet dinghy. 12 x 5 ft x 14 in. Built by Athol Taylor to the order of Ken Gourlay. First noted in October 1935 when competing at the Woodbridge Regatta. Advertised for sale in March 1937. By 1945 owned by Sam Purdon. Represented TAS in the 1946 Stonehaven Cup, helmed by Sam Purdon. By 1948 owned by Mick Purdon. Represented TAS in the 1949 Stonehaven Cup held in Adelaide. Represented TAS in the 1950 Stonehaven Cup held in Melbourne, helmed by Mick Purdon. By 1952 owned by A. Tate, by 1958 owned by J. White.

1936. *Brilliant*. Schooner. 42 x 10 x 6 ft. Built to the order of Neil Campbell and launched on 24 September 1936. Designed by Sparkman and Stephens. Sailed to NSW in April 1937 with the unfortunate loss of Athol Taylor off Gabo Island. Subsequently sold in Sydney. Later purchased by B. E. Warming of Adelaide, SA. By 1954 returned to TAS and owned by Mac Foster. Competed in the 1954 and 1960 Sydney to Hobart yacht races.

1936. *Aero (Viking)*. Cadet dinghy. 12 x 5 ft x 14 in. Built to the order of N. Johnston and first noted on the Derwent in October 1936. Advertised for sale in August 1938. Advertised for sale in October 1946. Renamed *Viking* in 1947. By 1948 owned by K. R. Lowe, by 1950 owned by H. D. Calvert, and by 1957 owned by G. C. Johnston.

1937. *Seamew*. Heavyweight sharpie. 19.6 ft. Built to the order of F. Peacock and launched on 20 January 1937. By 1944 owned by P. J. Cerutty. By 1958 owned by Bryan Horne (sailed by Brian Lewis).

1937. *Albatros*. Heavyweight sharpie. 19.6 ft. Built to the order of B. G. Jones and launched on 20 January 1937. By 1944 owned by C. Batten of the Tamar Yacht Club. By 1948 owned by J. R. Burton, and by 1950 owned by D. J. Wilson. Advertised for sale in April 1951. In 1952 owned by N. Attrill. Advertised again for sale in May 1953.

1937. *Petrel*. Heavyweight sharpie. 19.6 ft. Built to the order of P. A Canning and launched on 20 January 1937. Still owned by P. A. Canning in 1944. By 1946 owned by G. Stephenson. By 1950 owned by P. C. Fowler, P. Hindrum and P. Tardrew; by 1951 owned by P. C. Fowler. Advertised for sale in March 1953. By 1962 owned by the First Derwent Sea Scouts.

1937. *Grebe*. Heavyweight sharpie. 19.6 ft. Built to the order of J. T. Joyce and launched on 20 January 1937. Sailed by Max Muir in the 1937-38 season. Advertised for sale in August 1939 for £40, possibly purchased by A. Wiesmann. By 1945 transferred to the Tamar Yacht Club and owned for several years by Charlie Rose. By 1949 owned by Bill Tyson. By October 1951 owned by Trevor Graeme.

1937. *Sealark*. Heavyweight sharpie. 19.6 ft. Launched by February 1937. Finished first in the sharpie race at the 1937 Royal Hobart Regatta, helmed by J. C. Grubb. Finished third at the 1938 Australian Sharpie Championship held in Hobart. Advertised for sale in October 1939. By 1944 owned by Ray Claridge of the Tamar Yacht Club. Owned by B. Neville in 1961.

1937. *Sea Gull.* **Heavyweight sharpie**. 19.6 ft. Hull built to the order of H. E. Baily of the Mersey Yacht Club. Still owned by H. E. Baily in 1948.

1937. *Osprey.* **Heavyweight sharpie.** 19.6 ft. Launched in time for the 1937-38 season and built to the order of Ken Gourlay. Advertised for sale in March 1938, likely purchased by K. Dallas. By 1944 owned by Casey Brothers. Advertised for sale in May and September 1950. Again for sale in February 1954.

1937. *Kareela.* **Yacht.** 35 x 9 ft. Built to the order of Gahey Brown, rear commodore of the Royal Yacht Club of Tasmania and launched in late 1937. By 1944 owned by A. J. Shield. Transferred to Melbourne, VIC, in 1947.

1938. *Vagabond.* **Heavyweight sharpie.** 19.6 ft. Keel and frames built to the order of R. Masterman, commodore of the Mersey Yacht Club. Boat completed by Hugh Millbourne of Devonport and launched in November 1938. Likely sold following Masterman's death in 1940 to C. Lamprey. By 1942 owned by R. Rooney of Devonport. Purchased by J. Higgs in January 1945. Advertised for sale in May 1946. By October 1947 owned by Athol Knight. Purchased by Max Williams in October 1948.

1938. *Sirocco.* **Yacht.** 44.2 x 10.5 x 6 ft. Built to the order of Charles Davies and launched on 5 October 1939. Designed by Sparkman and Stephens of New York, USA. In October 1944 transferred to Sydney, NSW, and subsequently purchased by K. Gabler. Advertised for sale in February 1957. Later transferred to Melbourne, VIC. Still in existence. Since 2000 owned by Krissy and John Mackintosh of Batemans Bay, NSW. Returned to Hobart to feature at the 2015 Australian Wooden Boat Festival and has since remained on the River Derwent.

1946. *Ben Boyd (Ronnell).* **Fishing boat.** 57 ft. Built to the order of James Alderton of Cremorne, NSW and launched in January 1946. Renamed *Ronnell* and owned by the Rattenbury family of the Tasman Peninsula by late 1946 and for many years thereafter. Later transferred to VIC and then back to TAS. Still in existence; advertised for sale in 2017.

1946. *Silver Cloud II (Seaflyer).* **Motor launch.** 42 x 11 x 5 ft. Built to the order of H. A. Nichols. Designed by Max Creese, with assistance from Messrs. N. Pulfer and R. Cooper. Owned by H. A. Nichols until 1950. Possibly renamed *Seaflyer* and owned by the Robbie family of Hobart in the 1950s. Transferred to Sydney, NSW, in the 1970s.

1947. *Marauder.* **Yacht.** Built for Geoff Cripps. Later owned by H. C. Butler for many years and following A. Gibson. Subsequently transferred to QLD.

1948. *Fulmar.* **Heavyweight sharpie.** 19.6 ft. First noted on the River Derwent in January 1949, owned by Peter Donovan. Advertised for sale in March 1951 and again in February 1953.

1949. *Te Lua.* **Yacht.** Kiwi class yacht. Built to the order of David Brumby and launched in January 1949.

1974. *Bill Leitch.* **Barge.** 27 ft. 10 ton displacement. Steel. Designed and built to the order of IXL Timber. Used for timber recovery following flooding of Lake Pedder and Lake Gordon. Transferred to SA in 1983 and used to recover logs in Lake Bonney over a 10-year period.

Battery Point boat and ship yards (circa 1937). Courtesy Jock Muir Family Collection.

Ernest "Jock" Muir

One of Australia's acclaimed 20th century boat builders and designers, Jock Muir first embarked on a career in tin smithing at the height of the Depression, sailing and learning the craft of boat building in his spare time. Having won the Stonehaven Cup for cadet dinghies in 1933, Jock moved on to successfully compete in the 16 ft skiff and heavyweight sharpie classes, and following the local cruiser class. In 1937 he built the deep-sea cruiser *Westwind* in the backyard of his Battery Point home. During World War II Jock moved to Sydney where he set up a boatyard business. A few years later illness forced him and his family to return to Hobart. By 1948 Jock was on the mend and, following his life's dream, established a boatyard at Battery Point. Up until Jock's retirement in 1987 more than 35 vessels were built here, including some of the finest blue-water racing yachts in the country. During this period Jock also designed approximately 100 vessels. With a reputation as an exceptional sailor established in his teens, Jock continued his meteoric rise at the helm throughout his career. He competed in the Sydney to Hobart Yacht Race 19 times, notably winning the race on line honours or handicap five times. Jock's legacy continues to this day in the many vessels he built and/ or designed that are still in existence, as well as via the Muir family's boatyard at Battery Point which remains in operation.

Ernest "Jock" Jack Muir was born on 22 October 1914 at his parents' residence of 164 Bathurst Street, Hobart. He was the eldest child of Ernest (Ernie) and Elsie Muir (nee Haigh). As a toddler Jock and his family moved to 39 Colville Street, Battery Point, where his brother Arthur Maxwell (Max) was born on 3 April 1916. Three more children were born to Ernie and Elsie Muir in the years that followed: Wallace (Wally) born 1918, Bessie born 1922 and Donald (Don) born 1926.

Continuing the Muir family's maritime legacy, Jock's father Ernie spent much of his early working life at sea employed on interstate trading vessels, including the barque *Natal Queen* and later the schooner *Handa Isle*. Ernie was notably one of 12 crew rescued from the *Natal Queen* when the vessel was wrecked in Adventure Bay, Bruny Island, in June 1909.

By 1919 Ernie was working as a telegraph linesman and the Muir family had moved to 6 Sloane Street, Battery Point. Ernie had also taken a lease out on Betsey Island, located at the mouth of the Derwent estuary, likely supplementing his family's income through harvesting of the island's rampant rabbit population. A few years later the growing Muir family moved to 12 St Georges Terrace, Battery Point, and following to 18 Queen Street, Sandy Bay. By the 1930s the Muir family had returned to Battery Point and were living at 42 Colville Street.

Battery Point

Growing up a stone's throw from the Battery Point boatyards meant that Jock Muir witnessed some extraordinary events as a child. One of his earliest memories was as a five-year old being on board the 153 ft three-masted schooner *Amelia J* during its launch which took place on 31 July 1919. The vessel was built to the order of Henry Jones and Company by Henry Moore at the Battery Point shipyard owned by Kennedy and Sons and was intended for the interstate trade. Jock's uncle Alfred Haigh worked on the *Amelia J* during the vessel's construction. Notably *Amelia J* has the honour of being the longest vessel ever constructed at Battery Point.

Jock also significantly notes in his biography *Maritime Reflections* that he would wander down to Percy Coverdale's Battery Point yard most days after school, often in company with life-long friend Neall Batt. Here Percy would appease the pair's appetite and interest in the craft of boat building. They would also rub shoulders with up-and-coming boat builders, including Athol Taylor and Chook Newman.

Launch of the *Amelia J* at Battery Point.
Courtesy *Tasmanian Mail*, 7 August 1919.

Cadet Dinghies and Model Yachts

Other drivers and influences of Jock Muir's future career path include participation in the cadet dinghy class, beginning in 1929. Jock's first boat was the *Mayfly* which his father Ernie had purchased from Chook Newman for £20. Jock began the 1930/31 season racing in a new cadet dinghy, *Kittiwake*, which Ernie had commissioned Skipper Batt of Battery Point to build at a cost of £40. By December 1930, with only a few races under his belt in the new vessel, Jock was noted to be "consistently brilliant" and considered a contender for the state's Stonehaven Cup team, the national championship for cadet dinghies.

True to form Jock was selected to represent Tasmania in the 1931 Stonehaven Cup, the event held in Hobart in February of that year. Though Jock and crew failed to place, they did well at the event and undoubtedly gained valuable skills and knowledge. Capping off a great season, Jock won the Royal Yacht Club of Tasmania's champion pennant for cadet dinghies in August 1931, amassing £13 in prize money throughout the season. He also claimed the title the following season. The 1931/32 season saw Jock's younger brother Max racing in the cadet dinghy class, competing in *Mayfly*. Like Jock, Max proved an exceptional helmsmen from the get-go.

Unfortunately a lack of funds prevented the Tasmanian contingent from attending the 1932 Stonehaven Cup, held in Western Australia. However, funds were made available the following year to send one team to the national event, with Jock and crew (comprising Bill Humphreys and Alf Gough) selected to compete in *Kittiwake*. Travelling by steamer to Melbourne and then by train to Adelaide, the three boys were accompanied by Skipper Batt and crew of the 21 footer *Tassie III*, who were travelling to Adelaide to compete in the Forster Cup. At the event *Kittiwake* won both the first and second heats, thus clinching the national title without the need for a third heat. Jock and crew were ceremoniously congratulated upon arrival back in Hobart.

During this period Jock Muir also began competing in model yacht events: 50 inch boats which participants followed in chaser dinghies. In May 1933, for example, he received several prizes at the Royal Yacht Club of Tasmania's annual award ceremony for his helmsmanship of Col Snook's model *Sunbeam II*. Continuing his dominance with model yachts, Jock also won the pennant and several prizes for A class model yachts that season (and in subsequent seasons), racing *Storm Bird* and *Storm Bird II*.

By now too old to compete in the cadet dinghy class, Jock graduated to the 16 ft skiff class, winning the championship pennant in *Wee Davie* in his inaugural season (1933/34). Age restrictions meant that Jock was unable to defend his Stonehaven Cup title. However, the 1934 Stonehaven Cup, held in Sydney in January of that year, did feature a Muir. Three boats were selected to represent Tasmania at the national event: *Kittiwake* (helmed by Max Muir), *Rangare* (helmed by George Gibson) and *Kiwi* (helmed by E. O'May). Jock's younger brother Max Muir finished equal third at the event, with the title going to *Rangare*. Max, in *Kittiwake*, was selected as Tasmania's sole representative to compete for the 1935 Stonehaven Cup in Melbourne where he finished first, successfully returning the cup to the state.

School and Apprenticeship

Academically, Jock Muir and his younger siblings attended school at Albuera Street Primary. In grade six, around the age of 12, Jock also attended the Battery Point Trade School, learning woodworking and technical drawing under instruction from Charles Snook one day per week.

A keen student, in January 1926 Jock received a scholarship to attend Hobart High School. Six years later, in 1932 at the age of 18, Jock was noted as undertaking courses at the Hobart Technical College in tin smithing, receiving credits in subjects such as theory and drawing, tin smithing calculations and practical tin smithing. These classes were taken as part of his apprenticeship in the metal fabrication industry with Charles Davis, at the time Tasmania's leading hardware firm. The height of the Depression meant that upon leaving school Jock was very fortunate to find an apprenticeship. Though it was not in his preferred area of employment, i.e., boat building and design, it was a job no less. Continuing to undertake classes at the Hobart Technical College as part of his apprenticeship, in May 1933 Jock was awarded the Cadbury-Fry-Pascall Pty. Ltd. prize for tin smithing.

Spare Time

Bent on not letting go of his dream, Jock Muir spent his spare time studying yacht design with Athol Taylor (who several years later established a boatyard at Battery Point with his brother Norm). Athol encouraged Jock to draft designs straight on to paper rather than making half models. Jock also built several dinghies during this period.

Out on the water, having graduated from both the cadet dinghy and 16 ft skiff classes, in late 1934 Jock began helming *Ventura* in the cruiser class. The introduction by the Royal Yacht Club of Tasmania in early 1936 of the 12 square metre class, or heavyweight sharpies as they were colloquially known, also saw Jock successfully return to racing smaller craft.

In mid-1936, after completing his tin smithing apprenticeship though still in the employ of Charles Davis as a sheet metal grader, Jock began building a 36 ft deep-sea double-ended cruiser in the backyard of his parents' home in Colville Street, Battery Point. The vessel's design merged that of two vessels that had visited Hobart in 1935, the *Ho-Ho* and *Te Rapunga*. The former was sailed by a trio of Norwegian adventurers in search of the missing Danish barque *Kbenhaven*. The latter, sailed by a German by the name of Captain George Dibbern, had won the Tasman Sea race from Auckland to Melbourne in January 1935. With the intention of undertaking a cruise of the Pacific in the vessel, Jock also completed courses in navigation.

Named *Westwind,* Jock Muir's cruiser was launched at the Hobart wharf in September 1937. He successfully sailed the vessel for several years in the local cruiser class, notably winning the 1938 Bruny Island Race on corrected time. Jock also used *Westwind* for local and interstate fishing and pleasure trips.

Opposite: *Westwind* under construction.
Courtesy Jock Muir Family Collection.

Westwind nearing completion in 1937.   Courtesy Jock Muir Family Collection.

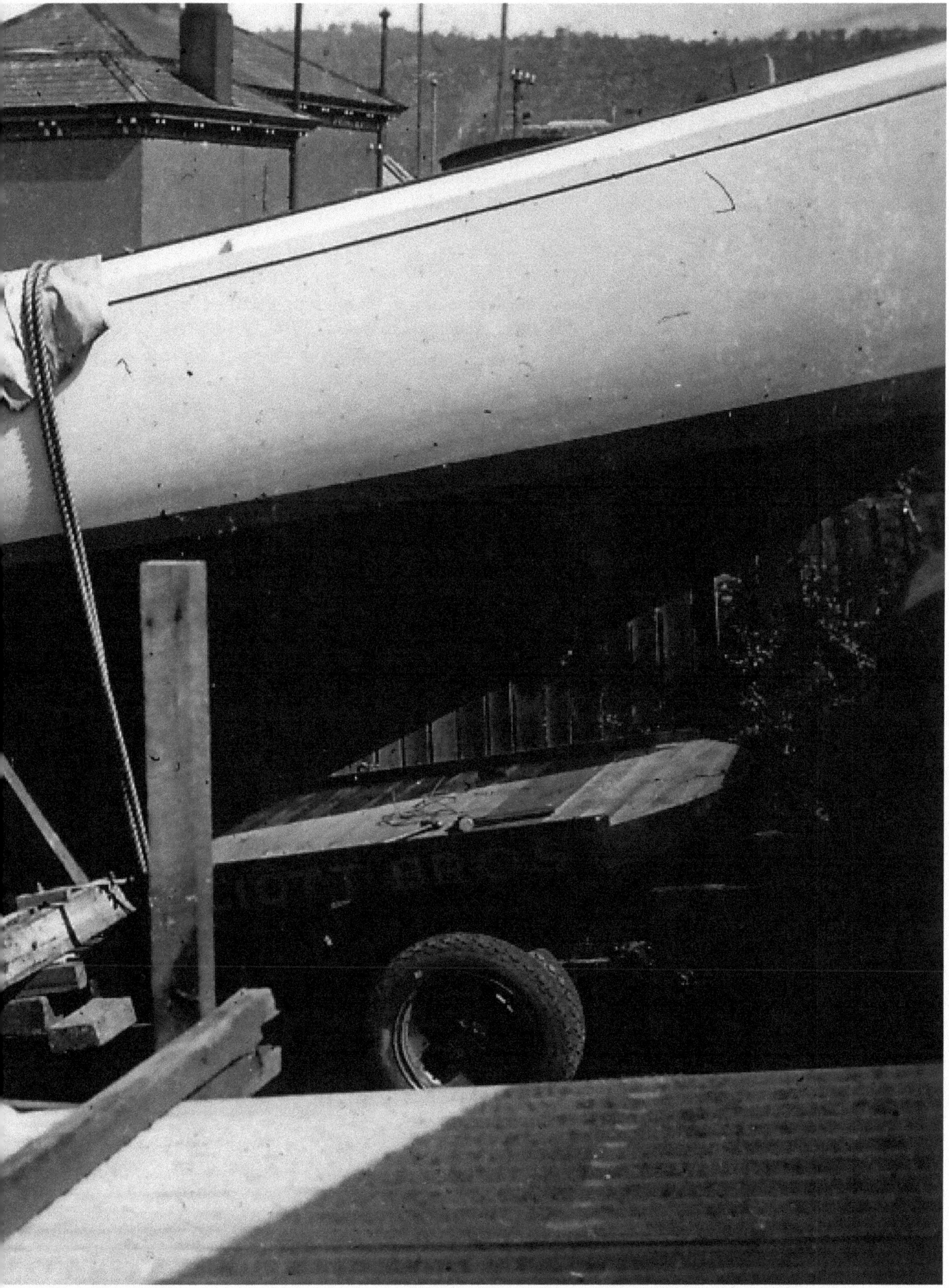

Jock Muir built *Westwind* with the intention of cruising the Pacific. However, by the time he was ready to embark on this journey Jock had caught the eye of his neighbour Mollie McAllister. The couple married in Hobart on 26 April 1941. A month before their wedding, Jock had sailed *Westwind* to Sydney where the vessel was sold. The proceeds were used to finance the newlywed couple's relocation to the mainland.

Sydney

On 30 April 1941 Jock and his new bride Mollie flew to Sydney where Jock was keen to establish himself as a boat builder and designer. By January of the following year he had achieved this goal and was operating a boat building and brokerage business out of Mosman Bay. Subsequently joined by his youngest brother Don, as well as Tim Chambers of Sydney, the trio spent much of World War II building wooden lifeboats for the United States Army which were deployed in New Guinea.

Jock Muir at his boatyard in Sydney, New South Wales (1943).
Courtesy Jock Muir Family Collection.

A Return to Tasmania

In late 1944 Jock Muir began supervising construction of a fishing boat at Narooma on the New South Wales south coast. Disappointingly the work was not completed to Jock's high standard such that he and his family were forced to move to the region to complete the build. As the 45 ft vessel, *Wake*, valued at around £7,000, neared commissioning in early 1945 Jock was struck down with polio, a debilitating disease that saw him spend several months in hospital and dramatically limited his capacity to work and thus provide for his young family.

Though Jock left Tasmania with the intention of permanently settling in New South Wales, illness forced him and his family to return to Hobart in late 1945. Jock, his wife Mollie and their two young children (Lynette and John) moved in with Mollie's family at St Georges Terrace, Battery Point, while Jock convalesced and the couple prepared for the birth of their third child (Ross).

Gradually regaining back his strength, Jock Muir began placing advertisements in the local classifieds for second-hand bandsaws, tilting tables and 3-phase electric motors. He also began reconditioning marine diesel engines and advertising them for sale. Around this period Jock received an order from an interstate buyer for a large fishing cruiser. With the help of his brother Wally, along with Alan Cracknell and Bruce Griggs, and later Bill Foster, construction of the vessel took place in a paddock off 52 Queen Street in Sandy Bay. Though Sandy Bay was quite populated at the time, Jock notes in his biography that a cow ate the original line plans of the vessel!

By December 1946 Jock Muir's health had recovered enough to enable him to crew on board Colin Philp's 20 ton welded steel sloop *Southern Maid* in that year's Sydney to Hobart Yacht Race. Also on board were Colin Philp, Max Creese (later boat builder of Battery Point), Huon Watchorn, Robert Hedley and Ron Doolan. It was the second time the Sydney to Hobart Yacht Race had been held and the first of 19 Christmases that Jock would spend away from home preparing for the race.

Westward

After competing in the Sydney to Hobart Yacht Race where *Southern Maid* finished a commendable seventh on handicap out of 18 vessels, Jock Muir continued to develop his boat building business. Regrettably the sale of the fishing cruiser he was building fell through. Thankfully George Gibson, Jock's long-time friend from his cadet dinghy sailing days, was able to take over the order. The 42 ft Bermuda-rigged cutter *Westward* was launched on 6 September 1947, estimated to have cost over £4,000 to build.

Jock Muir saddled up for more races on board *Westward*. First was the Royal Yacht Club of Tasmania's inaugural 174 mile Maria Island Ocean Race where the vessel, skippered by owner George Gibson, finished first. Jock's father Ernie and two of his brothers were also on board as crew. Next came the 1947 Sydney to Hobart Yacht Race with Jock navigating *Westward* second across the line and first on handicap. It proved another successful Muir family venture with Jock's father Ernie and his brothers Wally and Don also on board.

Westward under construction in Queen Street, Sandy Bay.
Courtesy Jock Muir Family Collection.

A Battery Point Boatyard

In March of 1948 Jock Muir returned to Sydney, this time delivering Max Creese's yacht *Mavis* to her new owner. It would prove the first of many delivery trips Jock would make over the course of his career.

Following the delivery of *Mavis*, Jock set about establishing a boatyard at Battery Point, petitioning the Hobart City Council for approval to erect a sawbench in a fibro shed located on the foreshore off Napoleon Street to the north side of Taylor Brothers. While waiting for approval Jock received an order for a new yacht which he began building in the same paddock off Queen Street, Sandy Bay, where *Westward* was built. Here Jock also began construction of a 29 ft motor boat, *Pinjarra*, built to the order of the Bastick family. Completed at Battery Point by January 1949, a subsequent owner decades later noted the text "WWF 1948" carved in a deck beam of the vessel which can only be identified as the initials of Bill Foster, the yard's cheeky apprentice. During this period Jock also continued to act as broker for the sale of second-hand vessels and reconditioned marine engines.

Lass O'Luss

The first vessel launched from Jock Muir's newly-established Battery Point boatyard was the racing sloop *Lass O'Luss*, built to the order of John Colquhoun, a yachtsman of Sydney. Jock's nephew Bill Foster relays the story that the keel, stem, sternpost, forefoot and moulds were constructed in the paddock off Queen Street. They were then transported to Jock's new Battery Point yard along with a demountable shed containing a large saw. When Percy Coverdale arrived at his neighbouring boatyard the next morning and looked over at Jock's new yard, he could not believe his eyes. There stood a small saw shed, along with the keel and frames of a 41 ft yacht!

With Jock's brother Max now employed at the yard, having served his time with Percy Coverdale and then worked at Purdon and Featherstone during World War II, Jock and his team laboured with great drive and energy to complete John Colquhoun's vessel with the intention of racing her in that year's Sydney to Hobart Yacht Race. Based on a design by Robert Clark of England, *Lass O'Luss* was launched on 4 December 1948. John Colquhoun sailed the vessel to Sydney a few days later, with a crew including Don Muir, arriving just in time to prepare for the race back to Hobart.

With *Lass O'Luss* complete, Jock too sailed to Sydney on board *Westward* to compete in the 1948 Sydney to Hobart Yacht Race. The vessel went on to finish fifth across the line and first on handipcap, equalling her success with the previous year's race. The newly-built *Lass O'Luss* was forced to retire off St Helens owing to a crew member requiring immediate medical attention.

More Orders, More Boats

With *Westward* and *Lass O'Luss* under his belt, Jock Muir continued to gain local and national attention for the construction of fast and reliable ocean-going cruisers. Two more orders were received from yachtsmen of Sydney. These were for the 47 ft *Waltzing Matilda,* built to the order of Phil Davenport and launched on 2 July 1949, and the 47 ft *Patsy*, built to the order of A. C. Cooper and launched on 4 April 1950. The *Waltzing Matilda* was designed off *Westward* with the main difference being that the vessel had a counter stern whereas *Westward* had a large tuck stern. The two vessels also had slightly different lines below the water. In contrast, *Patsy* was designed by Laurent Giles, a world-renowned naval architect emanating from the United Kingdom.

Several smaller boats were built at Jock Muir's Battery Point boatyard during this period. These include two heavyweight sharpies, *Tawaki* and *Kittihawk*. Both were built by Jock's younger brother Don, an employee of the yard, and launched in early 1949 and October 1949, respectively. A commercial crayfishing dinghy was built by Bill Foster in early 1950 to the order of Bill Wisby of Bruny Island. In September 1950 Bill Foster and Don Muir built the sharpie *Skimmer* for Ediss Boyes. This particular vessel won the 1951 Australian Sharpie Championship, held in Brisbane, with a crew consisting of Ediss Boyes, Geoff Omant and S. Nichols. *Darter,* another heavyweight sharpie was launched in September 1950, built by Bill Foster and Don Muir to the order of Neil Campbell. Finally the cadet dinghy *Sirocco* was built by Max Muir to the order of David Boyes and launched by November 1950.

Waltizing Matilda. Courtesy Tasmanian Archive and Heritage Office.

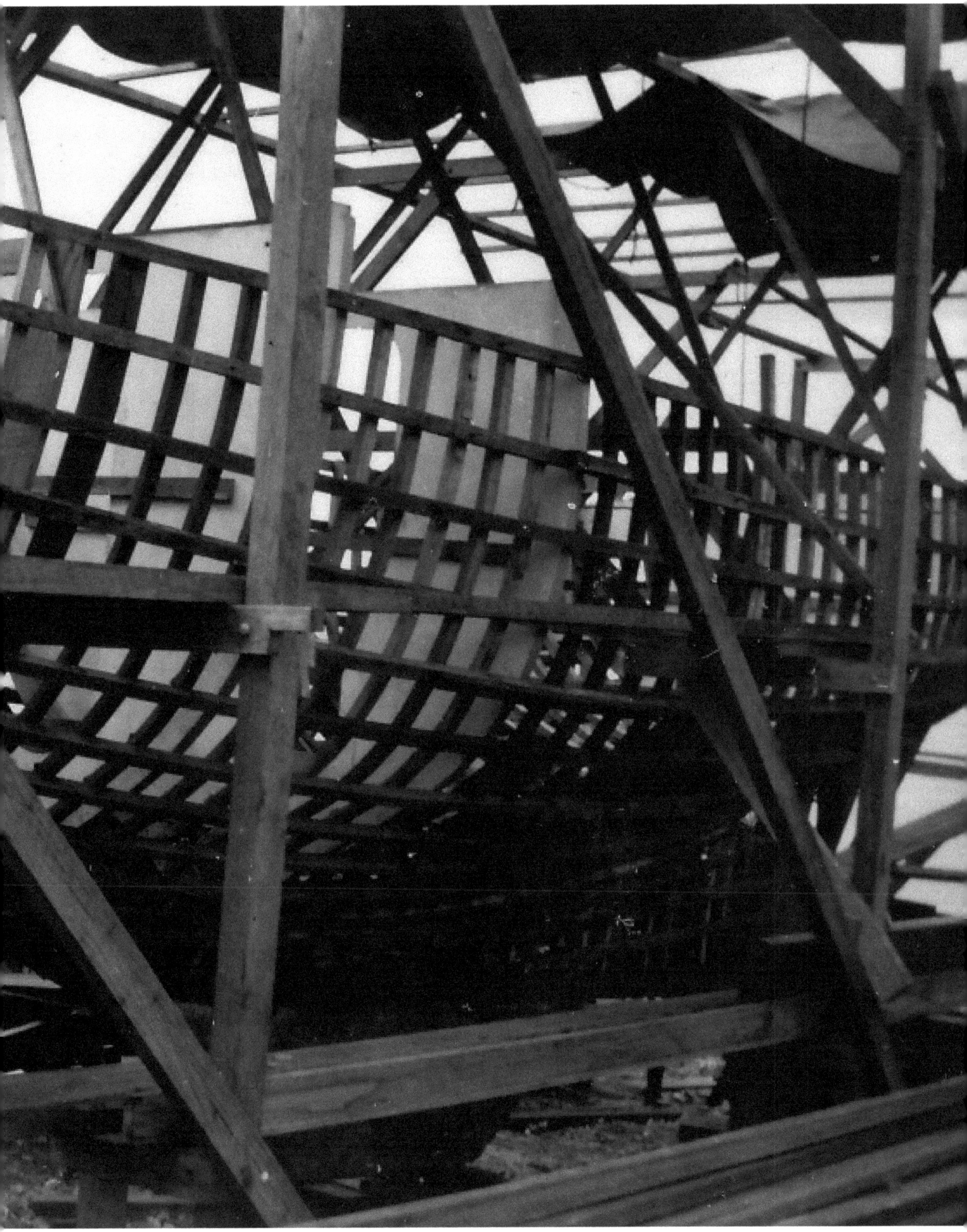

Two Sydney to Hobart Yacht Races

Commensurately earning a reputation as one of Australia's best deep-water helmsmen, Jock Muir, along with his brother Don, were invited to crew on board *Waltzing Matilda* in the 1949 Sydney to Hobart Yacht Race. With Jock at the tiller, the vessel finished first across the line (and second on handicap) following a dramatic three-way battle up the River Derwent with *Margaret Rintoul* and *Trade Winds* in near calm conditions.

The following year Jock Muir skippered Guy Rex's *Mistral V* (built at Battery Point by Purdon and Featherstone) in the Sydney to Hobart Yacht Race. His younger brother Wally was also on board. The vessel finished second across the line and third on handicap out of a fleet of 16.

Crew of *Mistral V* that competed in the 1950 Sydney to Hobart Yacht Race.
Left to Right: Wally Muir, Max Hansen, Joe Palmer, Bruce Cottier, Tony Parkes, Ron Ikin, Jock Muir (skipper), Guy Rex and Dudley Burridge.
Courtesy Guy Rex Collection (Suzanne Rex).

The 1951 Federal Budget

With a well-earned reputation and a well-established boatyard, Jock Muir's future business prospects appeared sound. Large orders continued to arrive. In March 1951 Jock was commissioned to build a 50 ft canoe-stern cutter for Len Nettlefold. A few months later he was asked to complete a 41 ft fishing boat for Leon Scarf. Named *Helen S*, the vessel had been designed and partially built by Alan Norman and was launched from Jock's Battery Point yard in June 1951. Another new order came in for the fishing boat *Marie Laure*, completed in mid-1951 for the Dunbabin family of Dunalley. An order for an ocean racing sloop was also received in July 1951 from Des Ashton of New Zealand (who at the time was stationed in Rabaul, Papua New Guinea), with aspirations of competing in the Sydney to Hobart and trans-Tasman races.

In September 1951, however, something beyond Jock Muir's control with serious implications for his business was released: the Federal Budget. Treasurer Sir Arthur Fadden introduced a budget that called for large increases in income, sales and other taxes. In particular, the budget increased the sales tax on pleasure boats from 10 to 33 per cent effective immediately.

Marie Laure under construction.
Courtesy Jock Muir Family Collection.

Given the substantial increase in sales tax, prospects for new recreational orders, particularly yachts, became grim. Instead Jock Muir focussed his attention on completing the vessels he had underway. Des Ashton's 33 ft racing sloop, *Lahara*, was launched on 8 December 1951. Despite little time available to test out the vessel's capabilities, Jock skippered *Lahara* in the 1951 Sydney to Hobart Yacht Race, finishing seventh across the line and second on handicap.

Two more vessels were completed in 1952. The 25 ft fishing boat *Evelyn* was built to the order of Alf Barnett of Binalong Bay and launched in January of that year. One of the biggest luxury cruisers built in Hobart for many years, Len Nettlefold's cutter, *Van Diemen*, was launched on 2 May 1952.

A New Slipway

With the bane of the federal sales tax on vessels jeopardising new business, in 1952 Jock Muir decided to diversify, laying a second slipway capable of accommodating vessels up to 75 ft in length and weighing up to 70 tons. It proved a wise decision. The slip supplemented the yard's boat building income nicely and became an integral part of the business in the decades that followed. As part of the slipping process, Jock Muir produced more than 1,000 slipping plans over his career, including profile sketches of vessels that were slipped at the yard. The work was a serious operation, Jock regarding the hauling of customers' vessels to be one of the utmost responsibilities of his profession.

Lahara under construction.
Courtesy Jock Muir Family Collection.

Wild Wave

On 11 March 1953 another vessel designed by Jock Muir was launched, built by Lindsay and Geoff Keats at Rose Bay, just across the river from Hobart. Named *Wild Wave*, the 47 ft cutter was considered a sister ship to *Waltzing Matilda*.

Not only did Jock supervise the vessel's build but he also skippered *Wild Wave* in the 1953 Sydney to Hobart Yacht Race. Other crew members included John Bennetto, Dudley Burridge, Peter Attrill, Basil Chipman, Keith Ratcliffe, Peter Crawford and joint owners Lindsay and Geoff Keats. After leading for most of the race, the vessel finished first across the line, with Jock Muir stating in the local press that "… the win was his best yet". The win also marked the first time in the race's history that a yacht built in Tasmania, owned by Tasmanians and skippered by a Tasmanian had won the event. In celebrating the win Jock even hinted about retiring from competitive ocean racing.

However, the jubilation was short-lived. A protest was lodged by the skippers of two entrants, *Josephine* and *Nimbus*, regarding an incident that occurred during the start of the race on Sydney Harbour. Following five hours of deliberations, the race committee upheld the protest and *Wild Wave* was stripped of line honours and disqualified from the race.

Though accepting the decision with grace, a disappointed but determined Jock Muir immediately announced that he would definitely be competing in the next Sydney to Hobart Yacht Race, postponing any thoughts of retirement.

Wild Wave on the Derwent
Courtesy Maritime Museum of Tasmania.

The 1950s

Back at his Battery Point boatyard, the years immediately after the Australian federal government increased the sales tax on pleasure vessels saw Jock Muir begin to advertise 10 ft marine-ply dinghies for sale in the local press. New orders were relatively subdued. The only large vessel completed in 1953 was the 34 ft British-designed racing sloop *Fantasy* which was launched on 12 December 1953, built to the order of Dudley Burridge and Stan Brown, both of the Huon.

In April 1954 Jock completed the fit-out, including construction of decks and interior furnishings, of the 56 ft motor launch *J Lee M,* which had been built at Triabunna by Jim Jones to the order of Reg Morrison of Strahan. The vessel was designed by fellow Battery Point boat builder Max Creese with the purpose of towing up to 200 tons of floating logs between the Gordon River and Strahan. It was also intended for use in the local tourism trade, at the time an industry in development.

Next off the slipway at Jock Muir's yard was the 40 ft game fishing boat *Blue Seabird*, built to the order of Len Lawrence of Sydney. This particular vessel was launched in 1954 and delivered to Sydney by Jock and crew after an 84 hour non-stop passage driven by the vessel's 5 LW Gardner diesel motor.

In early 1955 Jock completed *Mistral VI*, a 26 ft Sparkman and Stephens designed light-displacement cruiser built to the order of Guy Rex. The vessel marked the third Sparkman and Stephens designed vessel Guy Rex had commissioned to be built by the various boat builders of Battery Point.

In a departure from many of the cruising yachts built at Jock Muir's yard to date, the 52 ft pilot launch *Captain Mackenzie*, built by contract to the Launceston Marine Board, was launched in 1956. Designed by Bruce Thompson, a local naval architect, the vessel was based at the Low Head Pilot Station in Tasmania's north for many years.

J Lee M nearing completion.
Courtesy Jock Muir Family Collection.

Jack Earl's *Maris*

In late 1958 Jock Muir completed the 36 ft yacht *Maris* for maritime artist Jack Earl of Sydney who had previously sailed the double-ended ketch *Kathleen Gillett* in the first Sydney to Hobart Yacht Race, and in which he undertook a circumnavigation of the world. Designed by Alan Payne, *Maris* was one of the first vessels built to Payne's Tasman Seabird design. Constructed of Huon pine over hardwood ribs and backbone with the hull planks splined, *Maris* also marks the first vessel in which Jock Muir employed this planking method.

The Earl family lived on board *Maris* for five years, sailing thousands of miles throughout the Pacific, including to North America. Nearly 60 years later Jack Earl's granddaughter Tiare Tomaszewski and Lord Howe Islander John Green are joint owners of this remarkable vessel. Over its lifetime *Maris* has covered more than 300,000 nautical miles.

Launch of *Maris*.
Courtesy Jock Muir Family Collection.

MARIS

More Sydney to Hobart Races

Throughout the 1950s Jock Muir remained an active competitor in the Sydney to Hobart Yacht Race. Determined to overcome the disappointment of disqualification after skippering *Wild Wave* first across the line in the 1953 race, Jock joined the crew of John Palmer's 57 ft Sydney-based cutter *Even* as co-skipper for the 1954 race. Although the vessel's hull was savagely attacked by a 12 ft shark during the race's final stages, *Even* finished first across the line, 20 minutes ahead of the Livingstone family's *Kurrewa IV*. It was a victory that Jock savoured for the rest of his life, particularly given the previous year's disheartening outcome.

Jock Muir did not compete in the 1956 or 1957 Sydney to Hobart yacht races, opting to spend two of very few Christmases at home with his family. The 1958, 1959 and 1960 Sydney to Hobart races, however, saw him on board the 65 ft cutter *Kurrewa IV* as sailing master. Though forced to retire from the 1958 race after springing a leak 50 miles off Gabo Island, the 1959 race saw *Kurrewa IV* finish second across the line, and the 1960 race saw the vessel go one better, finishing first. All told, between 1947 and 1960 Jock competed in the Sydney to Hobart Yacht Race ten times, skippering yachts to victory (either first across the line or first on handicap) five times: quite a remarkable achievement.

The 1960s

There was a four-year gap between the launch of *Maris* and the launch of the next big boat from Jock Muir's Battery Point boatyard. During this period the yard continued to undertake slip, valuation, survey and repair work. Several vessel delivery trips were also undertaken to the mainland. A few smaller boats were additionally built, including for Jock's children who were just getting into competitive sailing.

The early to mid-1960s saw six larger vessels and several smaller vessels launched in the space of four years from Jock Muir's yard. These include the racing cruisers *Salacia, Narawi, Bindaree* and *Balandra*.

The 41 ft Sparkman and Stephens designed racing cruiser *Salacia*, built to the order of Bob Rusk of Sydney, was launched in early 1962. In March of the following year Jock Muir launched the 35 ft sloop *Narawi*, built to the order of Robert H. Minter and Jock Simpson, two solicitors of Sydney. She was the first of several vessels built to Jock Muir's Abel Tasman 64 design.

In 1962 Ross Muir, Jock's 16-year old son, joined the boatyard as an apprentice. Ross' first major job was working with Dave Wardrop on Graham Blackwood's 31 ft sloop *Bindaree*, a light-displacement double-chine Van der Stadt. The vessel was launched the following year.

In November 1963 the 34 ft police boat *Alert* was launched from Jock Muir's Battery Point yard, having taken a year to complete. This particular vessel was constructed under the supervision of Bill Foster and built at a workshop in New Town, owing to lack of space at Jock's boatyard. It was transported to Battery Point just prior to launch.

In late November 1965 the 46 ft Camper and Nicholson designed racing yacht *Balandra* was launched. In his biography, *Maritime Reflections,* Jock Muir describes the vessel as one of the most beautiful boats he had ever been involved with. Built to the order of Robert Crichton-Brown of Sydney over a period of eight months, *Balandra* was constructed of Honduras mahogany, double skin, on pre-laminated and cold-moulded frames. The vessel went on to finish second across the line in both the 1965 and 1966 Sydney to Hobart yacht races. After delivering the newly-completed *Balandra* to Sydney, Jock was on board for the return leg to Hobart during the 1965 race, along with his friend Neall Batt. *Balandra* also won the 1967 Admiral's Cup as part of the Australian team.

Balandra finishing a Sydney to Hobart Yacht Race. Courtesy Maritime Museum of Tasmania.

During the mid-1960s two fishing boats were launched from Jock Muir's yard: the 31 ft *Gwynne-B* and the 42 ft *Dorothy Fay*. The former was built to the order of Alf Barnett of Binnalong Bay and launched in 1964. The latter was built to the order of Arnold White of Bicheno and launched in 1965.

More smaller vessels were built at Jock's boatyard during the mid-1960s. These include the cadet dinghy *Venom*, built by Ross Muir and Bruce Darcey and launched in September 1963, and the cadet dinghy *Kittiwake II*, which Jock built for his youngest son Greg, and launched in September 1965. Both vessels continued the Muir family's triumph at the Stonehaven Cup with Ross winning the event in 1964 at the helm of *Venom,* and Greg winning the event in 1967 at the helm of *Kittiwake II*.

This period also coincided with the lightweight sharpie era. Ross Muir built *Venom* in 1965 and then *Venom II* in 1966. He successfully helmed both vessels at the Australian Sharpie Championship over a period of several years.

More Large Vessels

The late 1960s continued to be a busy period for Jock Muir's boatyard. The fishing boat *Nambucca* was launched in 1967. Then followed a Top Hat design that was christened *Chindrina*. The vessel was built for Herbert Frey by Dave Wardrop, Ross Muir, Max Muir and Jim Groves and launched in late 1967. The 32 ft motor sailer sloop *Lady Nelson* was built to the order of Robert Robe (Jr) of New York, USA, and launched in early 1969. Designed by Jock Muir, this particular vessel was delivered to Sydney and then trans-shipped to New York.

The 1970s

Into the 1970s Jock Muir continued to undertake vessel delivery voyages and slip and repair work. Two large vessels were also built: *Trevassa* and *Astrolabe*. Of a similar design to *Waltzing Matilda*, the 48 ft cruising yacht *Trevassa* was purchased by Russell Duffield of Sydney part-way through construction and launched in 1971. At the time Russell Duffield owned *Patsy*, which Jock had built in 1950. Jock received this vessel as part-payment for *Trevassa* and sailed her in the 1971 Southern Cross Cup. In 1972 Jock entered *Patsy* in the inaugural Melbourne to Hobart west coaster. The 31 ft Lidgard designed sloop *Astrolabe* was built to the order of Bob Gear of Hobart and launched in 1973.

Notably the last vessel Jock Muir built was the cadet dinghy *Kittiwake III*, which he completed in 1975, built to the order of John Ross for his son Craig. The Muir family's Battery Point boatyard remained in operation however. With the closure of Purdon and Featherstone's nearby yard, the Muir boatyard picked up a lot of slipping business, not that Jock welcomed the demise of the historic slip.

Trevassa at Barnes Bay in 2016.
Courtesy John Muir.

Boat Designs

In addition to the building and slipping of vessels at his Battery Point boatyard, throughout his career Jock Muir also designed approximately 100 vessels built by other builders. These include cruising and racing yachts, power boats and fishing boats.

The first boat constructed to one of Jock's designs was the 41 ft fishing cruiser *Fiona,* built by brothers J. and E. Boyle at New Town over a 15-month period and launched in December 1947. Next came *Southern Gem*, a sloop of similar lines to *Westward*, built by one Jock's employees, Alan Cracknell. Launched on 26 March 1949, the vessel took over two years to complete and was constructed in the backyard of Cracknell's home at 71 York Street, Sandy Bay.

At least seven vessels were built to the same design as Jock Muir's ocean-going cruiser *Waltzing Matilda*, launched in 1949. In addition to *Wild Wave*, previously mentioned in this chapter, these include *Solquest*, built by Max Creese at Battery Point to the order of Len Staples and launched in 1956; two vessels built in California; *Manutara*, built by Salthouse and Logan of Auckland, New Zealand, and launched in 1962; and finally a vessel built from steel in Queensland.

The first vessel constructed to Jock Muir's Abel Tasman 64 was the sloop *Narawi,* which he launched in March 1963. Three more vessels were subsequently built to this design at other yards. These were *Kaiulani*, built by Wilson Brothers at Cygnet in 1966 to the order of Linsday Masters of Melbourne; *Pono*, built in New Zealand; and *Sagan,* built near Cygnet in 1985 by owner Derek Shields of Gardners Bay.

Jock Muir also designed more than 20 fishing vessels, six of which he built at Battery Point. One of the best-known fishing boats built elsewhere was the 60 ft *Donita,* built by Wilson Brothers at Cygnet for Geoff Martin of Victoria and launched in 1958.

Additional boats designed by Jock Muir include Tim Chesterman's yacht *Lady Gillian*, built by Mick Drake at Triabunna and launched in 1980, and the *Crusade,* a 36 ft fishing boat built by Barry Wilson for Ron Stevens.

Sydney to Hobart Yacht Races

Between 1946 and 1971 Jock Muir competed in 19 Sydney to Hobart yacht races, his final race on board *Patsy* which he had built in 1950. Jock's race record is exceptional. He finished first across the line three times and first on handicap twice. He also finished second, either across the line or on handicap, five times.

Delivery Trips

Throughout his career Jock Muir was involved with the delivery of many vessels to the mainland, including those which he built. Surveys and valuations also formed part of the boatyard's business. As with his other records, Jock's notes on his delivery trips are meticulous. The first vessel he was involved in delivering to the mainland appears to have been Max Creese's 42 ft yacht *Mavis*, which Jock and crew delivered to her new Sydney-based owner in March 1948.

In May 1950 Jock delivered the newly-completed Laurent Giles designed *Patsy* to Sydney, along with A. C. Cooper (the vessel's owner), two of the boatyard's apprentices (Bill Foster and Adrian Dean), and Ted Domeney. The following year, in July 1951, Jock was sailing master on board the 65 ft staysail schooner *Mistral II* during its delivery from Sydney to Hobart for new owner Jack Paine. In May 1953 Jock sailed Guy Rex's *Mistral V*, built by Purdon and Featherstone at Battery Point, to Melbourne from where it was trans-shipped to Hong Kong. The following year saw delivery of the 40 ft fishing vessel *Blue Seabird* to Sydney, which Jock had built for Len Lawrence.

The latter years of the 1950s were also busy in terms of vessel deliveries. In June 1957 Jock Muir and crew (comprising Wally Muir, Barry Croft and Mac Foster) delivered the 45 ft fishing vessel *Pendella* to Port Chalmers, New Zealand, the trip marking Jock's first across the Tasman. In June 1958 *Wild Wave* was delivered to Melbourne. On board were John Gilliam, Alf Gough, Bruce Griggs, David Boyes and a Mr Stevens. In November 1958 the *Catalina* was delivered to Melbourne. The following month saw the 33 ft yacht *Renene* delivered to the same location. Crew on board for this particular voyage were Lawrence Ford, Tom Prober and John Muir.

Jock Muir's Battery Point boatyard showing the *J Lee M* being fitted out.
Courtesy Jock Muir Family Collection.

Also in the late 1950s Jock Muir delivered the cruiser *Bikini* (ex *Mavourneen*) to Williamstown, Victoria, with a crew comprising Alf Gough, Leo Gough, Mick Purdon and Ernie Muir. The vessel struck a whale while crossing Bass Strait, though fortunately was not damaged.

1959 saw at least three vessels delivered to the mainland. In March 1959 Jock Muir and crew (comprising Allan Morgan, Dudley Burridge, Frank Goyre, Kevin Mooney and John Muir), delivered the racing sloop *Fantasy* to Melbourne which Jock had completed in 1953. In September 1959 Jock delivered *Valiant* to Melbourne. Also on board were Ross Muir, John Muir, Lawrence Ford, Geoff Balcolmbe and Barry Tinker-Casson. Jock's detailed notes for this specific voyage include points awarded for "yodelling," also known as sea sickness, with Ross Muir scoring 10 points, John Muir scoring 8 and Barry Tinker-Casson scoring 6. A month later the *Sea Breeze* was delivered to Devonport with a crew comprising Jock Muir, B. Skolds, Lionel Barber and the vessel's builder Tom Pilkington.

In November 1960 Jock delivered the 39 ft cutter *Anita* to Melbourne. Also on board were the vessel's owner Alan Cheetham, along with Maynard Meppin, Alf Gough and John Muir. In 1962 Jock sailed the newly-completed Sparkman and Stephens designed *Salacia* to Sydney along with owner Bob Rusk. In November 1963 the *Tuna W*. was delivered to Melbourne. In mid-1963, Jock delivered the newly-built sloop *Narawi* to Sydney with the vessel's two owners also on board.

The mid-1960s saw Jock Muir deliver the Sparkman and Stephens designed *Trilby II* to Melbourne with Ross Muir, Greg Muir, Andre van Nieuwenhuysen and Adam Brinton. In late 1965 *Balandra* was delivered to Sydney with Jock remaining on board for the return trip as part of that year's Sydney to Hobart Yacht Race. Also on board was his good friend Neall Batt. In 1969 Jock and crew delivered the motor sailer sloop *Lady Nelson* to Sydney for trans-shipment to New York.

Succession and Retirement

In 1970 Jock Muir made his eldest son John a part-owner of the Battery Point boatyard. In 1978 the pair were joined by Jock's middle son Ross. At this time Jock and John down-sized the boat building business. They then undertook major alterations to the site, including adding a second floor to the main building and erecting a new building alongside for a sail loft. Up until this point Ross had been working nearby at a yard operated by Sam and Mick Purdon. Here Ross undertook boat repairs, boat building, rigging, sail making and chandlery, working with Michael and George Grainger. The trio relocated all of the inventory to the new Muir's boatyard site. The revitalised Muir Boatyard thus became a "one-stop shop" for boat sales, chandlery, sail making, spares and rigging, slipping, moorings, service and boat repairs. Under the chandlery, Jock's youngest son Greg moved his own company in 1977, Yacht Distributors, selling production yachts, catamarans, sailing dinghies and associated recreational sailing equipment. Adjacent was John Muir's own business, Muir Engineering – Muir Winches, established in 1968 as Muir Diesel Services.

Jock Muir remained working at his Battery Point boatyard until 1987. His brother Max had retired several years prior, in 1984. Jock's retirement coincided with Ross Muir's departure for Queensland where he opened a chandlery at Manly. From 1987 to 1990 the Muir Boatyard was operated by John Muir and his business partner Jeff Gordon. Since this time the boatyard has been wholly owned by John Muir and his wife Wendy.

In the 1990s the downstairs portion of the Muir Boatyard workshop was leased to several boat builders, including Lindsay Woods, Gordon Stewart and Kevin "Ginger" Argent. Working at the site between 1993 and mid-1996 Gordon Stewart operated a boat building and repair business. Vessels he built during this period include a state championship winning sabot for Clare Brown (named *Chocolate Eclare*), a mirror dinghy for Jock Campbell, a Whithall-style recreational rowing boat, an American-style 20 ft ketch-rigged sharpie (designed by Alan Payne), and a pair of hulls for a solar-powered boat designed by Incat. The latter was built for a national competition held on Lake Burley Griffin in Canberra, which it won. Kevin Argent leased the property after Gordon Stewart where he built several small dinghies, likely some of the last boats to be built at Battery Point.

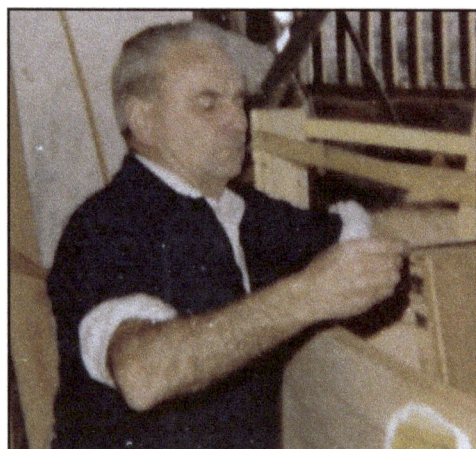

Jock Muir building *Kittiwake III* in 1975.
Courtesy Jock Muir Family Collection.

In recent years the Muir Boatyard has undergone a renaissance. Doyle Sails and Chandlery and Boat Sales Tasmania have moved in, bringing new life to the old boatyard.

Jock Muir died in Hobart on 29 November 1995 at the age of 81. His wife Mollie died on 17 July 1998. The couple is survived by their four children: Lynette, John, Ross and Greg.

Vessels Built by Jock Muir and Muir Boatyard Employees and Leaseholders at Battery Point (1937 – 1990s).

1937. *Westwind*. Ketch. 36 x 11 ft. Deep-sea double-ended built for Jock Muir's own use in the backyard of his parents' house, 42 Colville Street, Battery Point. Based on the design of the *Ho-Ho* and *Te Rapunga*. Launched in September 1937. Participated in the cruiser class and used for local and interstate pleasure and fishing cruises. Sold in March 1941 to Jack Capell of Sydney, NSW. By 1945 owned by F. H. Clapp, by 1952 owned by Dr F. A. Bellingham, in 1966 owned by William Gray, in 1969 owned by Malcolm Evans. Still in existence. Since 1997 owned by Chris Dicker of Cairns, QLD, and fully restored.

1947. *Westward*. Yacht. 42 x 12 x 6.2 ft. Cruising yacht built in a paddock off 52 Queen Street, Sandy Bay, by Jock Muir who was also the vessel's designer. Built to the order of a fisherman of NSW but purchased part-way through construction by George Gibson of Hobart. Launched on 6 September 1947. Competed in the 1947 Sydney to Hobart Yacht Race, finishing 2nd across the line and 1st on handicap. Won the 1948 Sydney to Hobart Yacht Race on handicap. Sold to Loris Solomon of Geelong, VIC, in June 1950. Won the Queenscliff to Devonport race in December 1950. By the mid-1950s owned by Bert Robilliard of VIC and competed in the 1958 Sydney to Hobart Yacht Race. Subsequently purchased by Stan Field of Maryborough, QLD, who owned the vessel for more than 50 years. Still in existence, donated to the Maritime Museum of Tasmania in 2010 and moored in Hobart.

1948. *Lass O'Luss*. Yacht. 41.5 x 9.5 x 6.5 ft. Built to the order of John Colquhoun of Sydney, NSW, based on a design by Robert Clark of the UK and launched on 4 December 1948. Participated in the 1948 Sydney to Hobart Yacht Race, though forced to retire. Participated in eight more Sydney to Hobart yacht races between 1949 and 1967. Notably finished 2nd across the line (and 3rd on handicap) in 1951. In 1961 purchased by Bill Psaltis of the Cruising Yacht Club of Australia, NSW. Advertised for sale in Sydney in 1976 and 1978. Still in existence, owned by W. Wawn of Sydney, NSW.

1949. *Pinjarra*. Motor boat. 29 ft. Built to the order of the Bastick family and likely launched in January 1949. Advertised for sale in June 1950. Subsequent owners include the Murdoch, Bales and Holder families followed by Andrew Perkins. Later sold to a Mr Dicker and then to the Bennett family. Wrecked at One Tree Point, Bruny Island.

1949. *Tawaki*. Heavyweight sharpie. 19.6 ft. Built by Don Muir. First noted on the River Derwent in February 1949. In January 1951 owned by Tom W. Edwards. Represented TAS in the 1952 Australian Sharpie Championship held in Melbourne, helmed by Don Muir. Advertised for sale in October 1953. By 1958 owned by Kevin Livingstone.

1949. *Waltzing Matilda*. Yacht. 47 x 12.1 x 6.5 ft. Built to the order of Philip Davenport of Sydney, NSW, based on Jock Muir's *Westward* design. Launched on 2 July 1949. Took line honours and finished 2nd on handicap in the 1949 Sydney to Hobart Yacht Race. The first Australian yacht to compete in the Fastnet Race, finishing 5th on corrected time (in her division) in the 1951 event, after sailing to England via the Strait of Magellan. Following, sailed to Europe and the Americas with her travels immortalised in Philip Davenport's book *The Voyage of Waltzing Matilda*, published in 1953. Later sold to Robert Barry of Philadelphia, USA. Lost in the Atlantic Ocean 100 miles west of the island of St Vincent in December 1968; all hands saved.

1949. *Kittihawk*. Heavyweight sharpie. 19.6 ft. Built by Don Muir and launched in October 1949. Sailed by a QLD representative at the 1950 Australian Sharpie Championship held in Hobart, and sold to D. Perrins of QLD immediately following the competition.

Vessels Built by Jock Muir and Muir Boatyard Employees and Leaseholders at Battery Point (1937 – 1990s).

1950. Dinghy. Commercial crayfishing dinghy built by Bill Foster, the yard's apprentice, in early 1950 for Bill Wisby of Bruny Island.

1950. *Patsy (Patsy of Island Bay)*. Yacht. 46.7 x 10.5 x 7.5 ft. Designed by Laurent Giles. Built to the order of A. C. Cooper, vice commodore of the Sydney-based Cruising Yacht Club of Australia and launched on 4 April 1950. Advertised for sale in February 1966. Purchased by Russell Duffield of NSW and competed in the 1968 to 1970 Sydney to Hobart yacht races. Transferred to Jock Muir in 1971 as part-payment for *Trevassa*. Competed in the 1971 Sydney to Hobart Yacht Race with Jock Muir and his son John on board. Finished 2nd in the inaugural (1972) Melbourne to Hobart Yacht Race. Sold in November 1975 to Gordon Beattie of Hobart. In 1997 purchased by Glen Nicholson and restored. Still in existence; since 2010 owned by Geoff McIntosh of Sydney, NSW.

1950. Dinghy. 9.6 ft. Built by Bill Foster as a tender for *Patsy*.

1950. *Skimmer*. Heavyweight sharpie. 19.6 ft. Built by Bill Foster and Don Muir to the order of Ediss Boyes and launched in September 1950. Won the 1951 Australian Sharpie Championship held in Brisbane with a crew of Ediss Boyes, Geoff Omant and S. Nichols. Represented TAS in the 1952 Australian Sharpie Championship held in Melbourne, helmed by Ediss Boyes, finishing 2nd. Represented TAS in the 1953 Australian Sharpie Championship held in Perth, helmed by Ediss Boyes, finishing 2nd. Represented TAS in the 1954 Australian Sharpie Championship held in Sydney. In September 1954 sold to W. Shearman. Owned by Kevin Livingstone circa 1959 and subsequently transferred to Launceston. Restored in Hobart in the early 2000s and on display at the Wooden Boat Centre, Franklin until 2014. Still in existence, sold in April 2016 to Terry Lean of the Huon.

1950. *Darter*. Heavyweight sharpie. 19.6 ft. Built by Bill Foster and Don Muir to the order of Neil Campbell. Launched in September 1950. Finished 2nd at the 1952 Australian Sharpie Championship, held in Melbourne, helmed by Dick Ikin. Competed in the 1954 Australian Sharpie Championship held in Sydney. By 1958 owned by D. L. Willing. By 1960 owned by Robert Clark.

1950. *Sirocco*. Cadet dinghy. 12 x 5 ft x 14 in. Built by Max Muir to the order of David Boyes and launched by November 1950. Represented TAS in the 1953 Stonehaven Cup held in SA, helmed by David Boyes. Represented TAS in the 1954 Stonehaven Cup held in VIC, helmed by David Boyes. By 1955 owned by J. G. Turner, by 1961 owned by P. A. Monoghan, by 1962 owned by V. Marsland, by 1964 owned by Peter Makepeace. Part of the Royal Yacht Club of Tasmania's complement of cadet dinghies in the 1990s. Possibly still in existence; last noted at Bicheno (condition unknown).

1951. *Helen S*. Fishing boat. 41 ft. Designed and partly-built by Alan Norman to the order of Leon Scarf of Victoria. Completed by Jock Muir and launched in June 1951.

1951. *Marie Laure*. Fishing boat. 28 ft. Launched in mid-1951 to the order of the Dunbabin family of Dunalley, TAS. Remained in the Dunbabin family's possession for several generations.

1951. *Lahara*. Yacht. 33 x 9 x 5.5 ft. Sloop. Built to the order of Des Ashton of Papua New Guinea and launched on 8 December 1951. With Jock Muir as sailing master, finished 7th across the line and 2nd on handicap in the 1951 Sydney to Hobart Yacht Race. Finished 2nd in the 1952 Trans-Tasman Race, 44 minutes behind *Lady Bird*. Finished 14th across the line in the 1956 Sydney to Hobart Yacht Race. Advertised for sale in March 1957. Advertised for sale in October 1983. Later owned by Ray Joyce. By the 1990s owned by P. Ashe and competed in the 1994, 1995 and 1996 Sydney to Hobart yacht races.
Still in existence; currently owned by Mike Warner of Sydney, NSW.

1952. *Evelyn*. Fishing boat. 25 x 8 4.2 ft. Built to the order of Alf Barnett of Binalong Bay and launched in January 1952. Later owned by Des Singline. Wrecked at Picnic Bay, TAS on 18 June 1971. At the time of loss owned by Wayne Kirkland.

1952. *Van Diemen*. Ketch. 50 x 13.9 x 5.5 ft. Built to the order of Len Nettlefold and launched on 2 May 1952. Designed by Jock Muir. Remained in Nettlefold's possession until his death in October 1971 and retained by his family, competing in the 1971 Sydney to Hobart Yacht Race with R. F. Hickman as skipper. Sold to John Colquhoun and transferred to Sydney, NSW, arriving in July 1973. Later purchased by Carl and Caressa Gonsalves. Still in existence; owned by Ian Begg and under restoration at Palm Beach, NSW.

1953. *Fantasy*. Yacht. 34 x 9 x 5.5 ft. UK-designed racing sloop built to the order of Dudley Burridge and Stan Brown, both of the Huon, and launched on 12 December 1953. Competed in the 1955 and 1956 Sydney to Hobart yacht races. Sold to Frank Eyre of Melbourne, VIC, in March 1959. Later transferred to Sydney, NSW.

1954. *J Lee M*. Motor launch. 56 x 14 ft. Built by Jim Jones of Triabunna to a design by Max Creese and fitted out by Jock Muir for owner Reg Morrison. Launched in April 1954. Used to tow logs between the Gordon River and Strahan, and in the tourism trade. Still in existence; owned by Reg Morrison's nephew Alan Morrison and based at Kettering, TAS.

1954. *Blue Seabird*. Fishing boat. 40 ft. Built to the order of Len Lawrence of Sydney, NSW. Possibly later transferred to SA.

1955. *Mistral VI*. Yacht. 26 ft. Sparkman and Stephens designed light-displacement cruiser built to the order of Guy Rex. Later owned by Dr William Wilson of Hobart. Then purchased by Jack Fitzgerald, and in 1968 by Dr William Wilson. Later owned by Dr Norm Wood of Hobart. Still in existence; located in southern TAS.

1956. *Captain Mackenzie*. Pilot launch. 52 x 12 x 6 ft. Gaff-rigged. Built for the Launceston Marine Board as a pilot launch. Designed by Bruce Thompson. Based at the pilot station at Low Head, TAS, for several years. Sold to Trevor Brown of Hobart and used for the Maatsuyker Island mail run. Sold to pilot services in Sydney, NSW, for the Torres Strait service off Cairns, QLD. By 1989 noted to be in Southport, QLD, and owned by Harry and Carol Littler. Still in existence; located in VIC.

1958. *Maris*. Yacht. 36.5 x 9.5 x 4.7 ft. Built to the order of maritime artist Jack Earl of Sydney, NSW. Designed by Alan Payne. Launched in late 1958. Sailed extensively by the Earl family throughout the Pacific. Competed in two Sydney to Hobart yacht races. By the 1970s, and for many years, sailed by Ian Kiernan. Competed in five more Sydney to Hobart races. Still in existence, based in Sydney, NSW, and jointly owned by Jack Earl's granddaughter Tiare Tomaszewski and Lord Howe Islander John Green.

Vessels Built by Jock Muir and Muir Boatyard Employees and Leaseholders at Battery Point (1937 – 1990s).

1959. *Mitzi*. Dinghy. International cadet dinghy built by Jock Muir for his sons. Competed in Sandy Bay Sailing Club events. Sailed by Greg Muir in the inaugural Australian Championship for International Cadets, held in Melbourne, VIC, in 1962.

1960. *Aristotle*. Motor launch. 25 ft. Built to the order of Lindsay Masters to a design by Don Muir.

1962. *Salacia*. Yacht. 41 ft. Built for Bob Rusk based on a Sparkman and Stephens design. Later sold to Arthur Byrne of Sydney, NSW. Advertised for sale in Sydney in September 1982. Still in existence and located at Pittwater, NSW.

1963. *Narawi*. Yacht. 35 x 9.5 x 6.4 ft. Sloop. Built to the order of Robert Minter and Jock Simpson, two solicitors of Sydney, NSW. First of several vessels built to Jock Muir's Abel Tasman design. Noted to be present on Sydney Harbour by October 1963. Sailed competitively by Robert Minter for several decades. Advertised for sale multiple times in the mid to late 2000s, though remained in the Minter family's possession. By 2016 owned by Andrew Minter, Robert Minter's son, and refurbished at Palm Beach, NSW. Ran aground off Lion Island near Pittwater, NSW, in late June 2016, all on board safe. Could not be salvaged.

1963. *Alert*. Police Launch. 34 ft. Built to the order of Tasmania Police by Muir boatyard employees Bill Foster, Dave Wardrop, Fred Dennis and Ross Muir at a workshop in Lenah Valley and launched from Battery Point in November 1963. Still in existence; located at Lindisfarne Bay, TAS.

1963. *Venom*. Cadet dinghy. 12 x 5 ft x 14 in. Built initially by Ross Muir and Bruce Darcey at Lenah Valley then transferred to Battery Point where Ross Muir finished the work. Won the 1964 Stonehaven Cup held in Hobart, helmed by Ross Muir. Competed in the 1965 Stonehaven Cup held in Adelaide, helmed by Ross Muir. In 1965 sold to Steve Masters of Hobart. In 1968 transferred to VIC. Still in existence, currently on display at the Royal Melbourne Yacht Squadron, VIC.

1963. *Bindaree*. Yacht. 31 ft. Built by Dave Wardrop and Ross Muir at North Hobart and launched from Battery Point. A light-displacement double-chine Van der Stadt built to the order of Graham Blackwood, a solicitor of Hobart. Competed in the 1964 Sydney to Hobart Yacht Race, though forced to retire.

1964. *Gwynne-B*. Fishing boat. 31 ft. Built to the order of Alf Barnett of Binalong Bay. Still in existence; advertised for sale in 2017. Moored at the Motor Yacht Club of Tasmania in Lindisfarne, TAS.

1965. *Venom*. Lightweight sharpie. Built by Ross Muir and launched in September 1965. Competed in the 1966 Australian Sharpie Championship held in Sydney, helmed by Ross Muir. Sold to a buyer from NSW that same year.

1965. *Dorothy Fay*. Fishing boat. 42 x 12.9 x 6.4 ft. Built to the order of Arnold White of Bicheno and launched in May 1965. Capsized and sank off Schouten Passage on 3 August 1975; all hands saved.

Opposite: One of Jock Muir's slipping plans.
He produced over 1,000 slipping plans during his career at Battery Point.
Courtesy Jock Muir Family Collection.

1965. *Balandra.* **Yacht.** 46 x 12 x 7 ft. Sloop. Launched in late November 1965. Built to the order of Robert Crichton-Brown of Sydney to a Camper and Nicholson design. Finished 2nd across the line in both the 1965 and 1966 Sydney to Hobart yacht races; the former with Jock Muir on board as crew. Competed for Australia and won the 1967 Admiral's Cup. Also competed in the 1969 Southern Cross Cup. Between 1968 and 1989 participated in eight more Sydney to Hobart yacht races. From 1970 owned by the Army Eastern Command. By 1977 owned by Randolph Carpenter. By 1980 returned to Hobart and owned by Russell Piggott. Purchased by Gerd Hennicke in 1985 and Jamie Saunders in 1992. Still in existence; currently under restoration.

1965. *Kittiwake II.* **Cadet dinghy.** 12 x 5 ft x 14 in. Built by Jock Muir for his son Greg and launched in 1965. Competed in the 1965, 1966 and 1967 Stonehaven Cups. Won the 1967 Stonehaven Cup held in Hobart, helmed by Greg Muir with David Norman and David Cook as crew. Later transferred to VIC. Still in existence.

1966. *Venom II.* **Lightweight sharpie.** Built by Ross Muir at Battery Point and finished at Dave Wardrop's shed in North Hobart. Built for Ross' own use. Competed in the 1967 Australian Lightweight Sharpie Championship held in Hobart. Competed in the 1968 Australian Lightweight Sharpie Championship held in Melbourne. Competed in the 1969 Australian Lightweight Sharpie Championship held in Port Moresby, Papua New Guinea. Transferred to Sydney in the early 1970s.

1967. *Red Jacket.* **Cadet dinghy.** 12 x 5 ft x 14 in. Built by Ross Muir to the order of a customer from VIC.

1967. *Nambucca.* **Fishing boat.** 47 x 14.5 x 7.2 ft. Designed by Ray Kemp. Built for a syndicate from north TAS who later cancelled the order. Continued on speculation and sold to Tim Bailey and Alan Yates, both Bicheno-based fishermen. Destroyed by fire off Stoney Head, TAS, on 6 February 1997. At the time owned by Paul Morton.

1967. *Chindrina.* **Yacht.** Top Hat design built for Herbert Frey by Dave Wardrop, Ross Muir, Max Muir and Jim Groves. Built of strip-planked King Billy. Launched in late 1967.

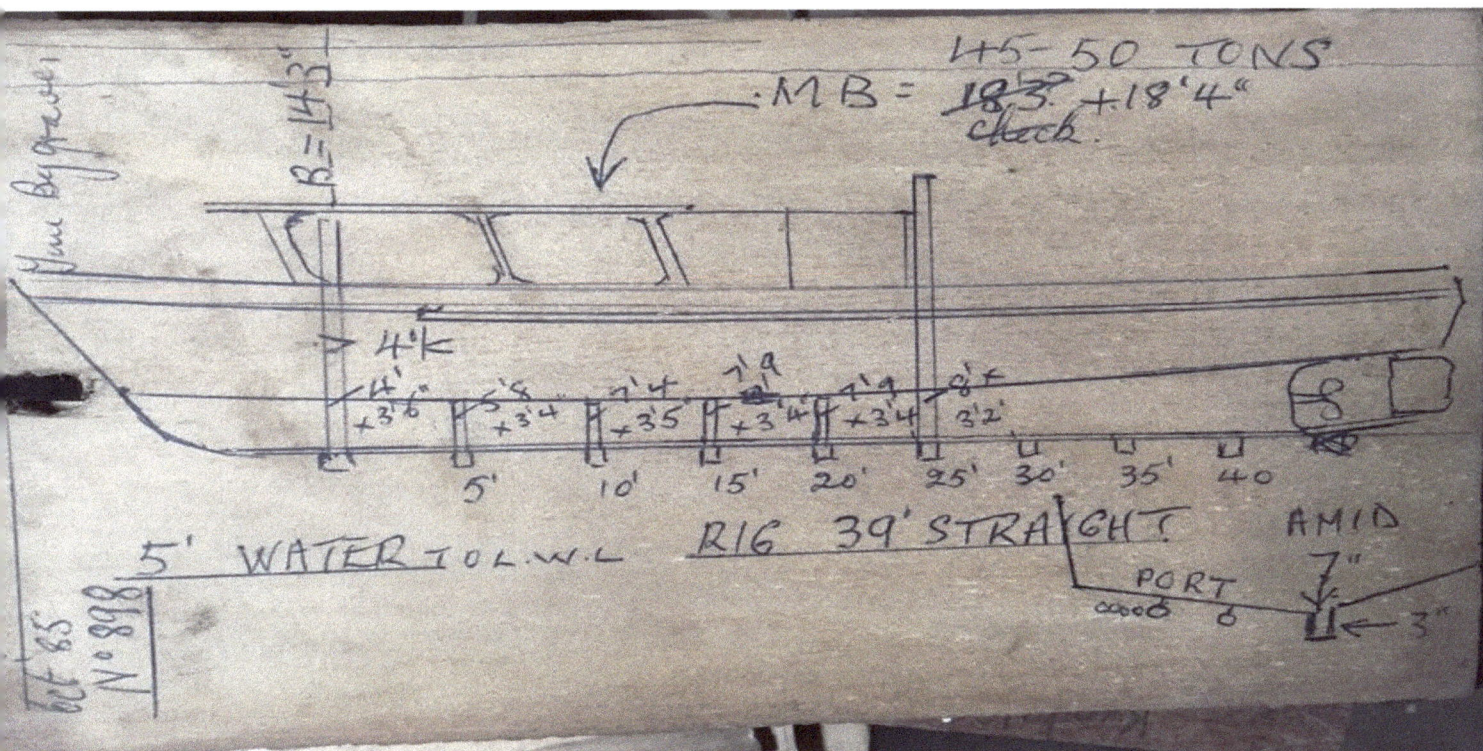

Vessels Built by Jock Muir and Muir Boatyard Employees and Leaseholders at Battery Point (1937 – 1990s).

1969. *Lady Nelson*. Yacht. 32 x 10 x 4.5 ft. Sloop. Designed and built by Jock Muir for Robert Robe (Jr) of New York, USA. Trans-shipped to North America. Still in existence; based in Boston, USA.

1971. *Trevassa*. Yacht. 48 x 12.2 x 7 ft. Designed and built by Jock Muir on speculation. Purchased by Russell Duffield of Sydney, NSW, just prior to completion and launched in 1971. Competed in five Sydney to Hobart yacht races between 1972 and 1990. Still in existence; in 2012 purchased by Jock Muir's four children (from the Duffield family), returned to Hobart and restored.

1973. *Astrolabe*. Yacht. 31 x 10 x 8 ft. Lidgard designed cold-moulded sloop built to the order of Bob Gear of Hobart. Purchased by Wesley McMaster and moved to Port Moresby, New Guinea in 1978. Later returned to Hobart. Still in existence; currently owned by Peter Bosworth of Hobart.

1975. *Kittiwake III*. Cadet dinghy. 12 x 5 ft x 14 in. Built to the order of John Ross for his son Craig. Later owned by Alf Gough for his son Robbie, and following was sailed by John McCley and Jason Muir. Part of the Royal Yacht Club of Tasmania's complement of cadet dinghies in the 1990s. Still in existence; recently purchased by Greg Muir and Kenn Batt of Hobart.

Aerial view of Hobart, including Battery Point (circa 1950s). Courtesy State Library of Victoria.

1990s. *Chocolate Eclare.* **Dinghy.** Sabot dinghy built by Gordon Stewart for Clare Brown. Won a state championship.

1990s. Dinghy. Mirror dinghy built by Gordon Stewart for Jock Campbell.

1990s. Boat. Whithall-style recreational rowing boat built by Gordon Stewart.

1990s. Sharpie. 20 ft. American-style ketch-rigged sharpie built by Gordon Stewart to a design by Alan Payne.

1996. Hulls. A pair of hulls built by Gordon Stewart for a solar-powered boat designed and built by Incat Australia Pty. Ltd. of Derwent Park, TAS, and named Hull 039. In April 1996 raced by Robert Clifford and won a six hour national solar competition held on Lake Burley Griffin in Canberra, ACT. Still in existence; on permanent display at Incat's facility in Derwent Park, TAS.

Late 1990s. Dinghies. Various dinghies built by Kevin Argent.

Maxwell (Max) Creese

Born and raised in Hobart, Max Creese began building yachts as a teenager before embarking on a career as a builder and contractor. Yet his passion was in designing and building boats and in 1948, at the age of 37, he established his own yard at Battery Point. Here, up until his retirement in 1990, Max built more than 40 vessels, including ocean racing yachts, fishing boats and motor cruisers, over half of which remain in existence. He also designed more than 20 vessels, including fishing boats and motor sailers, that were built by professional and amateur boat builders in and around Hobart and at Cygnet. Known for his meticulous work, Max Creese's boats developed a solid reputation both locally and interstate and were particularly sought after in Sydney. Equally matched was Max's commitment to the sport of yachting. He competed in four Sydney to Hobart yacht races, including the first race held in 1945, and was a popular and consistently successful competitor in local yacht races for many decades.

Maxwell (Max) Mark Creese was born on 21 July 1910 at his parents' residence of 182 Brisbane Street, Hobart, the second of six children born to Henry and Maud Marion Creese (nee Martin). He was a third generation Tasmanian hailing from a family well-embedded with nautical occupations.

Though Max's father worked at the Government Printing Office, his uncles were very active in the local maritime community. Max's uncle Joseph Creese, for example, was for many years master of the intercolonial trading barques *Pet* and *Kassa*. After a decade-long stint as deputy harbourmaster of the Port of Hobart, Joseph Creese became lighthouse keeper of Deal Island, Iron Pot, Bruny Island, and finally, Goose Island lighthouses.

Another uncle, William Creese, built the cutter yacht *Inez* in 1885. This particular yacht was built in the backyard of his home in Macquarie Street, Hobart. Also built by William Creese were the yacht *Myrtle*, launched in 1889, and the fishing boat *Mildura*, launched in 1890. The latter was built for William Creese's own employment in the fishing industry. Another yacht built by William Creese, the *Monsoon*, was launched in 1890. All three vessels were built in the backyard of Captain Joseph Creese's home in Kelly Street, Battery Point. In 1895, following the loss of the *Mildura*, William Creese built the 42 ft fishing smack *Venture*.

Opposite: The Battery Point Trade School, on the corner of Hampden and Sandy Bay roads (circa 1960s). Courtesy Tasmanian Archive and Heritage Office.

A third uncle, Mark Creese, was a successful builder and contractor in the Hobart area, and was heavily involved in the Master Builders Association. In his younger years Mark Creese was also an active local yachtsman. A fourth uncle, Robert Creese, built model yachts during his youth, despite being nearly blind.

In addition to these maritime pursuits, over many decades the various kin of the Creese family were regular participants in local sporting clubs and events, including those associated with football, cricket, rowing and badminton. Max Creese's father Henry was a prominent local cricketer.

Natural Aptitude

From an early age Max Creese showed an interest and aptitude in mathematics. He had a yearning to become an architect, yet the practicalities of the Depression and the need to earn a living and help support his family saw Max veer towards a trade. In December 1923, as a 13-year old pupil of the Goulburn Street State School, Max was awarded a special prize for his woodworking skills. The award was given by Charles Snook, supervisor of the Battery Point Trade School, located on the corner of Sandy Bay and Hampden roads. Here Max, along with students from other local primary schools, undertook specialised classes one day a week in woodworking and technical drawing. The school appears to have been somewhat of a breeding ground for several of Battery Point's talented boat builders. Continuing to do well at school, in 1927 Max Creese received a credit for carpentry and joinery (theory and calculations, trade drawing and practical) from the Hobart Technical School.

The First Yacht

Outside of school hours Max Creese played several sports, including football with his older brother Harry. Yet much of his spare time was consumed by an interest in sailing and building boats. In September 1926, at the age of 16, Max and Harry launched the B class yacht *Monsoon*, built in the backyard of their home, 182 Brisbane Street, Hobart. The duo likely were helped in the design and building of *Monsoon* by family and friends, including A. Oliphant, as well as their uncle Mark Creese, who in the year prior had built the 12 ft cadet dinghy *Inez* for his two sons Jack and Eric. Showing his industriousness, Max Creese was noted as having made the *Monsoon*'s sails. With a talent for sewing, this practical handiness would later see him sew clothes for his children.

Though initially described in the press as a "very nice little boat," the *Monsoon* was also noted to have been designed to an out-of-date plan. Owing to this fact the yacht was considerably slower than her peers, resulting in many lacklustre performances. Still, the vessel proved an extremely worthwhile endeavour for Max and his brother Harry, both in terms of developing skills in building and maintaining a yacht, as well as sailing one. In October 1928, for example, Max and Harry were noted as having made several modifications to *Monsoon*, resulting in the yacht being more competitively placed within the B class. During this period the vessel was also often helmed by veteran yachtsman Fred Latham, who not only served as a mentor to the teenage Creese brothers but also steered the yacht to many key victories.

Monsoon under construction at 182 Brisbane Street, Hobart.
Courtesy Sandra Wilson.

Monsoon (circa late 1920s).
Courtesy Sandra Wilson.

Mavis

In the mid-1930s Max and Harry Creese sold *Monsoon* to their cousin Eric Creese and began building a larger, faster yacht. Based on a design modelled off Percy Coverdale's *Ninie* and A. R. Cumming's *Yeulba*, the 42.5 ft *Mavis* was built by Max in his spare time, once again in the backyard of his parents' home in Brisbane Street, Hobart. Complete with a modern Bermuda-style mainsail, the *Mavis* joined the local sailing fraternity in October 1937. With Max at the helm, the vessel immediately gained a reputation as one of the more consistent boats in her class, a reputation which the *Mavis* maintained for many years.

House Carpenter turns Boat Builder

During the period that Max Creese built the *Mavis* he also established his career as a local builder and contractor, likely gaining experience working with his uncle, Mark Creese. Towards the end of World War II, however, Max joined the Battery Point shipbuilding firm of Purdon and Featherstone, where he helped in the construction of several harbour defence launches and sea ambulances.

Mavis under construction. Courtesy Sandra Wilson.

ADDITION TO DERWENT SAILING FLEET

MODERN "A" CLASS YACHT, owned by Mr. Max Creese, and launched in Constitution Dock at the week-end. It was designed and built by the owner in his leisure time, and was christened Mavis by Mrs. Creese. Its length overall is 42ft. 6in., beam 8ft., and draught 5ft. 4in., and it will have modern Bermudan rig.

Mavis off Battery Point just after launch.
Courtesy Guy Rex Collection (Suzanne Rex).

Post World War II

As World War II came to an end Max Creese returned to the building trade and set about expanding his business. In September 1945 Max announced his intention to apply for permission to erect an electric saw bench at his workshop, 61 Molle Street, Hobart. During this time Max Creese also partnered with Fred "Rufus" Chamberlain, a local bricklayer, to undertake building projects, the pair regularly advertising for carpenters and labourers in the local press.

Coinciding with this period Max Creese sold his yacht *Mavis* to E. T. Domeney, a prominent local yachtsman. Intent on building a bigger, faster yacht, the local press noted that Max was to start work on an 8 metre yacht; a new class of vessel on the verge of establishment in Australia and proving popular overseas. The yacht was built in the backyard of Max's house at 36 Marieville Esplanade, Sandy Bay. By November of 1946 work on the vessel was well-underway with Max's older brother Harry helping with construction. However, with no yacht of his own until the vessel was complete, Max continued his active involment in yacht racing, often taking the helm of borrowed vessels, including his ex-yacht *Mavis*.

The Birth of an Ocean Race

With a keen interest in blue-water racing, in December 1945 Max Creese sailed to Sydney on board Percy Coverdale's *Winston Churchill* to compete in the first ever Sydney to Hobart Yacht Race. Other crew members included Jerry Chamberlain, brothers Neall and Ken Batt, and Keith Wilson. It is doubtful that any of them realised the auspiciousness of the race they were about to partake in. With only nine yachts competing, no-one could have predicted that the event would evolve into one of the world's most coveted, arduous yet illustrious yacht races.

On 2 January 1946, after seven days at sea, the *Winston Churchill* and her sea-weary crew arrived back in Hobart to a warm welcome of more than 600 people. Despite finishing second across the line and third on handicap, Percy Coverdale stated he was "very disappointed" in the outcome. Yet this piqueness soon turned into a resolve to compete in the race again, not only for Percy but also for many of his crew. Max Creese in particular would sail in three more Sydney to Hobart races during his life time.

A Busy Year

1946 proved to be a busy year for Max Creese. In addition to his professional and sailing commitments, Max also became involved in yacht club administration. In August 1946, he was appointed to the committee of the Derwent Sailing Squadron, a position he would hold for several years. In the late 1940s and early 1950s he was appointed rear commodore. In November of 1946 the Cruising Yacht Club of Australia appointed Max an honourary measurer of Tasmanian boats competing in that year's Sydney to Hobart Yacht Race.

A Second Sydney to Hobart

The 1946 Sydney to Hobart Yacht Race saw Max Creese again competing, this time as a crew member on board Colin Philp's 55 ft welded-steel sloop *Southern Maid*.

Launched just a week prior to departing for Sydney, the vessel was designed and built by Colin Philp at Sandy Bay and was notably one of the first welded-steel vessels built in Tasmania and the only steel craft to compete in the Sydney to Hobart race that year. One of 19 yachts in the race, the untried and untested *Southern Maid* finished a credible fourth across the line.

Crew of *Southern Maid* that competed in the 1946 Sydney to Hobart.
Left to Right: Max Creese, Colin Philp, Jock Muir, Ron Doolan,
Robert Hedley and Huon Watchorn. Courtesy *The Mercury*, 16 December 1946.

Launch of *Southern Maid* at Sandy Bay Beach in December 1946.
Courtesy Maritime Museum of Tasmania.

Another 8 Metre Yacht

Perservering as a builder and contractor, in December 1947 Max Creese was commissioned to build an 8 metre yacht for his friend E. T. Domeney, owner of the *Mavis* and a staunch proponent of the XA class, first established in 1944, where the 8 metre yachts were intended to race. Though Max's own 8 metre yacht was still under construction, the fact that he was commissioned to build a similar yacht is indicative of Max's quality of craftsmanship, reputation and work ethic.

Finally, a Yard of His Own

The start of 1948 saw Max Creese continuing to develop his building business. In March he was awarded a tender for £7,729 to build a factory for McKay and Henry Pty. Ltd. of Hobart. However, with an increasing reputation for building and designing yachts, and professional experience in the boat building trade under his belt, in April 1948 Max announced in the local press his intention to become a boat builder. His passion had always been in boat building, and at the age of 37 he set about making it a reality.

Max Creese's new boatyard was located along Napoleon Street, Battery Point. The site was previously in the possession of the late Albert "Tucker" Abel, and in the 19th century was owned by the Risby family.

The *Sandra*

Four months after announcing his entrée into professional boat building, on Saturday 14 August 1948 Max Creese launched his own 8 metre yacht, *Sandra*, at King's Pier, Hobart. Named for his eldest daughter, the vessel was built to Max's own design and was the first yacht of her type constructed in Tasmania.

The *Sandra* joined the R class (which had recently merged with the XA class) and immediately lived up to expectations, not only winning the Royal Yacht Club of Tasmania's Maria Island Ocean Race held in October 1948, but also breaking the race record. The Sydney to Hobart Yacht Race was the next major event on Max Creese's agenda for his new yacht *Sandra*. With Max at the helm, the yacht left Hobart for Sydney on 11 December 1948, only a few hours after competing in a local pennant race. It proved an eventful trip as *Sandra* broke a tiller in heavy seas. Still, the vessel was ready by race day and lined up on Sydney Harbour as one of 18 competitors overall and one of six Tasmanian yachts. After a gallant race, *Sandra* finished third across the line to Sir Claude Plowman's *Morna* and Frank Barlow's *Mistral II* and was notably the first of the Tasmanian yachts to finish.

Back in Hobart, *Sandra* remained a standout on the Derwent, winning several class pennants, as well as many local regatta races. The vessel also won the 1949 Maria Island Ocean Race.

The First Boat Launched at Battery Point

On 4 June 1949 the first of many boats built by Max Creese at his Battery Point boatyard was launched. The 8 metre yacht *Erica J*, built to the order of E. T. Domeney, commodore of the Derwent Sailing Squadron and one of Tasmania's best-known yachtsmen, slid down the cradle into the Derwent joining the *Sandra* and C. E. Davies' *Norske* in the local R Class. Considered a sister yacht to the Norwegian designed *Norske*, the *Erica J* was intended for off-shore racing out of Hobart, as well as local pennant races.

Below and right: A series of photos showing construction of *Erica J* at Battery Point, including John Lucas working on the vessel's mast. Courtesy Maritime Museum of Tasmania.

Another Tasmanian First

Immediately following the launch of the *Erica J*, Max Creese and his employees, including John Lucas and Jack Hansen, set to work building another Tasmanian first, a Tumlaren racer-cruiser, a new class of yacht gaining traction on the mainland. Built to the order of Ken Gourlay, the 27.7 ft *Malaren* was launched on 1 October 1949, the hull and deck built in just six weeks. Designed by Knud Reimers of Sweden, the yacht was the 20th Tumlaren class boat in Australia and proved an impressive participant in the local second division cruiser class for several years.

More Boats

Late 1949 saw Max Creese build a Rainbow class dinghy, *Jill*, for his 11-year old son Peter. The vessel was launched the same day as the Rainbow class dinghy *Crusin Susan* which Max built for Walter Loney. The following year Max and his employees launched a 27 ft motor cruiser, *Snowgoose*, built to the order of Howard Wright of Melbourne to a design by Jack Savage. The boat was built over seven months, Max assisted by John Lucas and Jack "Turk" Bridge. *Snowgoose* was delivered to the mainland in March 1950 by Max Creese, his son Peter and two crew.

Having solidified himself as a professional boat builder, in 1951 Max Creese reinstated his house building operations by applying to the Hobart City Council to erect a 2 hp electric sawbench at his Napoleon Street boatyard as part of a joinery operation. He also advertised for carpenters, joiners, tradesmen, and apprentices. This move was likely precipitated by a slowdown in the boat building trade, the result of a shortage of materials and rising costs. The latter was a direct result of then federal treasurer Sir Arthur Fadden introducing a budget in 1951 that increased the sales tax on pleasure boats from 10 to 33 per cent, effective immediately. Max (and his employees) would often return to the building trade when boat work waned in the years and decades that followed.

Still, work at the boatyard continued. On 26 October 1951 the 35 ft *Terra Nova,* named for Scott's Antarctic exploration vessel, was launched, the second vessel Max Creese built to the order of Ken Gourlay. She was a light-displacement cruiser intended for the larger yacht class. Designed by Alan Payne, a naval architect of Sydney, *Terra Nova* immediately set the pace within Hobart's yachting precinct, taking line honours in the 1951 Bruny Island Race. *Terra Nova* also competed in the 1952 Sydney to Hobart Yacht Race.

During the early to mid-1950s Max Creese built several Huon pine dinghies, including one advertised for sale in 1954. In addition, he assembled a 98 ft lighter to be used to carry limestone from Southport to the Carbide works at Electrona, south of Hobart. Launched in June 1954 and comprising parts imported from the Fairmile Construction Company in Surrey, England, this particular vessel, named *Ida Bay*, has the distinction of being the first all-welded steel commercial vessel assembled in Tasmania, capping off another first for Max Creese and his employees.

Terra Nova at Battery Point. Jack "Turk" Bridge and John Lucas at the stern. Barry Wilson at the bow. Courtesy Maritime Museum of Tasmania.

The Mid to Late 1950s

Following the launch of the *Ida Bay*, the mid to late 1950s proved an exceptionally busy period for Max Creese with at least nine boats launched from his Battery Point boatyard. These include the *Solquest*, *Tregenna*, *Molly Ann*, *Seaman* and *Southerly Buster*. Two Dragon class yachts, *Sandra II* and *Ann*, were also built during the late 1950s. The 17 ft work boat *Little Patti* is additionally credited as being built by Max Creese during this period.

The 38 ft yacht *Solquest* was launched in 1956, built to the order of Len Staples of Hobart to a design by Jock Muir, fellow boat builder of Battery Point. The vessel was built with the specific intention of sailing to North America where Staples and his family intended to settle.

Courtesy *Australian Women's Weekly*, 15 May 1957.

WHITE-PAINTED *Solquest* looks small beside other craft at a Sydney jetty. The yacht, of 15 tons, was built to a special design for its six months' voyage.

They'll sail Pacific i
15-ton yacht

By
CYNTHIA
STRACHAN
staff reporte

● Life on the ocean wave will become a six months' reality for an Australian family who leave Sydney this month to voyage to America in a 15-ton yacht.

THEY are Mr. Len Staples, his wife, Joyce, and sons, Len, jun., aged 7, and Wayne, 4, who are making the voyage with Pilgrim Father determination to settle in the United

she'd be able to keep the menus interesting and varied from the well-appointed galley of the yacht, which has a 160-gallon fresh-water tank.
A Melbourne girl, Mrs. Staples had never set foot in a boat until she married her

ture for the Staples', who have never been overseas.
"Although we are not scared, we all have a healthy respect for the sea, and we have our fingers crossed that the Pacific will live up to its peaceful name," said Mrs.

"I hope the voya be rough," she said. reasonably good sai we haven't been on a this before, and the occasionally have b sick.
"Still, think how ful it will be follo sun," she said. "Th we named the yacht I can't wait for those

In 1957 Max Creese completed the 33 ft fishing boat *Tregenna*, built to the order of "Bunny" Thomas of Orford at a cost of £4,500. Based on a design originating in the United States, the vessel was considered somewhat unorthodox amongst the local fishing fleet in that she had a planing hull and was fitted with a 100 hp diesel engine making *Tregenna* twice as fast as conventional fishing vessels.

In January 1958 Max Creese launched the Dragon class yacht *Sandra II* at the Hobart wharf, built with his son Peter over a three-month span in the backyard of their house at Sandy Bay. It was one of the first Dragons to be built in Tasmania. The class was fast gaining momentum both in Tasmania and across the country, helped by its selection as one of five sailing classes at the 1948 Olympic Games held in London, and the Duke of Edinburgh donating the Prince Philip Cup in 1952 for what would become the principal interstate racing series. The *Sandra II* was launched just in time for Max Creese to compete in the Prince Philip Cup, held in Hobart in February 1958.

Another boat completed by Max Creese in 1958 was the 25 ft yacht *Molly Ann*. The vessel was built to the order of Bob Taylor, based on a design by Taylor's brother, E. R. Taylor of Sydney.

Rounding out the decade, the 35 ft yacht *Southerly Buster*, the third vessel built by Max Creese to the order of Ken Gourlay, was launched in 1959. Designed by Alan Payne, *Southerly Buster* competed in the 1960 Sydney to Hobart Yacht Race.

The Dragon class yacht *Ann*, built to the order of Ediss Boyes, was also launched in 1959, as was the yachting world cadet dinghy *Mistral VII*, built for Charles Rex, Guy Rex's son.

Sandra II being launched at the Hobart wharf. Courtesy Sandra Wilson.

A New Technique

1960 saw Max Creese adopt the innovative glued-seam method of building ocean racing yachts. The 36 ft yacht *Seaman*, launched in 1960 and built to the order of Colin Philp based on Philp's own design, was the first vessel Max constructed using this method. *Seaman* went on to compete in the 1962 and 1964 Sydney to Hobart yacht races with Max Creese on board for the 1962 race. Also constructed using this method was the 38 ft yacht *Palana*, built of strip-planked King Billy to the order of R. J. Shield of Huonville based on an Arthur Robb design. Launched in 1961 and built specifically to contest the Sydney to Hobart Yacht Race, *Palana* went on to compete in the 1962, 1963 and 1965 races.

Seaman at Battery Point with Colin Philp on board. Courtesy Sandra Wilson.

Above: *Palana* coming off the slip at Battery Point.
Below: *Palana* on the River Derwent.

Courtesy Steven Shield.

The 1960s

Three more yachts were launched from Max Creese's Battery Point yard in the 1960s. These were *Con Moto*, *Huon Lass* and *Mistral IX*. Launched in 1963, the 35 ft *Con Moto* was built to the order of Barrie Foster based on a Peter Cole design. The 40 ft *Huon Lass* was launched in 1965, built to the order of Hedley Calvert based on a design by Robert Clark of England. The vessel went on to compete in the 1966, 1967, 1968 and 1971 Sydney to Hobart yacht races. The Cole-Luders designed 40 ft classic yacht *Mistral IX* was built to the order of Guy Rex and launched in 1966.

Huon Lass on the River Derwent. Courtesy Maritime Museum of Tasmania.

The 1960s also saw the launch of a motor launch, *Thalassa,* and two fishing boats, *Seahund* and *Leillateah,* from Max Creese's Battery Point yard. *Thalassa,* completed in 1966, was built to the order of Trevor Stokes. The fishing boat *Seahund,* also launched in 1966, was built to the order of Ken Petith. The fishing boat *Leillateah,* launched in November 1968, was built to the order of Fred and Robert Clifford to a collaborative design by Max Creese and Robert Clifford; the latter also assisting with the build.

Three lightweight sharpies were built by Max Creese during the early 1960s: *Vega* for Kevin Livingstone, *Ulinga* for Bill Shearman, and *Black Marlin* for Mike Cummins, as well as a Rainbow class dinghy built by Max's apprentice Robert Laughlin to the order of Ian McKay.

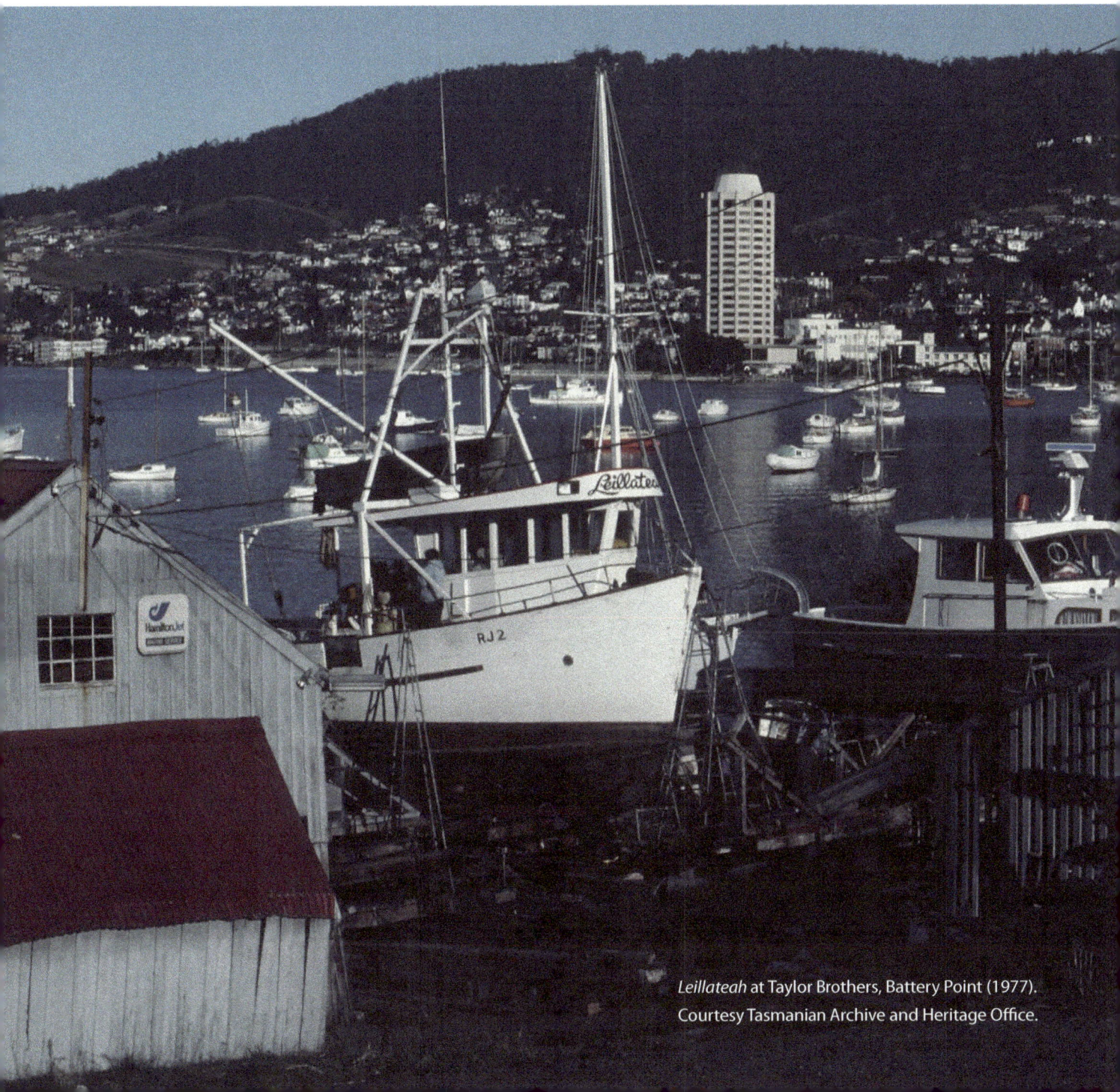

Leillateah at Taylor Brothers, Battery Point (1977).
Courtesy Tasmanian Archive and Heritage Office.

Peter Creese (left) and Ron Crawford (right) working on *Mistral IX*.
Courtesy Guy Rex Collection (Suzanne Rex).

Preparing for launch of *Mistral IX*.
Courtesy Guy Rex Collection (Suzanne Rex).

Launch of *Mistral IX*. Courtesy Guy Rex Collection (Suzanne Rex).

Two More Ocean Racers

The early 1970s saw two more ocean racing yachts launched from Max Creese's Battery Point yard. The 37 ft Huon pine ocean cruiser *Maria* was built by Max and his son Peter to the order of Dr Des Cooper of Hobart. She was designed by Sparkman and Stephens of New York and launched in July 1970. The *Maria* competed in the 1970 Sydney to Hobart Yacht Race. The following year she was one of three yachts to represent Australia in the World One Ton Cup held in Auckland, New Zealand.

Another vessel of a Sparkman and Stephens design, the 35 ft Huon pine sloop *Nike,* was built by Max Creese to the order of Charles E. Davies and launched on 18 October 1973, taking 12 months to complete. Very full towards the stern, *Nike* was considered somewhat unorthodox in appearance. Her hull was built from three layers of strip- planked quarter-inch Huon pine, two running diagonally and one horizontally, producing a very light but strong skin. *Nike* was built specifically for racing and competed in the 1973, 1974 and 1975 Sydney to Hobart yacht races.

Maria at Battery Point. Courtesy Maritime Museum of Tasmania.

Max Creese and Charles E. Davies with *Nike* at Battery Point.
Courtesy *The Mercury*, 19 October 1973.

Motor Cruisers

In June 1972 Max launched the motor cruiser *Toheroa*, built for his own use and to his own design. Now approaching 65 years of age, the mid to late 1970s saw Max Creese continue to design and build boats. In 1973 the 48 ft steel fishing boat *Hewardia II* was launched. The vessel was designed by Don Muir who also helped with construction. In 1974 the 30 ft cruiser *Alkira* was completed, built to the order of Ken Newham. The vessel was fitted out at Taroona and launched in September 1975. That same year the motor cruiser *Lantara*, built to the order of Geoff Cripps, and the motor cruiser *Jantina,* built to the order of a Mr Coleman, were launched. Four years later Max Creese launched the 25 ft motor launch *Fantasy* based on a Hartley design.

Toheroa at Bellerive Yacht Club (2017). Courtesy Warren Cripps.

The Last Boats

In 1978 Max Creese launched another 48 ft fibreglass fishing boat, *Hewardia*, built to a design by Don Muir who also helped with construciton. In 1981 Max Creese and George Burrows completed a 20 ft pulling boat, a replica of the 19th century ferry boats used on the River Derwent. Named *Ramping Lion*, this particular vessel was later acquired by the Australian National Maritime Museum. The following year Max Creese launched the 45 ft fibreglass fishing boat *Tata*, designed by Don Muir.

The last boat built by Max Creese at his Battery Point boatyard was the 40 ft ocean racer/ cruising yacht *Tradition*. Launched in 1984, the vessel was built to the order of David Gough to Max's own design. *Tradition* went on to compete in the 1984, 1988, 1990, 1991, 1992 and 1994 Sydney to Hobart yacht races.

Tata under construction. Courtesy Michael Muir.

Boat Designs

Max Creese designed many vessels for many purposes throughout his career as a boat builder, and also prior to establishing his boatyard at Battery Point. These include the motor launch *Silver Cloud II,* built by Taylor Brothers at Battery Point in 1946; the 60 ft motor launch *J Lee M,* built at Triabunna by Jim Jones and fitted out by Jock Muir at Battery Point in 1954; and the steel fishing boat *Vansittart,* built by Purdon and Featherstone at Battery Point to the order of Nigel King and launched in 1969.

Geoff Cuthbertson built at least six vessels at his Montagu Bay slip to Max Creese designs. These include the 36 ft motor sailer *Islander II,* built to the order of John Wignall and launched in 1968; the 32 ft motor sailer *Halycon,* built to the order of Noel Cox and launched in 1971; the yacht *Chinook,* launched in 1973; the 40 ft motor sailer *Stardust,* built to the order of Roger Richards and launched in 1975; the 43 ft motor sailer *Vagabond,* built to the order of Graham Wignall and launched in 1975; and the motor sailer *Jendiri,* built to the order of Rod Baron and launched in 1978.

So admired were Max Creese's motor sailers that four more were built to his designs by Wilson Brothers at Cygnet. These were the 41 ft *Liberty,* built to the order of David Boyes and launched in 1975; the 41 ft *Beyond,* built to the order of Picton Hay and launched in 1976; the 42 ft *Solution,* built to the order of Geoff Abel and launched in 1980; and the 41 ft *Sea Quella,* built to the order of Guy Cole and launched in 1986.

Max Creese also designed two fishing boats built by Wilson Brothers at Cygnet, both to the order of Ken Hunn. These were the 65 ft *Gaye Glenn* (now *Storm Boy*), launched in 1969, and the 75 ft *Wilsons Pride,* launched in 1973.

Other vessels built in and around Hobart to Max Creese designs include the 39 ft yacht *Moonraker,* built by E. McVilly and Bruce Darcey and launched in 1970; the 35 ft motor cruiser *Just Flo,* built by Hilton Coad and launched in 1979; the 36 ft cruiser *Genioso,* built by Darryl Ridgeway and launched in 1980; the fishing boat *Waubs Bay,* built by Trevor Hardstaff at Rokeby and launched in 1980; and the motor cruiser *Montagu,* built by Robert Laughlin and launched in 2005. A production fibreglass catamaran hull dinghy of 10 ft was also designed by Max Creese in the 1970s. The vessels were manufactured and sold by John Fleming of Sandy Bay. Many still exist today as boat tenders.

Additional Projects

Beginning in the 1970s, Max Creese's son Peter became increasingly involved in the boatyard business. Peter had started work at the yard in 1953 at the age of 15 after completing a year as an apprentice builder with Gillham Brothers. He then completed his apprenticeship at the boatyard. After spending several decades working alongside his dad building boats, in 1970 Peter took on supplementary work offsite. Of particular note was maintenance work associated with Transport Commission vessels, including the *Lady Wakehurst, Lady Ferguson, Birngana, Man On* and *Melba.* Other projects Peter Creese managed were the fitting out of coastal trading vessels, including the *Joseph Banks, Straitsman* and *Blythe Star,* and the slipping of vessels for the Tug & Lighterage Company at the Domain slipyard.

Legacy

Max Creese semi-retired following the completion of *Tradition* in 1984, and formally retired in 1990 at the age of 80. His Battery Point boatyard was subsequently sold. Max Creese died six years later on 25 December 1996. His wife Mavis predeceased him by 12 years, dying on 16 July 1984. Max was survived by their three children: Peter, who worked with his father for 35 years up until 1988, Sandra and Jill. Sandra's husband Barry Wilson also worked for Max Creese at Battery Point for many years.

Over his lifetime Max Creese earned a well-deserved reputation as a builder of high quality boats that is still echoed in the maritime circles of Tasmania and interstate. Many of the vessels he built remain actively in existence, including the 8 metre yachts *Sandra* and *Erica J*, launched in the late 1940s. Max's first-class repution was further enhanced by his ability to intuitively design fast racing yachts, handsome cruising motor sailers, and efficient deep-sea fishing vessels. Many of these vessels also remain in existence.

Islander II. Courtesy Nick Connor.

Vessels Built by Max Creese and Employees at Battery Point (1949 – 1984).

1949. *Erica J.* **Yacht.** 49 x 8.2 x 6.5 ft. 8 metre yacht built for E. T. Domeney to a Norwegian design. Intended for off-shore and local pennant racing. Challenged for several Sayonara cups in the 1950s. Transferred to Sydney, NSW, in 1962. Advertised for sale in Sydney in August 1970, later returned to TAS, then transferred back to Sydney. Still in existence. In 2011 transferred to the United Kingdom and refurbished by new owner David Myatt. Most notably raced in the International 8 Metre World Championships in 2012 in Cowes.

1949. *Malaren.* **Yacht.** 27.7 x 6.2 x 4.3 ft. Tumlaren class yacht built to the order of Ken Gourlay. Designed by Knud Reimers of Sweden. First of its class built in Tasmania and the 20th Tumlaren class yacht in Australia. Launched on 1 October 1949. Competed in the second division cruiser class for several years. In March 1951 shipped to Sydney, NSW, having been purchased by W. A. Marr. Possibly renamed *Glyn Ayr*.

1949. *Jill.* **Dinghy.** Rainbow class dinghy built for Max Creese's son Peter. Competed in Sandy Bay Dinghy Club events. Sold to Geoff Balcolmbe in the early 1950s.

1949. *Cruisin Susan.* **Dinghy.** Rainbow class dinghy built for Walter Loney. Launched the same day as *Jill*. Competed in Sandy Bay Dinghy Club events. Won the Tasmanian championship in 1951.

1950. *Snowgoose.* **Yacht.** 27 x 8.5 ft. Built to the order of Howard Wright of Melbourne, VIC, to a design by Jack Savage. Remained in Wright's possession until 1965 when sold to Dr John Noonan. By the mid-1980s owned by Michael Blair, Peter Cox and Robert Stephens of the Royal Brighton Yacht Club. In 1994 sold to Peter Blake. Following restoration, sold to Peter Gunnerson in 1996 and then to Peter Galbally in 2009. Sold back to Peter Blake in 2010. Still in existence; located in Melbourne, VIC, and undergoing restoration by owner Richard Blake, Peter Blake's son.

1951. *Terra Nova.* **Yacht.** 35 x 7.6 x 5.7 ft. Built to the order of Ken Gourlay. Designed by Alan Payne. Competed in the 1952 Sydney to Hobart Yacht Race. Advertised for sale in September 1954. Still in existence, currently in Lakes Entrance, VIC, having been purchased in 2009 by two classic yachting enthusiasts. A previous owner, Rob Pearce, was a noted Melbourne surgeon who spent a significant amount of resources restoring her. He sadly lost his life in the Kinglake bushfire in February 2009.

1954. *Ida Bay.* **Lighter.** 98 x 24 ft. Welded-steel commercial barge assembled from parts imported from the Fairmile Construction Company in Surrey, England. Used as a lighter to carry limestone from Southport to the Carbide works at Electrona. By 1960 registered to T. M. Lipscombe Pty. Ltd, by 1964 registered to Alginates Pty. Ltd., by 1971 registered to the Derwent Tug Company Pty. Ltd.

1950s. **Dinghy.** 10.5 ft. Huon pine, fitted with an engine. Advertised for sale in April 1954.

1956. *Solquest.* **Yacht.** 38 x 12 ft. Designed by Jock Muir. Built to the order of Len Staples of Hobart with the specific intention of sailing the vessel to North America where Staples and his family intended to live. Sailed from Sydney in May 1957, arriving in Alameda, California, USA, in September 1958. By the early 1960s owned by Ralph Muravez, a businessman of Burbank, California, USA. Wrecked on Cedros Island, 250 miles southwest of San Diego, California, USA, in January 1963 during a storm; all hands saved.

1957. *Tregenna*. Fishing boat. 33 x 9.5 x 6 ft. Built to the order of Bunny Thomas, a fisherman of Orford, based on an American design. Later owned by Dougie Russell.

1958. *Sandra II*. Yacht. 29.2 x 6.4 ft. International Dragon class yacht built by Max Creese for his own use. Designed by John Anker. Launched in January 1958 at the Hobart wharf. Sold to Don Calvert in 1963. Competed in the Prince Philip Cup, held 1963 in Adelaide, SA. Later transferred to Melbourne, VIC. Still in existence, restored in 2009 by Greg Blunt of Williamstown, VIC, for Ron House. Currently at Metung, Gippsland Lakes, VIC, and part of the large Dragon fleet looked after by Terry Grundy.

1958. *Molly Ann*. Yacht. 26.9 x 8.7 ft. Built to the order of Bob Taylor to a design by Taylor's brother, E. R. Taylor of Sydney. Considered similar in design to a Dragon. Still in existence; based in southern TAS and recently advertised for sale.

1959. *Southerly Buster*. Yacht. 35 x 10 x 4.8 ft. Built to the order of Ken Gourlay. Designed by Alan Payne. Competed in the 1960 Sydney to Hobart Yacht Race. A few years later, transferred to Sydney. Advertised for sale in Sydney in October 1970. Possibly renamed *Free*.

1959. *Ann (Joanne)*. Yacht. 29.2 x 6.4 ft. International Dragon class yacht. Built to the order of Ediss Boyes. Designed by John Anker. Competed in several Prince Philip Cup races in the 1960s. Later named *Joanne*.

1959. *Mistral VII*. Dinghy. Yachting world cadet dinghy built for Charles Rex, Guy Rex's son.

1950s. *Little Patti (Allegro Non Troppo)*. Work boat. 17 ft. For many years used as a workboat on Bruny Island and owned by the Whayman family. Purchased by Ross James in 2001, extensively restored, and renamed *Allegro Non Troppo*. Sold in 2005 and believed to have been transferred to Melbourne, VIC.

1960. *Seaman (Seaman of Pittwater)*. Yacht. 36.1 x 10.1 ft. Designed by Colin Philp and built for Philp's own use. Competed in the 1962 and 1964 Sydney to Hobart yacht races. Has had several changes of owners. Still in existence; located in NSW.

1961. *Palana*. Yacht. 38 x 10.3 x 4.3 ft. Built to the order of R. J. Shield of Huonville of strip-planked King Billy to an Arthur Robb design. Built specifically to compete in the Sydney to Hobart Yacht Race. Participated in the 1962, 1963 and 1965 races. Advertised for sale in February 1969. Advertised for sale in Sydney in October 1984. Advertised for sale in Sydney in April 1989. Still in existence; possibly located in QLD.

1961. *Vega*. Lightweight sharpie. Built to the order of Kevin Livingstone.

1961. *Ulinga*. Lightweight sharpie. Built to the order of Bill Shearman.

1961. *Black Marlin*. Lightweight sharpie. Built to the order of Mike Cummins.

Vessels Built by Max Creese and Employees at Battery Point (1949 – 1984).

1963. *Con Moto.* **Yacht.** 35 x 10 x 5 ft. Built to the order of Barrie Foster based on a Peter Cole design. Advertised for sale in Sydney in 1967. Still in existence; in 2015 owned by John Lockett.

1964. Dinghy. Rainbow class dinghy built to the order of Ian McKay by apprentice Robert Laughlin.

1965. *Huon Lass.* **Yacht.** 39 x 10 x 6.4 ft. Built to the order of Hedley Calvert of the Huon. Designed by Robert Clark of the UK. Participated in several Sydney to Hobart yacht races. Transferred to Sydney in 1974. Still in existence. Moored at Pittwater, NSW, for several decades. Advertised for sale in 2016/2017.

1966. *Mistral IX.* **Yacht.** 40 ft. Built to the order of Guy Rex of Hobart. Designed by Luders Marine Construction Co. and Peter Cole. Purchased by Anthony Rundle of Devonport in 1974. Later transferred to Sydney. Still in existence. In 2016 sighted at Lovett Bay, NSW.

1966. *Thalassa.* **Motor launch.** Built to the order of Trevor Stokes.

1966. *Seahund.* **Fishing boat.** Built to the order of Ken Peddith.

1968. *Leillateah.* **Fishing boat.** 44.3 x 14.3 x 7.5 ft. Built to the order of Fred and Robert Clifford of Hobart. Later sold to Bill Denis. Sighted at Kettering, TAS, in 2016. In 2017 located at Triabunna.

1960s. Motor launch. 35 ft. Built to the order of Doug Bridges.

1970. *Maria.* **Yacht.** 37 ft. Huon pine ocean cruiser. Designed by Sparkman and Stephens. Built to the order of Dr Des Cooper of Hobart. Competed in the 1970 and 1971 Sydney to Hobart yacht races. One of three yachts to represent Australia in the One Ton Cup held in Auckland, New Zealand, in 1971. Advertised for sale in interstate papers in February 1973, though remained in Hobart. Still in existence, moored at Sandy Bay, TAS.

1972. *Toheroa.* **Motor cruiser.** 35 ft. Built and designed by Max Creese for his own use and launched in June 1972. Later owned by Peter Creese and transferred to QLD. Still in existence, in 2015 purchased by Warren Cripps of Hobart, an apprentice of Max Creese's at the time of her build, and returned to Hobart. Currently moored at Bellerive.

1973. *Hewardia II.* **Fishing boat.** 48 ft. Steel. Designed by Don Muir who also helped with construction.

1973. *Nike.* **Yacht.** 35 ft. Huon pine sloop. Designed by Sparkman and Stephens. Built to the order of Charles E. Davies. Launched on 18 October 1973, taking 12 months to complete. Built specifically for ocean racing. Competed in the 1973, 1974 and 1975 Sydney to Hobart yacht races. Advertised for sale in Sydney in 1976. Advertised again for sale in Sydney in 1988. Still in existence, currently owned by the Hunt family and sails with the Sydney Amateur Sailing Club.

1975. *Alkira.* **Yacht.** 30 x 10 ft. Third class cruiser built to the order of Ken Newham in 1974. Fitted out at Taroona and launched in September 1975. Moored at Oyster Cove for many years. Still in existence; currently owned by Jim Groves.

1975. *Lantara*. **Motor cruiser.** Built to the order of Geoff Cripps. Still in existence; moored in Hobart.

1975. *Jantina*. **Motor cruiser.** Built to the order of Bill Coleman. Subsequently owned by Len Shepard and Rohen Johnson. Still in existence, recently noted at Cygnet and owned by Andrew Askey.

1978. *Hewardia*. **Fishing boat.** 48 ft. Designed by Don Muir who also helped with construction. Built of fibreglass. Wrecked near Point Hibbs on the west coast of TAS in August 1989. At the time owned by Brian Colenso Wareham. All hands saved.

1979. *Fantasy*. **Motor launch.** 25 ft. Designed by Hartley. Made of marine ply. Built to the order of a customer from Dynnyrne, TAS.

1981. *Ramping Lion*. **Pulling boat.** 20 ft. Clinker built replica of the 19th century ferry boats used on the River Derwent. Built in conjunction with George Burrows. Still in existence, acquired by the Australian National Maritime Museum in the late 1980s.

1982. *Tata*. **Fishing boat.** 45 ft. Designed by Don Muir. Built of fibreglass using the Chopper Gun method. Sold to a Brisbane, QLD, owner and later sold to a fisherman from Canada. Still in existence.

1984. *Tradition*. **Yacht.** 40 ft. Built for David Gough. Competed in the 1984, 1988, 1990, 1991, 1992 and 1994 Sydney to Hobart yacht races. Still in existence, currently owned by Tim Gourlay and based in Hobart.

Tradition at Battery Point. Courtesy Sandra Wilson.

The Royal Yacht Club of Tasmania's Battery Point premises (circa 1960s).
To the left is Max Creese's boatyard. Courtesy Mick Purdon.

Purdon Brothers

Raised next door to the Battery Point slipyards, brothers Donald "Sam" and Allan "Mick" Purdon continued the maritime legacy of their paternal family. As teenagers Sam was apprenticed to Norm Taylor at his Battery Point boatyard while Mick was apprenticed to a local cabinet maker. During this period, like many of their peers, Sam and Mick Purdon spent much of their spare time sucessfully competing in the cadet dinghy and later heavyweight sharpie classes. Sam also excelled at football, playing over 100 games in the Tasmanian Football League for Sandy Bay. In 1951 Sam and Mick established a cabinet making business in a shed off 2 Napoleon Street, Battery Point. However, advances in fibreglass technology and its use in the boat building industry proved to be pivotal for the pair. In 1954 they began building 8, 10, 12, 13 and 14 ft fibreglass dinghies. The success of this enterprise saw Purdon Brothers later expand into the manufacture of fishing wells, shower bays and laundry troughs. Several wooden boats were also built by Sam and Mick Purdon in the many decades they spent working at Battery Point, including four heavyweight sharpies and the 32 ft motor cruiser _Barameda_.

The Purdon family is engrained in Battery Point's maritime history. In 1903, after several decades spent at the helm of commercial trading ketches that he built for the local river and coastal trades, Tom Purdon, the patriarch of the family, established a shipyard with Henry Featherstone at Battery Point, operating under the name of Purdon and Featherstone. Two decades later, in semi-retirement, Tom Purdon worked at a smaller yard off Derwent Lane with two of his sons, Tom (Jr) and Ernest Purdon, undertaking slip and repair work and building smaller vessels.

Until his tragic death in 1937 Ernest Purdon spent his life working at the family's Battery Point slipyard and during peak times was employed as a shipwright with Purdon and Featherstone. Ernest, his wife Lizzie and their growing family, comprising children William Thomas, Donald Max, Kathleen Rose, Arthur Richard, Reginald Allan, Trevor Ernest, Harold Hardy, Rex Hardy, Owen Ronald, Leo and Brian Edward, lived close by at 4 Napoleon Street (accessed off Derwent Lane).

Brothers Sam and Mick Purdon are the sons of Donald Max (Don) Purdon, grandsons of Ernest Purdon and the great grandsons of Tom Purdon. Sam, christened Donald Max after his father, is the eldest of the pair and was born at 60 Alexander Street, Sandy Bay, on 25 October 1929 to Don and his wife Maude (nee Burnett). Mick, christened as Allan John, was born to the couple on 19 March 1931. Three daughters followed: Lenna Marion (born 15 July 1932), Norma Eveline (born 20 November 1933) and Marion Patricia (born 30 December 1940).

Sam and Mick Purdon (circa 1934).

Father and Uncles

Though many generations of the Purdon family before him had undertaken careers in the maritime industry, and the family lived in Napoleon Street, next door to the Battery Point slipyards, Sam and Mick's father Don Purdon chose a white-collar career. Gifted academically, Don attended Albuera Street Primary with his siblings and in January 1920, at the age of 14, was awarded a place at the Hobart State High School. Following completion of his studies Don gained employment as a messenger with the Hobart division of the Commonwealth Meteorological Department. He would remain in the federal government's employ for his entire working life.

As with most Battery Point boys of their era, sport formed an integral part of Don Purdon and his siblings' free time. Despite living on the waterfront it was boxing rather than sailing or rowing that took up the bulk of their interests. Don and his brothers excelled at boxing and were successful amateur boxers in the 1920s and 1930s. Don Purdon, in particular, first shows up in the records in April 1923 when he represented the Naval Sports Club in a local boxing tournament. His older brother William also participated in the lightweight division. That same year Don Purdon made his debut at the Tasmanian Amateur Boxing Championships, reaching the semi-finals in the midget class. During this period the Purdon family's Battery Point boat shed became the location where intra and interstate boxers trained leading up to their matches.

The Purdon brothers were formidable opponents. William Purdon won the Tasmanian Amateur Boxing Championship in the lightweight class in 1924 and 1925. William was then selected to compete in the Tasmanian team at the Australasian Amateur Boxing Championships, held in Brisbane in September 1925, where he put up strong performances.

In 1925 Don Purdon began competing in the featherweight class, again making it to the semi-finals in the Tasmanian Amateur Boxing Championship. The following year Don Purdon won the state amateur featherweight title. Though no state championships were held in 1927 or 1928, he won the state amateur lightweight title in 1929. Don Purdon next represented Tasmania at the Australian Amateur Boxing Championship, held in Hobart in September 1929, where he finished runner-up in the lightweight class. Continuing his supreme performance in the ring, Don won the 1930 Tasmanian Lightweight Amateur Boxing Championship and finished runner-up in 1931.

It was the height of the Depression yet sport was one of the few entertainment outlets that appears to have grown in popularity during the era. In January 1932 Don Purdon sailed to Melbourne as part of the Tasmanian team to compete in the Australian Amateur Boxing Championship. Here he fought in the welterweight division. After hanging up the gloves, Don Purdon continued his involvement in the sport, becoming a referee and steward. He would later become heavily involved in the sporting activities of his two sons, Sam and Mick.

Home, School and Sport

Growing up in the 1930s was tough, particularly in Battery Point. The Depression affected the local community significantly and work was hard to come by. Employment at the nearby boat and ship yards was piecemeal at best with few new vessels built. Thankfully Sam and Mick's father Don had a stable job with the public service. The growing Purdon family also received support from relatives who lived close by, and in turn provided support in times of need. Sam, Mick and their family lived at 2 Napoleon Street; a one storey brick house known as "The Elms" and consisting of six rooms. The property had previously been owned by their great grandfather Tom Purdon. Next door, at 2a Napoleon Street, in a house known as "Glen Elm," lived their great grandmother Rosina, Tom Purdon's widow. At 4 Napoleon Street lived Sam and Mick's paternal grandparents Ernest and Lizzie Purdon.

Like many of their peers who were raised at Battery Point, Sam and Mick Purdon and their sisters attended school at nearby Albuera Street Primary, and in grade six the boys spent one day per week at the Battery Point Trade School learning woodworking and carpentry skills from Charles Snook. Both Sam and Mick also took piano lessons as youngsters at St Joseph's College, achieving several certificates from the Australian Music Examination Board. School football games also helped pass the winter months. Their sisters Lenna and Norma excelled at netball and hockey, respectively, and went on to represent Tasmania at several interstate carnivals.

Apprenticeships and Cadet Dinghies

After finishing school Sam Purdon was apprenticed to Norm Taylor at his Battery Point boatyard while Mick began an apprenticeship in cabinet making. It was the end of World War II and work at Taylor Brothers was steady. Vessels Sam Purdon was involved with during his apprenticeship include the 57 ft fishing trawler *Ben Boyd* (later named *Ronnell*), built to the order of James Alderton of Cremorne, New South Wales; the 42 ft motor launch *Silver Cloud II*, built to the order of H. A. Nichols to a Max Creese design; and the first class cruising yacht *Marauder*, built to the order of Geoff Cripps.

Commensurate with undertaking their apprenticeships Sam and Mick Purdon began sailing competitively. Sam's first boat was the cadet dinghy *Apex* which he won a trophy for in the 1943/1944 season. In December 1945 Sam's consistency at the helm of *Apex* saw him selected as one of three teams to represent Tasmania in the Stonehaven Cup to be held on Hobsons Bay, Victoria, in January 1946. The season saw younger brother Mick also start sailing in the cadet dinghy *Shamrock*. Mick was additionally named as an emergency for the 1946 Stonehaven Cup team.

Though none of the Tasmanian representatives went on to win the 1946 Stonehaven Cup, the boys gained valuable skills at the national event and were well-regarded by their interstate competitors. Later that year Sam Purdon won the Derwent Sailing Squadron's cadet dinghy pennant for the 1945/46 season.

The opening of the 1947/48 season saw Sam at the helm of the cadet dinghy *Conchra*, while Mick Purdon took the helm of *Apex*. Mick's consistency as skipper equalled that of his brother and resulted in him being selected to represent Tasmania at the 1949 Stonehaven Cup. Sam was unable to attend the event as he was by now over 19 years of age.

In February 1949 Sam Purdon sailed the heavyweight sharpie *Prion II* at the Bellerive Regatta. It was his first race in the 12 square metre class and *Prion II* finished second across the line. For the remainder of the season Sam continued to race *Conchra* in the cadet dinghy class, competing against brother Mick in *Apex*. Sam's superiority at the helm saw him awarded both the Royal Yacht Club of Tasmania and Derwent Sailing Squadron pennants that season. A fitting end to his last season in the class.

In April 1949 Sam sold *Conchra* to R. Stokes and set about building himself a heavyweight sharpie. Mick remained a standout in the cadet dinghy class and was selected to helm *Apex* in the 1950 Stonehaven Cup where he finished a credible third. The event was held in Melbourne in early January of that year.

Apex. Courtesy Sam Purdon.

Heavyweight Sharpies

In early October 1949 Sam Purdon launched his own heavyweight sharpie, *Swan,* at the foreshore of the Royal Yacht Club of Tasmania's premises at Battery Point. Less than two weeks later *Swan* finished second in the opening pennant race of the season. The next race saw *Swan* finish first. It proved the start of a very successful inaugural season for Sam, the first of several highlights being *Swan* winning the Tasmanian 12 Square Metre Championship in December 1949. A keen mentor, the local press noted Sam's dads' efforts in following him during the championship series, stating that Don Purdon rowed for miles in and out of the fleet during the three-race series to keep a close eye on his son's efforts.

In February 1950 the Australian championship for the 12 square metre class was held in Hobart. Sam, in *Swan*, was one of six boats selected to represent Tasmania at the event. Though still a newcomer to the class he excelled at the event, out-classing former state and national champions and future Olympians to be crowned the national champion; a triumphant achievement for Sam's first season in the class. Once again the efforts of Don Purdon, in following his son's progress in a dinghy during the race series, was recognised. Said to have rowed up to ten miles during one of the heats, in gales and torrential rain, Don Purdon was presented with a silver pewter engraved with "Greatest Rower on the Derwent" by the South Australian contingent.

In April 1950 Sam Purdon capped off another great season, claiming victory in the Derwent Sailing Squadron's champion helmsman race against several of Hobart's more prominent yachtsmen. Competing in Derwent class yachts, Sam took the helm of *Gnome* with a crew notably made up of dinghy boys, namely Mick Purdon, R. Lewis and K. Downie. That season Sam Purdon also won both the Derwent Sailing Squadron and Royal Yacht Club of Tasmania's pennants for the 12 square metre class.

Lack of funds and high transportation costs meant that the Tasmanian contingent for the 1951 Australian Sharpie Championship, held in Brisbane in January of that year, was restricted to just two boats. Despite being the national titleholder Sam Purdon was not automatically selected as part of the state team. Instead he had to compete against the best of the local boats to earn his selection. Disappointingly for Sam the two boats chosen were *Skimmer,* helmed by Ediss Boyes, and *Tattler,* helmed by Chook Newman. Not giving up on defending his national title, supporters of Sam Purdon established a special fund to raise money to send him to the event. One of Sam's most vocal ambassadors was his employer Norm Taylor. The Sandy Bay Football Club also assisted with the raising of funds, as did Michael Clennett, one of Sam's crew. Fortunately a little over a week later enough funds were raised to send Sam, his team and his boat *Swan* by air to participate in the event. Though the national title went to Ediss Boyes in *Skimmer*, Sam Purdon's effort to even get to the event proved worthwhile with *Swan* finishing runner-up.

Football

Coinciding with their participation in the cadet dinghy and heavyweight sharpie classes, Sam and Mick Purdon spent the winter months playing football. A standout in the position of rover, Sam's first year in the Sandy Bay senior team (1949), playing in the Tasmanian Football League, saw him finish runner-up in the club's best and fairest medal count. The following year Sam was selected in the southern team for the annual north versus south match. He was again picked in the southern side in 1952 and later that year was named one of the best rovers in the league when Sandy Bay won the grand final.

In July 1953 Sam was selected in a state team to play against Geelong, at the time the undeafeated team in the Victorian Football League. Though one of the best on ground, the Tasmanian team went down by 65 points to their mainland competitor. That same year the senior Sandy Bay team played in the grand final against New Town. Though losing by 11 points, Sam Purdon was again one of the best on ground, also kicking three goals.

Picked in the southern side in 1954, that year Sam also played in several intrastate games. He was additionally selected as a reserve in the Tasmanian team to play against an All-Australian amateur side. Active around the packs, the diminuitive rover came on in the last quarter during this particular game, helping his team to an overwhelming 53 point victory.

Sam Purdon remained a consistent performer in the Sandy Bay senior team for many years. All told he played more than 100 games in the Tasmanian Football League. Mick Purdon also began training with the senior team in 1953 and played with the reserves. Their father Don, always present on the side lines, acted as the senior team's trainer. After finishing his playing career with Sandy Bay, Sam Purdon went on to successfully coach country teams at Kingston and Kermandie.

Sandy Bay Senior Football Team. Sam Purdon is fourth from right.
Courtesy Tasmanian Archive and Heritage Office.

Purdon Brothers, Cabinet Makers

In addition to their sporting accomplishments, the early 1950s saw the two Purdon brothers set about establishing their own business. In May 1951 Don Purdon petitioned the Hobart City Countil for approval to build a concrete block workshop at his property, 2 Napoleon Street, to be used by Sam and Mick to establish a cabinet making business. The adjacent parcel of land, extending to the foreshore and used as a slipyard by the Purdon family for several decades, was at the time owned by the Royal Yacht Club of Tasmania and in use as a boat storage and slipway facility.

With approval to build the shed granted, Sam and Mick Purdon resigned from their places of employment and began taking on carpentry work, odd jobs and repairs, as well as making furniture and cabinets to order. During this period they also built an 11 ft clinker dinghy and four heavyweight sharpies (*Swan II, Waterwitch, Snowgoose* and *Darter II*). Having graduated from the cadet dinghy class, *Swan II* was built for Mick Purdon's own use and is first noted on the Derwent when competing at the Royal Hobart Regatta in February 1953. Two years later Mick was selected to represent Tasmania at the Australian 12 Square Metre Championship, held in Adelaide.

Fibreglass Technology

In 1954 Sam and Mick Purdon turned an idea to start developing fibreglass dinghies into a reality. The decision was to lay the foundation for the future of their business for the next two decades and also become their specialty. The technology, based on the use of glass fibres reinforced with plastic resins, was originally patented in 1936 by Owens Corning of Toledo, Ohio, USA. Being lightweight yet durable in construction, it was first used in boat making in the years following the end of World War II. By the early 1950s fibreglass was becoming increasingly accepted in the construction of dinghies. The watertight material allowed boats to be made as a single unit rather than from multiple lengths of wood pieced together. It also allowed for mass production of identical vessels as opposed to the previously accepted norm of made to order or custom builds. Fibreglass was revolutionary.

With wooden moulds made for them by neighbouring boat builder Max Creese, Sam and Mick Purdon set to work, initially building fibreglass dinghies of 10 ft in length. With demand growing and their increasing knowledge of working with the glass and resin products ever improving the quality of their builds, Purdon Brothers soon expanded their offerings. Between 1954 and 1972 the pair manufactured several thousand dinghies of various sizes: 8, 10, 12, 13 and 14 ft. Their best production rate was five dinghies per week, i.e., one per day, but on most weeks they averaged three dinghies. This is in stark contrast to the building of clinker wooden dinghies which would take approximately three weeks to complete. Though initial set-up costs were high and a fibreglass dinghy would sell for the same price as a comparably-sized wooden dinghy, the fact that more fibreglass vessels could be made in the same time period proved advantageous.

Sam Purdon. Courtesy Sam Purdon.

As their fibreglass boats became more popular, Sam and Mick Purdon would spend the winter months building up stock for their busiest period: Christmas. Often they would be out of stock as the end of the year neared. To offset the dinghy business, they also manufactured sailing craft, fishing wells, shower bays and wash troughs out of fibreglass.

Sam and Mick Purdon. Courtesy Sam Purdon.

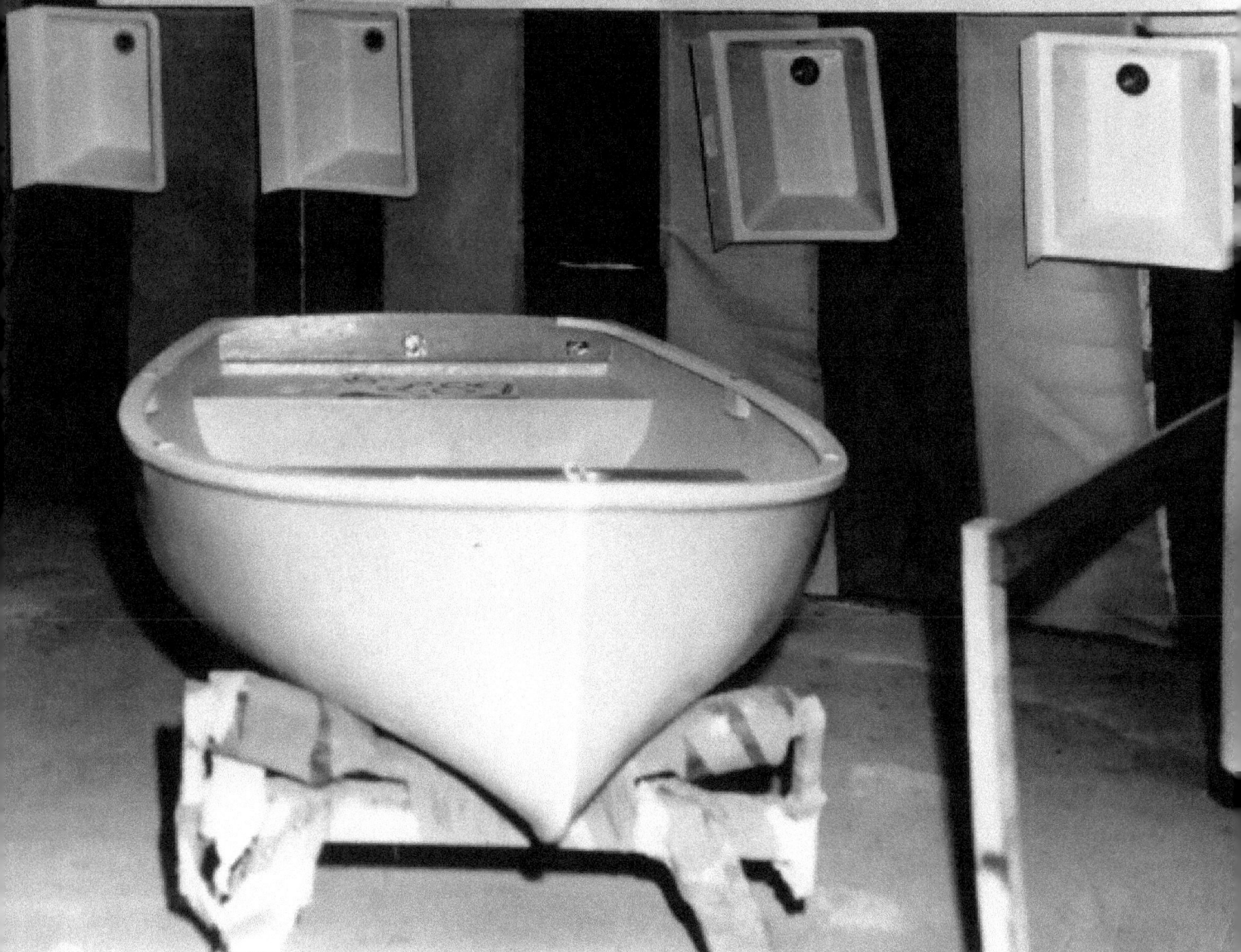

Purdon Brothers. Courtesy Sam Purdon.

More Changes

However, just as fibreglass technology replaced wooden materials in the manufacture of smaller vessels, its prominence in the boat building industry was also supplanted. Following the development of fibreglass, then aluminium came along. Though initially more expensive, aluminium dinghies eventually became cheaper and went on to price fibreglass dinghies out of the market. Demand for vessels built by Purdon Brothers declined commensurately. After three decades in operation, the pair finished manufacturing fibreglass dinghies in the early 1980s.

In the years that preceded their retirement, Sam and Mick, who by now owned the Napoleon Street slip previously used by the Royal Yacht Club of Tasmania, undertook repair work. The pair also went on the road, repairing fridges of fishing boats. Later Mick Purdon built canisters for Liferaft Systems Australia, a company established by Robert Clifford and others. Not giving up on their original trade, several wooden boats were also built at Battery Point during this period, including the last heavyweight sharpie, *Jabiru II*, and the 32 ft motor sailer *Barameda*. The latter was built in 1968 for Sam and Mick Purdon's own use. They retained ownership of the vessel for 44 years.

With a large slip all to themselves, Sam and Mick Purdon also leased portions of their Battery Point property to other tradesmen. In 1968 Ross Muir, a shipwright by trade, relocated from his father Jock's neighbouring yard to Purdon Brothers. Here he undertook boat repair work as well as the building of yachts and spares, rigging, sail making and chandlery. Both Michael and George Grainger worked for Ross Muir at Purdon's yard before the trio moved back to the Muir Boatyard in 1978. Still, at Purdon's slipyard Ross Muir built several vessels. Amongst them were the diamond class yacht *Venom*, which he sailed in numerous Australian titles throughout the 1970s, including those held in Hobart, Perth, and Melbourne.

Mick and Sam Purdon (2016). Courtesy Terry Lean.

Retirement

Sam and Mick Purdon retired from commercial boat manufacturing in 1982. They sold their slipyard property at 2 Napoleon Street in 1984. Pre and post retirement Sam and Mick Purdon have remained active participants in local yachting circles, both on and off the water. Recreationally and competively, the pair have enjoyed great success at the helm of several vessels. Mick, for example, skippered the Dragon class yacht *Janlyn* in the Prince Philip Cup championship series during the 1970s. In 1977 he won the Australian Dragon class yachting title in the yacht *Chip*, a first for Tasmania after two decades of participation at the national event. Mick Purdon was additionally a well-respected judge at over 50 Australian and international yachting events, served as commodore and vice commodore of the Derwent Sailing Squadron, president of the state sharpie and Dragon associations, as well as on Yachting Tasmania's rules committee. For these efforts, Mick was inducted into the Tasmanian Yachting Hall of Fame. Always the sportsman, Sam Purdon maintains an active lifestyle, playing golf several times a week. Both deserve strong applause for their contributions to Battery Point's maritime legacy, and their achievements to Australian yachting in general.

Barameda (2017).
Courtesy Colin Grazules.

Wooden Vessels Built by Purdon Brothers and Others at Battery Point (1949 – 1972).

1949. *Swan*. Heavyweight sharpie. 19.6 ft. Built by Sam Purdon for his own use and launched in October 1949. Won the Tasmanian Sharpie Championship in December of that year. Won the Australian Sharpie Championship held in Hobart in February 1950. Still sailed and owned by Sam Purdon in January 1951 and represented TAS in the 1951 Australian Sharpie Championship, held in Brisbane, finishing 2nd. Sold to K. McCoy of Adelaide, SA. Later owned by James Hardy who represented SA at several national championships, being runner-up three times and who went on to be knighted for his involvement with the America's Cup.

1950. *Sula*. Heavyweight sharpie. 19.6 ft. First noted on the River Derwent in November 1950. Owned by R. Purdon and A. Harris who were also her builders, with the assistance of Mick Purdon. Represented TAS in the 1952 Australian Sharpie Championship held in Melbourne, helmed by Ken Batt. Represented TAS in the 1954 Australian Sharpie Championship held in Sydney.

1951. Dinghy. 11 ft. Clinker. Built by Purdon Brothers.

1952. *Swan II*. Heavyweight sharpie. 19.6 ft. Built by Purdon Brothers for Mick Purdon's own use. First noted on the River Derwent in February 1953. By 1961 owned by P. C. Fowler of the Tamar Yacht Club.

1953. *Waterwitch*. Heavyweight sharpie. 19.6 ft. Built by Purdon Brothers to the order of Neil Campbell.

1954. *Snowgoose*. Heavyweight sharpie. 19.6 ft. Built by Purdon Brothers to the order of Val Button. Finished 1st at the 1961 Australian Sharpie Championship held in Hobart, helmed by Val Button.

1954. *Darter II*. Heavyweight sharpie. 19.6 ft. Built by Purdon Brothers to the order of Neil Campbell. 1957/1958 Tasmanian champion, sailed and owned by Mick Purdon. By 1961 owned by L. Bevis. Sybsequentlly transferred to the Tamar Yacht Club.

1959. *Jabiru II*. Heavyweight sharpie. 19.6 ft. Built by Purdon Brothers for Max Thorpe of the Cygnet Sailing Club. Notably the last heavyweight sharpie built in TAS. Still in existence, owned by Terry Lean of the Huon and recently restored.

1968. *Barameda*. Yacht. 32 x 10.5 ft. Motor sailer built by Purdon Brothers for their own use. After 44 years of ownership, sold in 2012. Still in existence, located in southern TAS.

Late 1960s. *Stratus*. Lightweight sharpie. Built by Ross Muir at Purdon Brothers' yard for Ross' brother John.

1972. *Venom*. Diamond class yacht. 9 x 3 m. Built by Ross Muir at Purdon Brothers' yard and launched in June 1972. Sailed by Ross Muir until 1978. Competed in the National Diamond Class championships held in Hobart in January 1974 and in Perth in January 1975. Converted to a junior offshore group yacht and sailed for a further two years. Sold to a buyer from Launceston, TAS. Caught on fire and sank on the Tamar River a few years later.

Opposite: The view from Purdon Brothers' yard (circa 1970s). Courtesy Richard Blundell.

1970s. Trailer sailer. 16 ft. Hartley designed. Built by Ross Muir to the order of Max Aird.

1970s. Runabout. 16 ft. Hartley designed plywood runabout built by Ross Muir.

1970s. Dinghy. Moth class dinghy built by Ross Muir.

1970s. Dinghy. Fireball class dinghy built by Ross Muir.

1970s. Dinghy. Rainbow class dinghy built by Ross Muir.

William (Bill) Foster

William (Bill) Foster grew up in Battery Point where the local streets and slipyards were his playground. After leaving school Bill was offered a boat building apprenticeship with his uncle Jock Muir who at the time was building boats in a paddock in Sandy Bay. Several years later the yard moved to Battery Point where Bill helped with construction of Jock Muir's early cruising yachts and also built smaller vessels. Following a stint on the north west coast and four years spent in Melbourne working for boat builder Jack Savage, Bill Foster returned to Hobart in the early 1960s. In 1964 he took out a lease on Percy Coverdale's Battery Point yard where, in addition to slip and repair work, a handful of vessels were built, including a replica of the 22 ft yacht *Trekka*. Though later employed with the Tasmanian Grain Elevators Board, Bill Foster has retained an interest in boat building, particularly in the decades since his retirement. Most notably Bill has been actively involved in the Wooden Boat School at Franklin and the five-year restoration effort of the trading ketch *May Queen*.

William (Bill) Frederick Foster was born at the Queen Alexandra Maternity Hospital, Battery Point, on 6 August 1932, the eldest of four children born to Frederick and Ellen Foster (nee McAllister). As a young child Bill and his family lived at 7 Colville Street, Battery Point, though by his teenage years the family had moved to 3 Colville Street; a more accommodating house for the growing Foster family.

At the time of Bill's childhood, Battery Point was a modest suburb. The small cottages that now boast million-dollar price tags were the tenanted homes of working-class families, predominantly living week to week. The workers were employed close by; at the wharves, at the jam factories and at the slipyards. A somewhat neglected suburb, the streets and footpaths of Battery Point were gravel, the gutters were cobblestone and, with the exception of a few cars, buses and horse-drawn carts, traffic was non-existent.

Reflecting on his childhood Bill Foster recalls the closeness of the local Battery Point community, which he refers to as more like a village, and that many members of the maternal and paternal sides of his family lived nearby. Bill's father was an upholsterer by trade. His mother was a sewing machinest and clothing maker. Unfortunately the Depression of the late 1920s and into the early 1930s resulted in Bill's dad being in and out of work. Frederick Foster was lucky to find work during this period, helping build the road up to Mount Wellington. In later years he was employed at Palfreyman's furniture store.

Children playing in Arthur Circus, Battery Point (circa 1930s).
Courtesy Tasmanian Archive and Heritage Office.

CONSTRUCTION'S
UPWAR
on the MOUNT WELLINGTO

LIMB
NIC HIGHWAY

A vivid impression of the rough nature of the country through which the mountain road is being hewn, and of the skilful grading that is being accomplished, is given by these progress pictures of construction on Mount Wellington high level. The scenic highway when completed will give to the Tasmanian capital a tourist-inducing asset ranking with the world's most famous high altitude motoring outlooks, and one outvying any elsewhere in the Australian Commonwealth.

A Childhood at Battery Point

From the age of five Bill Foster attended school at Albuera Street Primary. Two years later war broke out in Europe. Though air-raid shelters were built next door to Bill's school, he reflects fondly on a childhood filled with games such as marbles, cards, tops, chasings and cricket, often played in nearby Arthur Circus. Bill also notes that his dad would take him and his siblings to the Royal Hobart Regatta, among other annual events, where the speedboats were of special interest.

Weekends were often spent at the Napoleon Street slipyards, a favourite place to play. Since the working week constituted 44 hours per week, including Saturday mornings, the yards were empty by Saturday afternoon, particularly in winter, offering an ideal location for the local Battery Point kids to roam. The only exception was Percy Coverdale who could always be found working at his yard, usually with the door left open. None of the fences that separated the yards were in good condition, thereby allowing easy access between the yards. Bill recalls that the smell of the timber, pine, oils and paints was something to behold.

Mentors and Teachers

Bill Foster's family, particularly his uncles on the McAllister side, were multi-skilled tradesmen, involved in woodwork, plumbing and general metal work. Bill has fond memories of spending time with his uncle Dave McAllister who worked at Purdon and Featherstone's shipyard along the Battery Point foreshore. The yard was extremely active during World War II building several sea ambulances and harbour defence launches. Bill also notes that he would often call into the McAllister house, on St Georges Terrace, on his way home from school and watch the progress of a yacht his uncle Don McAllister was building in the backyard. Taking five years to complete, the 38 ft cruising yacht *Kalua* was launched on 9 September 1944.

It was around this time that Bill attended the Battery Point Trade School one day per week where, under the instruction of Charles Snook, he was taught woodworking and technical drawing. Bill recalls that he would attend the school every Thursday during grade six. The morning of the class would be spent learning to draw models while the afternoon would be spent making them in the workshop. Each boy had his own bench and rack of tools on the wall. Huon pine was generally the material of choice and was readily available for the pupils to use. Though Mr Snook was quite stern and took no nonsense, Bill remembers this class as a highlight of his primary school years and still has a footstool that he made.

After finishing primary school, Bill Foster spent several years at the Hobart Junior Technical School, located between Bathurst and Liverpool streets in the city.

Opposite: Crew on board the *Patsy* for its delivery trip to Sydney in May 1950. Left to Right: E. T. "Ted" Domeny, Adrian Dean, Jock Muir and Bill Foster. Courtesy Bill Foster.

First Sailing Experiences

Bill Foster first built a "boat" with a mate in the backyard out of a sheet of galvinised iron. The pair nailed the bow onto a piece of vertical timber and shaped the stern out of an end of an apple box. Any gaps were filled with tar that they sourced from the edge of the road on a hot day. The "boat's" auspicious launch was from Short Beach, with Bill and his friend subsequently rowing the vessel around the boats moored off the Battery Point slipyards. Bill notes that neither he nor his friend could swim, nor was the "boat" fitted with any safety devices.

The first sailing experience Bill remembers was on board Ralph Featherstone's yacht *Plimsoll* which Bill's uncle Jock Muir, later boat builder of Battery Point, often borrowed. It was the first of many outings Bill would enjoy on the water with his extended family.

First Jobs

Following the end of World War II, and with Bill performing well in school, a friend of the Foster family offered him a job at a solicitor's office. Bill recalls that it only took a few days to realise that he did not enjoy licking stamps, folding letters and delivering them around Hobart! In fact several weeks into this new position, the firm suggested that he might like to find alternate employment.

In 1946 Bill was offered a much more suitable position, working for his uncle Jock Muir as an apprentice boat builder. At the time Jock was building the 42 ft Bermuda-rigged cutter *Westward* in a paddock off 52 Queen Street in Sandy Bay. The vessel, built for George Gibson, was launched on 6 September 1947. Following came the 29 ft motor boat, *Pinjarra*, built to the order of the Bastick family. During this period Bill also crewed on board the Max Creese-built yacht *Mavis* during its delivery to Sydney with Jock Muir at the helm. It was the first of several delivery trips that Bill would take with Jock over the years.

In 1949 Bill Foster built a Sydney Vaucluse Junior or VJ in the backyard of his home at Colville Street, Battery Point. The vessel was the first of its type to be built in Tasmania. Bill then helped Vic O'Brien complete the heavyweight sharpie *Tern*, launched in October 1950.

Bill Foster's Vaucluse Junior at Battery Point.
Courtesy Bill Foster.

Working at Jock Muir's yard, Bill Foster helped in construction of the racing sloop *Lass O'Luss*, built to the order of John Colquhoun. Work on this particular vessel began in the Queen Street paddock, though was moved to Jock's newly-established Battery Point boatyard in mid-1948 where it was launched on 4 December 1948. A few days later Bill was lucky enough to be on board *Westward* en route to Sydney to take part in that year's Sydney to Hobart Yacht Race. The vessel went on to finish fifth across the line and first on handicap; a tremendous honour for Bill who at the time was only 16 years of age.

Back in Hobart Bill set about helping with construction of the 47 ft cruiser *Waltzing Matilda*, built by Jock Muir to the order of Phil Davenport and launched on 2 July 1949. Next came the 47 ft cruiser *Patsy*, built to the order of A. C. Cooper and launched on 4 April 1950. Bill Foster also completed a commercial crayfishing dinghy to the order of Bill Wisby of Bruny Island during this period.

In September 1950 Bill Foster and Don Muir completed the sharpie *Skimmer,* built for Ediss Boyes. Another heavyweight sharpie built by the pair, *Darter,* was launched in September 1950, to the order of Neil Campbell.

Des Ashton's 33 ft racing sloop *Lahara* was the next big boat Bill Foster helped build at Jock Muir's yard. The vessel was launched on 8 December 1951. The following year saw the launch of the 25 ft fishing boat *Evelyn*, built to the order of Alf Barnett of Binalong Bay, and the luxury cruiser *Van Diemen*, built to the order of Len Nettlefold.

Bill notes that working conditions on the waterfront at the Battery Point boatyards were primitive to say the least. His time working for Jock Muir comprised a move from the Queen Street paddock to Jock's own boatyard at Battery Point. Though several small and large sheds and buildings were eventually constructed at Jock's yard, the majority of the boat building projects during Bill Foster's apprenticeship took place out in the open with workers exposed to the elements. The toilets were equally as primitive: long drops off the end of a walkway extending out into the Derwent. Tidal influences often saw the floors of these structures submerged. One can only imagine the possibilities of what could be seen floating around!

Still, Bill remembers the time he spent working for his uncle and mentor Jock Muir very fondly, both in terms of what he got to experience and what he learned. During this period Bill Foster also spent a lot of time learning the craft of boat building from Jock's younger brother Max.

Muir's Boatyard in 1951.
Courtesy Jock Muir Family Collection.

A Move to the North West Coast and then to Melbourne

In 1952, at the age of 20, Bill travelled to Penguin on Tasmania's north west coast to visit his friend Vic O'Brien. Following a few more visits to the area Bill decided to relocate permanently to Penguin. Though work was somewhat scarce Bill was offered a job as a carpenter where one of his first projects was on the Riana Area School. During this period Bill also met his future wife Shirley Aitken. The couple were married at Penguin on 9 June 1956.

Following their wedding Bill and Shirley Foster moved to West Ulverstone where they had bought a house. In the years since his arrival to the north west coast Bill had found employment at the Devonport slipyard working on construction of two fishing vessels. He also continued to build smaller vessels, including dinghies and a speedboat. Another position Bill Foster took on was working for Arch Kimberley's building and joinery company.

In 1958 Bill Foster moved his family to Victoria where he secured a job managing a small boatyard at Hastings. Though the work was enjoyable, it was not that consistent. The need to find more permanent employment precipated Bill's next move: a job as foreman at Jack Savage's Williamstown boatyard where he spent the next four years.

Back to Battery Point

In 1962 Bill Foster and his family relocated back to Hobart, initially moving in with Bill's parents in Colville Street, Battery Point. Bill immediately found work with his uncle Jock Muir. At the time Jock had been awarded a contract to build a boat for the Tasmanian Police Department. Having taken a year to complete, the 34 ft *Alert* was launched in November 1963. The vessel had been constructed under the supervision of Bill Foster at a workshop in New Town, owing to lack of space at Jock's boatyard, and was transported to Battery Point just prior to launch.

Alert. Courtesy Maritime Museum of Tasmania.

Percy Coverdale's Yard

Wanting to establish his own slipyard business, Bill Foster approached Eric Coverdale about the possibility of leasing Percy Coverdale's Battery Point yard. Percy had died on 29 March 1963, aged 81, and the property was under the management of Percy's brother Eric.

With a five-year lease agreed on, Bill Foster spent several months repairing the yard and getting the slip back to working order. The main slip was capable of accommodating boats up to 9 tons while the traverse accommodated vessels up to 2 tons. The work was soon steady and the yard full of boats requiring slipping or repairs. During this period Bill also found time to build several smaller vessels, including a rainbow class dinghy; a fireball class dinghy; two 12 ft cadet dinghies (*Guiding Star* and *Volante II*); a 30 ft plywood "Eventide," made to hull and deck stage; and a replica of John Guzzwell's 22 ft *Trekka* for Norm Sanders which was named *Tarema*.

As the end of the lease on the Coverdale yard approached, Bill Foster decided not to renew it. Instead in early 1968 he began working for the Tasmanian Stevedoring Company. It was the height of the fruit export industry and the work was busy. It also offered Bill and his growing family much needed job security.

However, after Britain joined the European Common Market in the early 1970s, Tasmania's apple exports fell drastically and Bill felt a need to find alternate employment sooner rather than later. Thankfully the Tasmanian Grain Elevators Board at the time were advertising for an executive officer. Bill Foster spent the next two decades working for this organisation.

Outside of work Bill was active in the Apex and Lions clubs, and the Sandy Bay Sailing Club. When his daughters showed an interest in sailing Bill built them an international cadet dinghy in a workshop at his home in St Georges Terrace, Battery Point. The vessel, *Chloe*, was launched in 1979. Several years later Bill took time off work to travel to Norfolk Island with his wife Shirley. Here Bill spent several months involved with the island's boat building activities, including restoration of a 28 ft launch.

Post-Retirement

Bill Foster retired from the workforce in 1992. Since this time he has been involved with numerous projects and activities, including building trophies for the Sandy Bay Sailing Club, the Royal Yacht Club of Tasmania, and the Cruising Yacht Club of Australia, among others; teaching at the Wooden Boat School at Franklin where Bill supervised construction of the *Lady Franklin*, *Atlas* and dinghies built to his own Foster10 design; and undertaking a three-week stint observing the weather on Maatsuyker Island.

Significantly Bill Foster was instrumental in the five-year restoration effort of the 19th century trading ketch *May Queen*. In 2003 these efforts were recognised by the World Ship Trust. In 2007 Bill Foster received the Order of Australia Medal for his services to the community, particularly relating to preservation and promotion of Tasmania's maritime heritage. Bill lives in Battery Point with his wife Shirley.

Vessels Built by Bill Foster at Battery Point (1949 – 1985).

1949. *Bobcat*. **Yacht.** Sydney Vaucluse Junior (VJ) yacht built in the backyard of Bill Foster's home at 3 Colville Street, Battery Point.

1950. *Tern*. **Heavyweight sharpie.** 19.6 ft. Built by Vic O'Brien and Bill Foster at Purdon's slipyard, Battery Point; the latter having taken over Rex Nichols' share in the boat prior to completion. Launched in October 1950. By 1958 owned by J. & P. Garde.

1964. *Futura*. **Dinghy.** Rainbow class dinghy built to the order of Barry Button.

1965. *Tarema*. **Yacht.** Replica of the 22 ft yacht *Trekka* that was sailed around the world in the 1950s by John Guzzwell. Built to the order of Norm Sanders of America. Trans-shipped to the USA. Between 1971 and 1983 owned by Gary Adams and sailed extensively around the Pacific.

1967. *Volante II*. **Cadet dinghy.** 12 x 5 ft x 14 in. By 1971 owned by P. M. Greeves, by 1975 owned by the Royal Yacht Club of Tasmania which retained ownership for several decades.

1967. *Guiding Star*. **Cadet dinghy.** 12 x 5 ft x 14 in . Built to the order of W. E. McIndoe and launched in 1967. Still in existence, has remained in the McIndoe family's possession and is located at Kingston.

1960s. **Dinghy.** Fireball class dinghy.

1960s. **Yacht.** 30 ft. Marine plywood "Eventide" built to hull and deck stage.

1979. *Chloe*. **Dinghy.** International cadet built at Bill Foster's home in St Georges Terrace, Battery Point.

1985. *Ellen*. **Dinghy.** "Foster 10" clinker dinghy built by Bill Foster at his home in St Georges Terrace for his daughter Helen's 21st birthday.

Tern off Battery Point. Courtesy Kim O'Brien

Opposite: *Ellen.*
Courtesy http://www.batterypointhall.org.au
(assessed September 2017).

Other Builders

In addition to the Battery Point boat builders profiled in the previous chapters, there are others who deserve special mention, including Robert Inches, Robert Kennedy, Fred Saunders and Don Muir. Also worthy of mention are those men who built boats in their backyards during spare hours, several of whom worked at the Battery Point boatyards during the day.

~~~~~~

Robert Inches

Robert Inches was born on 4 March 1849 at Hobart, the eldest son of eight children born to Thomas and Mary Inches (nee Garth). His father was a Scottish shipbuilder who emigrated to Australia in 1841. Two years later Thomas Inches partnered with James McLaren to establish a shipyard at Shipwrights Point on the Huon River, Tasmania. The pair went on to become pioneers of shipbuilding in the region, launching many ketches and barges that became the backbone of the local river trade, including the *Caledonia*, *Thistle*, *Fleetwing* and *Crest of the Wave*.

Following in his father's professional footsteps, Robert Inches learned the craft of shipbuilding at Shipwrights Point. In 1880 he purchased waterfront property along the southern end of Napoleon Street, Battery Point, for use as a shipyard. Here, up until his untimely death in 1904, Robert Inches built at least 19 vessels, including nine yachts and five ketches.

Of particular interest to this book are the vessels built by Robert Inches at his Battery Point yard in the 20th century. First, on 23 January 1900, the William Fife (Jr) designed yacht *Fairlie II* was launched, built to the order of F. N. Clarke. Next came the trading ketches *Swift* and *Olive*. The former was launched on 30 July 1900, built to the order of T. and J. Underwood of North West Bay to a design by Tom Purdon. Of a similar size, the *Olive* was built to the order of Auguste Nickel of the D'Entrecasteaux Channel and launched in early 1901. Both were intended for the Huon and Channel river trade.

In June 1901 Robert Inches was commissioned by the Tasmanian Timber Corporation to build a 50 ft oil launch for use at the company's Port Esperance mill. The vessel, *Oceana*, was launched on 14 December 1901. Next Robert Inches launched a yacht to the order of F. N. Clarke, again based on a design by William Fife (Jr). Named *Fairlie III*, the vessel was launched on 8 November 1902. Just over a year later, on 9 December 1903, Robert Inches launched what would be his final vessel, the 53 ft cutter *Dauntless,* built to the order of Alex McKay.

Robert Inches died at the General Hospital, Hobart, on 29 May 1904 at the age of 53. The following month his Battery Point shipyard, comprising two roods and 27 perches of property and 92 ft of water frontage, was advertised for sale. The yard also included a weatherboard house, two patent slips and three small jetties. The property was purchased by William Lucas in July 1904.

Left (Top): Robert Inches at the launch of *Oceana*. Courtesy *Tasmanian Mail*, 11 January 1902.
Right (Top) and Middle: Launch of *Oceana*. Courtesy *Tasmanian Mail*, 11 January 1902.
Bottom: Launch of *Fairlie III*. Courtesy *Weekly Courier*, 13 December 1902.

Removal of the patent slip at Battery Point. Courtesy *Illustrated Tasmanian Mail*, 24 August 1911.

Robert Kennedy

Robert Kennedy emigrated to Australia from Glasgow, Scotland, in 1859 at the age of 25. A ship's carpenter by trade, he established a shipyard on property located on the south bank of the Yarra River in Melbourne, Victoria. Here, over the next 25 years, in addition to repair and alteration work, Robert Kennedy was noted as building several vessels. These include a 60 ft steam punt, launched in 1873; the schooner *Wollamai*, launched in 1876; the 120 ft wooden paddle steamer *Tanjil*, launched in December 1877; and three 140 ton punts built in 1879.

Unfortunately the ongoing viability of Robert Kennedy's Yarra River shipyard was threatened by development. By January 1885 Robert and his sons had relocated to Tasmania, purchasing the Derwent Iron Works and Engineering Company from J. W. Syme. Located in Hobart at the New Wharf, the Kennedy family immediately set about establishing their customer base, advertising themselves as "Shipbuilders, Engineers, and Shipsmiths, Manufacturers of land and marine engines, boilers of all types, hoisting engines and cranes, bridges, girders, tanks and vats, and sawmill machiner, castings of every description in brass and iron; contractors' and iron work". Part of the Derwent Iron Works and Engineering Company's assets included the Battery Point shipyard and patent slip previously in the possession of John Lucas and prior to that by John Ross.

Upon establishing their business operations in Hobart, one of the Kennedy family's first projects was to supply ironwork for railway bridges being constructed across the Derwent near New Norfolk. In the years to come their work would be heavily associated with Tasmania's mining industry.

For many years the Kennedy family's Battery Point shipyard was busy with overhaul, alteration and repair work of vessels, particularly of steamships. In 1890 a silver lead ore smelter was also established on the site. Continuing the mixed-use of the property, Robert Kennedy and Sons built at least one vessel in the 20th century, the ketch *Aristides*, launched in August 1902 and built for their own use in interstate trade.

Robert Kennedy died on 15 May 1903 at his residence, "Ardmore", Davey Street, Hobart, and was buried at Cornelian Bay Cemetery. Though his sons maintained possession of the family's Battery Point shipyard until at least 1923, the patent slip, originally purchased from England by John Ross in the 1850s, was removed from the site to be relaid in Devonport in 1911. In the years that followed, the property was leased to various parties, including Henry Jones and Company for construction of their three-masted schooner *Amelia J* in 1919 (built by Henry Moore of Launceston and designed by Tom Purdon). The steamers *Excella* (built by John Dalgleish and launched in 1912) and *Rosny* (built by Fred Moore, brother of Henry Moore, and launched in 1913) were also constructed on the property.

Top (Left): Construction of *Amelia J* at Battery Point. Courtesy *Illustrated Tasmanian Mail*, 12 December 1918.
Top (Right): *Amelia J.* Courtesy State Library of Victoria.
Bottom (Left and Right): Launch of *Excella*. Courtesy *Illustrated Tasmanian Mail*, 14 November 1912.

Frederick (Fred) Saunders

Frederick (Fred) Saunders was born in Hobart on 10 April 1898, the first of five children born to Charles and Margaret Saunders (nee Dudley). His father was a carpenter and builder by trade and the family lived in several locations in and around Hobart.

After completing school and an apprenticeship at sea on board square-rigged sailing vessels, Fred Saunders followed in his father's professional footsteps and by the 1920s was working locally in the building trade. Around this period he also became involved in the Derwent Motor Boat Club.

The 1930s saw Fred Saunders become more prominent in the building trade, successfully completing several government tender projects, including building the fire station at New Norfolk. By World War II he was employed at the government shipbuilding yard at Prince of Wales Bay.

Frela. Courtesy Maritime Museum of Tasmania.

In January 1946 Fred Saunders began construction of a 65 ft steel trawler, the first of its kind to be built in Tasmania. With the work taking place at the Battery Point yard previously in the possession of Tucker Abel, Fred Saunders stated in the press that he had received contracts for three additional vessels to be built of similar construction.

On 17 September 1946 the first welded-steel vessel built in Tasmania was launched at Battery Point. Built by Fred Saunders to the order of Tasmanian Trawlers Pty. Ltd., the 65 ft *Diana* was intended for trawling and experimental fishing off the Tasmanian coast and into Bass Strait. Following the vessel's launch Fred Saunders immediately set to work on construction of a larger vessel.

On 29 December 1947 the 85 ft welded-steel ketch *Frela* was launched by Fred Saunders at Battery Point. Luxiourously appointed, the vessel was intended for the fishing trade though by 1948 was being used in the local tourist trade. In June 1949 Fred Saunders sailed the vessel to the Whitsunday Islands, Queensland.

It appears that neither Fred Saunders nor his vessel returned to Tasmania. He died in Maryborough, Queensland, on 12 October 1974 at the age of 76.

Donald (Don) Muir

Donald (Don) James Muir was born at Battery Point on 31 May 1926, the youngest of five children born to Ernest (Ernie) and Elsie Muir (nee Haigh). Don had three older brothers (Jock, Max and Wally) and an older sister (Bessie). The Muir family lived at 42 Colville Street, Battery Point, and like his siblings Don attended Albuera Street Primary School. He later attended the Hobart Technical College, undertaking classes in electrical wiring and technical drawing. As a teenager Don Muir competed in model boat racing and the local cadet dinghy class.

After completing school Don Muir moved to Sydney where he helped his brother Jock establish a boat building and brokerage business at Mosman Bay. Don also helped Jock with construction of the fishing trawler *Wake* at Narooma on the New South Wales south coast, launched in early 1945.

Several years later Don Muir returned to Hobart where he continued to work with his brother Jock, including building the cruiser *Westward* in a paddock off Queen Street, Sandy Bay. Don also participated in the 1947 Sydney to Hobart Yacht Race on board the vessel, finishing second across the line and first on handicap. It proved a successful Muir family venture, with Jock at the helm and their father Ernie and brother Wally also on board as crew.

In 1948 Don Muir helped Jock move his boat building operations to Battery Point where the racing sloop *Lass O'Luss* was launched on 4 December 1948. Don was also part of the crew that sailed the vessel to Sydney with owner John Colquhoun a few days after launch. Don then made the return trip to Hobart on board *Lass O'Luss* as part of that year's Sydney to Hobart Yacht Race.

1949 saw Don Muir make several vessel delivery trips to the mainland. First, with his brother Wally and their friend Keith Ratcliffe, the 35 ft yacht *Ungava* was sailed to Brisbane for owner A. S. Huybers. The voyage was reportedly the first time a yacht of such a small size had sailed from Hobart to Queensland. Next Don Muir, along with Ray Kemp and Barry Garth, delivered the 40 ft ketch *Colleen II* to Sydney on behalf of owner J. F. Willans. The year concluded with Don crewing on board *Waltzing Matilda* in the 1949 Sydney to Hobart Yacht Race. With his older brother Jock at the tiller, the vessel finished first across the line and second on handicap following a dramatic battle up the River Derwent with *Margaret Rintoul* and *Trade Winds*. Four months later Don Muir travelled to Queensland to helm *Ungava* in the Brisbane to Gladstone Ocean Yacht Race.

Several smaller boats were also built by Don at Jock Muir's Battery Point yard during this period. These include the heavyweight sharpies *Tawaki*, launched in early 1949, and *Kittihawk*, launched in October 1949. Don sucessfully sailed *Tawaki* over several seasons, including at the 1951 Australian 12 Square Metre Championship, held in Melbourne.

In September 1950 Don Muir teamed with Bill Foster to complete the sharpie *Skimmer,* built for Ediss Boyes. Another heavyweight sharpie built by the pair, *Darter,* was completed in September 1950 to the order of Neil Campbell. During this period Don also developed sail plans and interior drawings for boats whose hulls were designed by Jock Muir and built at the Muir boatyard, including for Des Ashton's racing sloop *Lahara*, launched in late 1951, and for Len Nettlefold's cutter *Van Diemen*, launched in May 1952.

In mid-1952 Don Muir skippered the 62 ft luxury motor cruiser *J'Attendrai* to Hobart from Sydney on behalf of new owner Dr V. R. Ratten. With a crew of six, bad weather resulted in the vessel taking 20 days to reach her destination.

In October 1953 Don Muir launched a new sharpie, *Sabre*. A success from the start, Don sailed *Sabre* at the 1954 Australian 12 Square Metre Championship, held in Sydney, and went on to win the Tasmanian championship later that year. He also sailed the vessel at the 1955 Australian 12 Square Metre Championship, held in Adelaide, and at the 1956 national championship, held in Hobart.

Workwise, the mid-1950s coincided with Don Muir leaving the Muir boatyard at Battery Point to set up his own business, reconditioning and selling marine engines and undertaking joinery work. After spending several years working out of his house in Colville Street, Battery Point, in 1963 Don Muir partnered with Frank Conway to establish Muir Marine in Argyle Street, Hobart, selling Mercury outboards and smaller boats to the leisure market. These included Caribbean fibreglass runabouts and De Havilland aluminium dinghies.

With business prospects favourable, in 1966 Muir Marine relocated to a new purpose- built facility on the waterfront at Napoleon Street, Battery Point. The property had previously been owned by the Kennedy family and also had been the site where John Ross' patent slip was installed in 1866. In 1967 a second building was constructed to provide for additional storage for Muir Marine and to support boat maintenance work.

Powercraft Marine in 1982. Courtesy Michael Muir.

In 1972 Don Muir's son Michael joined Muir Marine and later became its owner. The mid to late 1970s saw Muir Marine continue to sell and service Mercury outboards and a range of boats imported from interstate. 1978 saw the firm also begin to manufacture 6 metre fibreglass runabouts of which a total of 10 were produced. Designed by Michael Muir, the mould for the vessel was developed from a timber prototype built by neighbouring boat builder Max Creese.

In 1982 Muir Marine changed its name to Powercraft Marine. Between 1983 and 2003 the firm manufactured over 250 welded aluminium boats from 14 ft to 17 ft at its Battery Point premises. Driven by outboard motors, the vessels were purchased by abalone divers, commercial net fishermen, government departments, and private owners for leisure purposes. During this period aluminium fishing trawler storage bins were also produced.

Powercraft Marine was sold in 2003. Retailing operations subsequently diminished and the Battery Point buildings were used for storage.

Thoughout his career Don Muir continued to design boats. These include a 32 ft auxilary cruiser for C. Martin, launched in 1955; a 37 ft motor launch for P. Allnutt, launched in 1960; the motor sailer *Jacaranda,* built in 1960; the 32 ft motor sailer *Islander,* built by Geoff Cuthbertson to the order of John Wignall in 1962; a 25 ft motor sailer for Lindsay Masters named *Aristotle*; and the 36 ft yacht *East Wind*, which took owner John Tate seven years to build in the backyard of his home in Davey Street, Hobart, during the mid to late 1960s. Don Muir also designed several commerical fishing boats, including *Hewardia*, which was constructed of steel and built at Dunalley in 1970. Three more fishing boats were built next door to the Muir Marine premises at Battery Point in conjunction with Max Creese's yard. These were the 48 ft steel fishing boat *Hewardia II,* launched in 1973; the 48 ft fibreglass fishing boat *Hewardia,* launched in 1978; and the 45 ft fibreglass fishing boat *Tata*, launched in 1982.

Don Muir died on 29 December 2000 at the age of 74. His wife Ida (nee Savory) died in July of that same year. The couple were survived by their two children Michael and Jacqueline.

Don Muir and his father Ernie at the launch of *Hewardia* in 1978.
Courtesy Jacqueline Muir.

Powercraft Marine production fibreglass runabout (Seabird 600). Courtesy Michael Muir.

Backyard Builders

Backyard boat builders were quite common in Hobart and surrounds during the 20th century. Those that built vessels in the backyards of their homes at Battery Point include Bernie Berkshire, Bert Johnson, Don McAllister, Jack "Turk" Bridge, Henry "Chook" Newman, John "Jack" Hansen and Tom Pilkington.

Born in 1905, **Bernard (Bernie) George Berkshire** was a carpenter by trade who lived at 9 Kelly Street, Battery Point, in the 1930s with his wife Doreen. On 14 December 1935 Bernie launched a 42 ft fishing boat reported to embody the most modern ideas in ship construction. Taking only three months to complete, the vessel was built for Bernie's own use in the backyard of his Battery Point property.

By the late 1930s Bernie Berkshire and his family had moved to Negara Crescent, Goodwood, where several vessels were built in the backyard of their home which backed on to Prince of Wales Bay. These include the cruiser *Colleen* (launched in 1937), the cruiser *Colleen II* (launched in 1946 and later sold to Margaret and Denny King of Port Davey and renamed *Melaleuca*), and the cruiser *Colleen III* (launched in 1951). Bernie Berkshire also built the 45 ft Huon pine fishing boat *Lyndeene* in the backyard of his home at Goodwood. The vessel was launched on 22 February 1947 and built to the order of R. Denne for use in the crayfishing industry.

Born in 1900 and raised in South Street, Battery Point, **Bert Johnson** was a mariner by trade who served on numerous coastal trading vessels including the *Amelia J, Heather Belle* and *SS Zealandia*. He later found employment on engineering and construction projects. During the 1930s and 1940s Bert Johnson lived at 11 Arthur Circus, Battery Point, and from the 1950s at 51 Runnymede Street. In the backyard of these properties during spare hours Bert Johnson built over 40 dinghies which he advertised for sale. The vessels ranged from 8 to 14 ft. Two of the 14 ft dinghies were built to order of the Police Department. A 28 ft and a 40 ft motor boat were also built by Bert Johnson at Battery Point in conjunction with his brother John.

Over his lifetime Bert Johnson was also an avid collector of Tasmanian maritime paraphernalia, amassing over 500 photographs of vessels which he kept on display at his home. Many of these artefacts were later donated to the Maritime Museum of Tasmania of which Bert was a prominent member.

Born in 1912, **Don McAllister** was a plumber by trade and lived at 20 Cromwell Street in Battery Point. He was the brother-in-law of Jock Muir and the uncle of Bill Foster. Remembered for his trade skills and handiwork, over a five-year period during World War II Don McAllister built a 38 ft cruiser in the front yard of his mother's property (12 St Georges Terrace). The vessel, named *Kalua*, was built with assistance from Dave McAllister, Ernie Muir, R. Gibson and B. Taylor and launched at the Hobart wharf on 9 September 1944. A keen sailor, Don McAllister helmed the vessel in the 1946 Sydney to Hobart Yacht Race though was forced to retire owing to a faulty compass.

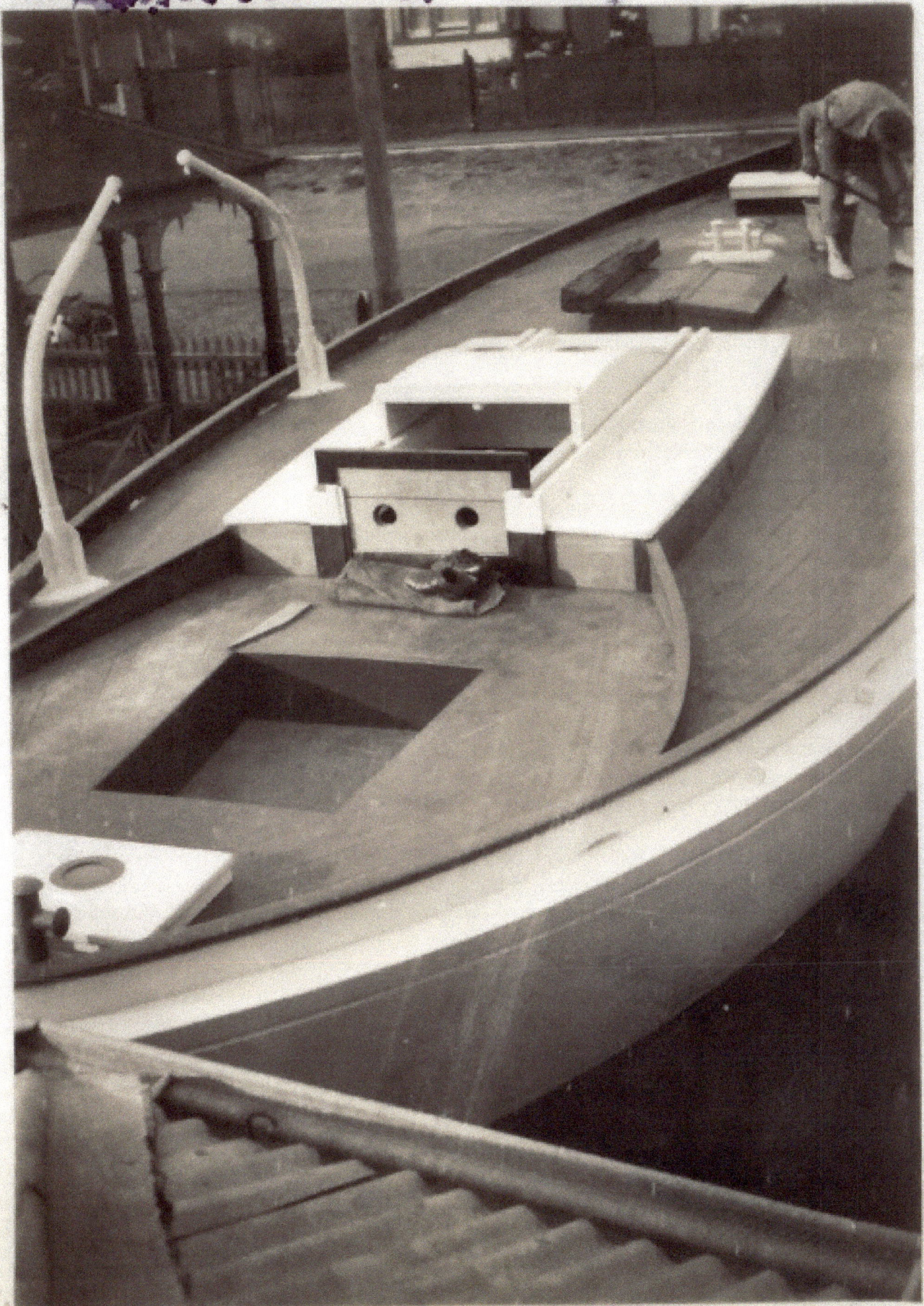

"A BEAUTIFUL CRAFT"

DON MC. ALLISTER

Don McAllister's *Kalua*. Courtesy Jock Muir Family Collection.

Born in 1924, **Jack "Turk" Bridge** lived at 40 Hampden Road, Battery Point, and during World War II served an apprenticeship at the government shipbuilding yard at Prince of Wales Bay, primarily building lifeboats. After the War he worked for Taylor Brothers at Battery Point and in 1951 moved to Max Creese's Battery Point yard where he remained for several decades.

The first vessel Turk Bridge is known to have built was the cadet dinghy *Turk*, launched in early 1944. The vessel was built in the yard of the Fazackerley family's home (9 Colville Street, Battery Point) which backed onto the Bridge's property. Two years later Turk Bridge completed the Derwent class yacht *Janus*, also built in the backyard of the Fazackerley family's Colville Street property. Assistance with the build was provided by John Nimmo, R. Taylor, Chook Newman and A. Ponsonby. *Janus* was launched on 12 October 1946 at the Hobart wharf and Turk Bridge had great success racing the vessel over many seasons.

In 1968 Turk Bridge completed a Dragon class yacht which he called *Janlyn* after his two daughters. The vessel was built in the backyard of his house at Lindisfarne.

Born in 1911, **Henry "Chook" Newman** spent his childhood at Battery Point and in his teenage years sailed model yachts and successfully competed in the newly-established cadet dinghy class. An outstanding helmsman, in 1924 Chook Newman skippered *Mayfly* in the inaugural Stonehaven Cup, held in Hobart, finishing equal first.

After completing school at Albuera Street Primary, Chook Newman served a boat building apprenticeship with Percy Coverdale. He went on to spend his entire career working at the Battery Point boatyards, including for Charlie Lucas, Taylor Brothers and Purdon and Featherstone.

In the late 1940s into the early 1950s Chook Newman had great success competing in the Derwent class and heavyweight sharpie class. He credited his achievements to the knowledge and experience handed down to him by his mentor Harry Batt.

In 1948, while living at 6 Waterloo Crescent, Battery Point, Chook Newman built the heavyweight sharpie *Jaeger*. He also helped Tom Pilkington build the sharpie *Tattler* in 1950. It was in this boat that Chook Newman, Tom Pilkington and Bill Burgess won the state title in 1952 and 1953 and competed nationally over several years.

John "Jack" Hansen was born in Williamstown, Victoria, in 1916, and arrived in Hobart as a teenager following his father's transfer to the Commonwealth Quarantine Service. In 1932 Jack Hansen began a cabinet making apprenticeship with Werner and Vallance. That same year he began crewing on board the B class yacht *Marie Jo*, and was in turn introduced to Skipper and Harry Batt. This meeting led to an invitation to sail on board *Weene*, which Jack Hansen did from 1932 until 1939.

During this period Jack Hansen began work at Purdon and Featherstone. He also found time, in 1937 at Skipper Batt's Battery Point workshop, to build the very successful heavyweight sharpie *Noddy* for Neall Batt. The following year Jack crewed on board *Tassie III* in the Forster Cup. Helmed by Harry Batt and taking place on the Derwent, the vessel went on to win the national event. Then in 1939, with Neall Batt's assistance, Jack Hansen built the cadet dinghy *Gumnut III* for Neall's brother Ken.

In late 1939 Jack Hansen enlisted with the Royal Australian Navy to serve in World War II. As a shipwright he was stationed at the HMAS Cerberus and HMAS Penguin naval bases in Victoria and New South Wales, respectively, and later saw worldwide active service on board the destroyer *HMAS Arunta*.

After the war Jack Hansen returned to Purdon and Featherstone at Battery Point and in 1947 commenced working for Max Creese at a neighbouring yard. With an interest in radio communications developed during the War, in 1950 Jack Hansen began working for Amalgamated Wireless (Australasia) Ltd., holding the position of service manager for 28 years.

Jack Hansen built several smaller craft during his spare time, including the heavyweight sharpie *Skull* for Ediss Boyes, launched in 1954, and the cadet dinghy *Taipan* for David "Jammy" Jones, launched in 1956. Jack was an excellent craftsman and also built many half models, including models of all of the America's Cup yachts. These are on display at the Royal Yacht Club of Tasmania.

Tom Pilkington, formally known as William James Thomas Piety Pilkington, was born on 22 October 1908 at "The Falls," now referred to as Lawitta, near New Norfolk in Tasmania. The Pilkington family had been farmers in the New Norfolk region for several generations. However just prior to World War I, Tom Pilkington moved with his family to Hobart where his father William found employment with Crisp and Gunn.

In October 1923 William Pilkington received permission from the Hobart Marine Board to erect a boat shed at Prince of Wales Bay. The Pilkington family lived nearby, in Lampton Avenue, Glenorchy. In 1924 William Pilkington began competing in local motor boat races in the *Rondee*. That same year he helped establish the Derwent Motor Yacht Club. With 33 members, the opening of the yachting season in October 1924 saw the Derwent Motor Yacht Club participating in manoeuvres. It was the first time a fleet of motor boats from a recognised entity had attended the event.

In October 1927 Tom Pilkington launched his first vessel, the 26 ft Huon pine motor launch *Melrose*, which had been constructed at Prince of Wales Bay over a 12-month period. Around this time Tom also started competing in dinghy races and took up rowing. By 1937 he had built and was competing in the heavyweight sharpie *Tui*. Two years later Tom launched the heavyweight sharpie *Kestrel* in which he competed nationally with Chook Newman and Bill Burgess as his crew. In 1938 Tom joined the Royal Yacht Club of Tasmania, remaining a member for the remainder of his life.

During World War II Tom Pilkington served with the Air Sea Rescue arm of the Royal Australian Air Force, and following his return to Hobart purchased land at 11 Marine Terrace, Battery Point. He worked close by at Purdon and Featherstone while he built a house on the property. A slip and jetty were later added.

In 1950, after an absence of several years from competitive sailing, Tom Pilkington began competing in the heavyweight sharpie *Tattler,* a boat he built in conjunction with Chook Newman and Bill Burgess at his Battery Point property. The vessel was launched in September 1950 and enjoyed success locally and nationally until early 1954 when it was sold to a buyer from South Australia. Next Tom Pilkington sailed *Imp* in the Derwent class.

Though self employed as a builder, in 1951 Tom Pilkington joined the Agricultural Bank of Tasmania and served as a senior building inspector until he retired in 1973. He was particularly proud of his efforts in helping many families rebuild their homes following the disastrous 1967 bush fires.

During the 1950s and 1960s Tom Pilkington built several vessels at his Marine Terrace property. These include the 34 ft Huon pine cruising yacht *Sea Breeze*, launched in 1956, and the 36 ft Huon pine motor sailer *Thomas Piety*, launched in the early 1960s and built for Tom's own use. This particular vessel was used to ferry the Royal family's mail, complete with security guards, to the *Britannia* during Queen Elizabeth II's visit to Hobart in early 1963.

Keen to return to competitive sailing, in 1965 Tom Pilkington built a Dragon class yacht which he also named *Thomas Piety*. Along with Turk Bridge's *Janlyn*, the vessel attended the 1968 Prince Philip Cup in Sydney, thanks to the Union Steam Ships Line providing them with a free passage. Tom continued to be involved in Dragons for many years, including serving (with Max Creese) as an official measurer in 1971 for the World Dragon Championships held in Hobart.

Other vessels built by Tom Pilkington at 11 Marine Terrace include the 38 ft motor sailer *Ruma*, launched in 1972, and the 30 ft strip-planked Huon pine motor boat *Ruby*, launched in 1975. In his eighties Tom also built two unfinished 38 ft cruisers. One was a King Billy diagonal-planked motor launch based on a Max Creese design. The other vessel was later finished by a new owner and named *Pindy Wirra*. In addition, Tom Pilkington built many small boats and dinghies, including a sabot dinghy and international cadet for his children and helped in the design of other vessels.

Tom Pilkington died on 9 June 2000 in Hobart at the age of 91. His son Tom Pilkington (Jr) continues the family's amateur boat building and sailing tradition.

Tattler at the 1953 Australian Sharpie Championship held in Perth.
Courtesy Ruby Pilkington.

Top: *Thomas Piety* under sail.
Bottom left: Tom Pilkington and Max Creese measuring Dragon yachts in 1971.
Bottom right: Tom Pilkington measuring a Dragon yacht in 1971.
All photos courtesy Ruby Pilkington.

Additional Vessels Built at Battery Point (1900 – 1980s).

1900. *Fairlie II.* **Yacht.** 37.5 x 8.6 x 5 ft. Built by Robert Inches to the order of F. N. Clarke based on a William Fife (Jr) design. Purchased by a local syndicate (Sharp and Company) in 1902, and several years later by Young, Dart and Mason. By 1912 purchased by a Mr Jameson of Westernport and transferred to VIC. Sailed out of the St Kilda Yacht Club, VIC, in the 1920s and 1930s. By the early 1940s, transferred to Sydney. Still in existence. Currently in Pittwater, NSW.

1900. *Swift.* **Ketch.** 53.4 x 15.4 x 4.7 ft. Built by Robert Inches to the order of T. and J. Underwood of North West Bay. Designed by Tom Purdon. Involved in the Huon and Channel trade. Wrecked off Cape Queen Elizabeth, Bruny Island, TAS, on 13 November 1935; all hands saved. At the time registered to Herbert Sward.

1901. *Oceana (Makira).* **Oil launch.** 53.5 x 10.5 x 5.5 ft. Built and designed by Robert Inches to the order of J. C. Kemsley of the Tasmanian Timber Corporation. Used in association with the company's Huon-based timber mill. Registered to Francis Rigby of Hobart in January 1912 as *Makira*. Transferred to NSW two months later. Purchased by Justus Scharff for the Solomon Island trade. In 1918 abandoned as unseaworthy and sold off in pieces at San Crostoval, Solomon Islands.

1901. *Olive.* **Ketch.** 49.2 x 14.1 x 4.1 ft. Built by Robert Inches to the order of Auguste Nickel of Long Bay (now Middleton). Involved in the Huon and Channel trade. Subsequent owners include the Pybus, Sward and Heatley families. Later converted to a fishing vessel and transferred to NSW, and following to Papua New Guinea.

1902. *Fairlie III (Nanoya).* **Yacht.** 40 x 11.4 x 4.5 ft. Built by Robert Inches to the order of F. N. Clarke based on a William Fife (Jr) design. Sold to W. A. Jorden of Hobart in 1904 and in mid-1905 to Tom Marshall of Sydney, NSW. Renamed *Nanoya* and spent several decades operating out of the Royal Prince Alfred Yacht Club. Several changes of owners and locations followed. Sailed to Europe in the late 1960s. Still in existence; currently located in Italy having been extensively restored.

1902. *Aristides.* **Ketch.** 80 x 21.9 x 7.1 ft. Built by Robert Kennedy and Sons for their own use. Employed in interstate trade. Purchased by the SA government in 1910. Subsequently purchased by Tom Spaulding and returned to TAS in 1929. Wrecked at Three Hummock Island, Bass Strait, in January 1940; all hands saved.

1903. *Dauntless.* **Cutter.** 53 x 16 x 6 ft. Built and designed by Robert Inches to the order of Alex McKay. Involved in the river trade. Later converted to a fishing vessel and owned by the Rattenbury family. Wrecked at the entrance to Port Arthur, TAS, on 27 April 1949; all hands saved. At the time owned by W. Spaulding of Dunalley.

1906. *Wietenah.* **Oil launch.** 40 x 8 x 4.5 ft. Built by J. Dent to the order of the Hobart Marine Board for use at one of its pilot stations.

1912. *Excella.* **Motor ferry.** 115 x 20 x 8.5 ft. Built by John Dalgleish and Sons at the Kennedy family's yard. Built to the order of James Rowe and Sons. Designed by Walter Reeks. Purchased by the Cygnet Steamship Company Ltd. in 1919. Remained in service up until the 1960s. Broken up in the 1990s.

1913. *Rosny.* **Steam ferry.** 110 x 26 x 10 ft. Built by Fred Moore at the Kennedy family's yard. Built to the order of the Rosny Estates and Ferry Company. By 1919 employed on Port Phillip Bay, VIC. Purchased by O'May Brothers in 1931 for use on the River Derwent. Later sold and moved to Launceston. Sunk while moored on the Tamar River, TAS, in July 1964.

1919. *Amelia J.* **Schooner.** 153 x 30.5 x 14.2 ft. Built by Henry Moore at the Kennedy family's yard. Designed by Tom Purdon. Built to the order of Henry Jones and Company and intended for interstate trade. Went missing in August 1920 en route to Hobart from Newcastle, NSW, on her second voyage. No survivors.

1920s - 1950s. Dinghies (40). 8 - 14 ft. Built by Bert Johnson at 11 Arthur Circus and later at 51 Runnymede Street, Battery Point. Two of the 14 ft dinghies were built to the order of the Tasmanian Police Department.

1926. Motor boat. 28 ft. Built by Bert Johnson and his brother John at 11 Arthur Circus, Battery Point.

1930s. Motor boat. 40 ft. Built by Bert Johnson and his brother John at 11 Arthur Circus, Battery Point.

1935. Fishing boat. 42 x 11 x 6 ft. Built by Bernie Berkshire in the backyard of his home at 9 Kelly Street, Battery Point. Launched at the Hobart wharf on 14 December 1935.

1944. *Turk.* **Cadet dinghy.** 12 x 5 ft x 14 in. Built by Jack "Turk" Bridge in the backyard of 9 Colville Street, Battery Point (Tas Fazackerley's house). First noted on the River Derwent in March 1944. Advertised for sale in May 1948. By 1951 owned by R. A. Johnson, by 1952 owned by N. R. Johnston. Advertised for sale in March 1953.

1944. *Kalua.* **Cruiser.** 38 ft. Built by Don McAllister over a five-year period in the front yard of his mother's Battery Point home (12 St Georges Terrace). Originally intended as a fishing vessel and based on a Norwegian design, launched on 9 September 1944. Competed in the 1946 Sydney to Hobart Yacht Race, though forced to retire owing to a faulty compass. In December 1948 sailed to Sydney, NSW, and advertised for sale. Purchased by John Tennant. Advertised for sale in November 1949 and sailed to Auckland, NZ, in April 1950. Later transferred to Hawaii, USA. Still in existence; owned by Juha Sironen and based in French Polynesia.

1946. *Janus.* **Yacht.** 24.5 x 6.7 x 4 ft. Derwent class yacht built in the backyard of 9 Colville Street (Tas Fazackerley's house) by Jack "Turk" Bridge. Assistance provided by John Nimmo, R. Taylor, Henry "Chook" Newman and A. Ponsonby. Launched on 12 October 1946 at the Hobart wharf. By the 1960s owned by P. C. Fuglsang; by the mid-1970s owned by A. A. Masters and R. C. Denholm, and subsequently by D. Gumley. In the 1980s owned by R. Farrington, and in the 1990s owned by W. J. Hodgman. Still in existence; located at Kettering, TAS.

1946. *Diana.* **Trawler.** 65 x 17 ft. Built by Fred Saunders and launched on 17 September 1946 from the Battery Point yard previously owned by Tucker Abel. Built to the order of Tasmanian Trawlers Pty. Ltd. and intended for coastal and Bass Strait fishing.

Additional Vessels Built at Battery Point (1900 – 1980s).

1947. *Frela*. Ketch. 85 x 19 x 8.5 ft. Built and designed by Fred Saunders. Launched on 29 December 1947 from the Battery Point yard previously owned by Tucker Abel. Luxuriously appointed, all-welded steel construction. Intended for the fishing trade, though by 1948 involved in the tourist trade. Sailed to the mainland in June 1949, spending several months sailing the Whitsunday Islands, QLD. Transferred to Sydney, NSW, and sold to the US government in April 1951 for use as a training ship in the Marshall Islands and Micronesia. Still noted to be in Micronesia in the late 1950s.

1948. *Jaeger*. Heavyweight sharpie. 19.6 ft. First noted on the River Derwent in October 1948, owned and helmed by her builder Henry "Chook" Newman. Represented TAS in the 1949 Australian Sharpie Championship held in Adelaide. Advertised for sale in April 1949 and in August 1949. By late 1949 owned by Neil Campbell and sailed by Dick Ikin. By 1951 owned by B. Balfe; by 1961 owned by P. Gee of Launceston.

1950. *Tattler*. Heavyweight sharpie. 19.6 ft. Built by Tom Pilkington at 11 Marine Terrace with assistance from Henry "Chook" Newman and Bill Burgess. Launched in September 1950. Helmed by Henry "Chook" Newman, represented TAS in the 1951 Australian Sharpie Championship held in Brisbane, the 1952 Australian Sharpie Championship held in Melbourne, the 1953 Australian Sharpie Championship held in Perth (finishing 2nd) and the 1954 Australian Sharpie Championship held in Sydney. Sold to R. Northey of Semaphore, SA, in February 1954. By 1958 owned by P. O. Cummings.

1952. *Shamrock*. Yacht. H28 class yacht. Built for Robert Davies by two cabinet makers under the watchful eye of Jock Muir. Completed and fitted out at Max Creese's Battery Point yard. Owned by J. Stuart in 1954. Currently located at the Hobsons Bay Yacht Club, VIC. Advertised for sale in July 2016.

1953. *Sabre*. Heavyweight sharpie. 19.6 ft. Built by Don Muir for his own use. First raced on the River Derwent in October 1953. Represented TAS in the 1954 Australian Sharpie Championship held in Sydney. Represented TAS in the 1955 Australian Sharpie Championship held in Adelaide. Still in existence, owned by Gordon Stewart and located in southern TAS.

1954. *Scull*. Heavyweight sharpie. 19.6 ft. Built by Jack Hansen to the order of Ediss Boyes who represented TAS in the 1956 Sharpie Championship held in Hobart, finishing 2nd. By 1961 owned by R. D. and W. R. Kilby.

1956. *Sea Breeze*. Yacht. 34 ft. Huon pine. Built by Tom Pilkington at 11 Marine Terrace. Transferred to Devonport, TAS, in October 1959.

1956. *Taipan (C. S. Burton)*. Cadet dinghy. 12 x 5 ft x 14 in. Built by Jack Hansen to the order of David "Jammy" Jones. Won the 1960 Stonehaven Cup. By 1961 owned by the Marsland family. Purchased by the Royal Yacht Club of Tasmania, likely in the late 1960s, and renamed *C. S. Burton*. In the early 1970s, sailed by Chris McIndoe.

1962. *Thomas Piety (Charlotte Rose)*. Motor sailer. 36 ft. Huon pine. Built by Tom Pilkington at 11 Marine Terrace for his own use. Later sold to the Peterswalds and renamed *Charlotte Rose*, then sold to Neil Batt and transferred to Melbourne. Still in existence, returned to Hobart in the early 1990s by owner Graham Gale.

1962. *Acacia*. Motor launch. 25 ft. Built by George, David, Peter and Frank Makepeace at 2 Clarke Avenue. Designed by Jock Muir. Still in existence; located at Kettering, TAS.

1965. *Thomas Piety (Gabriola, Quintessa, Gabriola II, Kylara)*. Yacht. 29.2 x 6.4 ft. Dragon class yacht built by Tom Pilkington at 11 Marine Terrace. Competed in the 1968 Prince Philip Cup held in Sydney. By 1970 owned by E. Pyke; by 1974 owned by B. E. Simpson; by 1979 owned by B. Freeman; by 1980 owned by Tom Loney; by 1990 owned by P. J. Hubbard; by 1992 owned by G. Pusta, P. Davis and K. Davis.

1967. *Bradypus*. Ketch. 35 ft. Cutter-rigged ketch built by Bruce Thompson at Gladstone Street, Battery Point and fitted out at Max Creese's yard. Designed by Charles Wittholz. Purchased by Caroline Langley and Rhondda Haldane in 1994.

1960s. Dinghy. Sabot dinghy built by Tom Pilkington at 11 Marine Terrace for his children.

1960s. Dinghy. International cadet dinghy built by Tom Pilkington at 11 Marine Terrace for his children.

1972. *Ruma (Canopus, Van Dieman)*. Motor sailer. 38 x 11 ft. Built by Tom Pilkington at 11 Marine Terrace to a Max Creese design. Sold in late 1974 to Professor Ellis and renamed *Canopus*. Initially moored off Sandy Bay then moved to Kettering. Later transferred to the Gold Coast, QLD, then to Sydney, NSW, and renamed *Van Dieman*. Still in existence; owned by Ron Kelly of Eden, NSW.

1975. *Ruby*. Motor boat. 30 ft. Huon pine. Built by Tom Pilkington at 11 Marine Terrace for his own use. Later sold. Still in existence; believed to be moored in Lindisfarne Bay.

1980s. Motor Cruiser. 38 ft. King Billy. Built by Tom Pilkington at 11 Marine Terrace though unfinished. Designed by Max Creese. Later sold to Max Smith of the Huon though remained unfinished. Eventually purchased by an ex-employee of Max Creese's and completed over a number of years.

1980s. *Pindy Wira*. Motor cruiser. 38 ft. Built by Tom Pilkington at 11 Marine Terrace though unfinished. Later sold and completed. Owned by Ross and Anita Petterd and sailed out of Kettering. Still in existence; owned by S. Youl and located in Hobart.

Janus. Courtesy Lynne Triffett.

Employees

In writing the history of Battery Point's 20th century boat builders and yards, it would be remiss not to include a list of employees. These men worked tirelessly, crafting boats with their hands often under adverse weather conditions. The hours were long and the work was hard. Machines were mostly non-existent. A typical yacht of 45 ft, for example, fully-rigged and ready for sea, took about 15,000 man hours to build, equivalent to seven men employed full-time for a year. The cyclical nature of the industry itself, where demand for boats peaked and declined over the decades, also meant that employees were often not certain of permanent, full-time work. Still these men persisted, and the outstanding quality of their work survives today, particularly in those vessels that are still in their prime. Though likely missing many names, the men and women who were employed at each of the Battery Point yards (and associated businesses) during the 20th century are acknowledged here.

Tucker Abel

Thomas Abel
Jack Abel

Percy Coverdale

Noel Bassett
Fred Coverdale
Jack Hansen
Henry "Chook" Newman
Max Muir
Athol Taylor

Max Creese

Jack "Turk" Bridge
Mike Burrows
George Burrows
Ron Crawford
Peter Creese
Warren Cripps
James Dewing
Brian Freeman
Jack Hansen
A. Kemp
Ray Kemp
Peter Keyes
Norman King
Shane Lansdell
Robert Laughlin
John Lucas
Bill McGuinness
Darryl Ridgeway
Barry Wilson

Bill Foster

Nil

Charlie Lucas

Ivar "Chips" Gronfors
Henry "Chook" Newman
F. Oldham
R. W. R. "Mick" Smith
Athol Taylor

Robert Inches

Fred Coverdale
Percy Coverdale
Charlie Lucas

William Lucas

Percy Coverdale
George Williams

Top: Fred Moore and employees involved in construction of the *Rosny*.
Courtesy *Illustrated Tasmanian Mail*, 31 July 1913.
Bottom: Purdon and Featherstone employees involved in construction of the *Cartela*.
Courtesy *Illustrated Tasmanian Mail*, 26 September 1912.

Jock Muir/Muir Boatyard

Alan Aitchison
Kevin "Ginger" Argent*
Hugh Auld
Ian Brett
Adam Brinton
Don Brown
George Burrows
Tony Chamberlain
John Champion
Peter Clarke
Alan Cracknell
Owen Cropp
Bruce Darcey
Adrian Dean
Fred Dennis
George Dingle
Mick Earl
Brett Evans
Malcolm Fergusson
Bill Foster
Graham Freeman
Alex Goodfellow
Jeff Gordon
Adrian Gorringe
Craig Grainger
George Grainger
Bruce Griggs
Jim Groves
Les Haines
Mike Igglesden
Rodney Jackman
Ray Kemp
Peter Keyes
Graham Mortyn
Eddie Mossop
Don Muir
John Muir
Max Muir
Ross Muir
Wally Muir
Alan Norman
Phil Poh
Andrew Price
Doug Russell

David Ryder Turner
Gary Smedley
Gordon Stewart*
Dave Wardrop
Rodney Watson
Duncan Wood
Lindsay Woods*
Paul Zuese
* Leaseholder

Muir's Chandlery**

Carol Ally
Faye Boon
Lionel Boon
Lyn Denehey
Peter James
Brad Knight
Bill Mills
Ross Muir
Tony Shearman
Graham Taylor
Robyn Wisby
**Purchased by Richard and Edward Fader.

Muir Diesel Services/Muir Engineering

Nick Fleming
Glen Gleeson
Bob Harper
Chris Michael
John Muir
Wendy Muir
Brett Ross
Brian Spencer

Muir Marine/Powercraft Marine

Frank Conway	Michael Muir
Simon Jennings	John Phillips
Gilbert McAllister	Alan Riley
Adrian McNally	James Searle
Don Muir	Rod Sherrin
Jacqueline Muir	Howard Stevens

Muir's Sail Loft

Craig Fox
Michael Cooper
Richard Goodfellow
Michael Grainger
Peter Jones

Purdon Brothers

Alan Aitcheson
Bill Barrow
Gordon Cherry
George Grainger
Michael Grainger
Ross Muir
Mick Purdon
Sam Purdon

Purdon and Featherstone

Hugh Auld
John Bennetto
Alfred Blore
Clyde Cannell
Gordon Cherry
R. Clark
Alan Cochrane
Max Creese
Bob Dodd
Edward Edwards
Clyde Featherstone
Henry Featherstone
Keith Featherstone
Richard Featherstone
Ray Freeman
Tony Gunton
John Harrod
M. Jackson
Eric Jacobson
Alan Johnson
O. Kalbfell
John Lucas
Alan Irvin

Rick Ivessa
Wally Murphy
George Neave
Geoff Maddock
Dave McAllister
Max Muir
Henry "Chook" Newman
Don Norton
Ken Owens
Robert Peacock
T. Phillips
Tom Pilkington
Ernest Purdon
Tom Purdon
Alex Quinn
Bert Quinto
G. Radford
Bruce Reynolds
Nick Rogers
Doug Russell
Les Schram
Charlie Scott
Geoff Seabrook
Bob Silberberg
R. W. R. "Mick" Smith
Wally Tame
Norm Taylor
Barry Wagner
G. Walter
Alan Whitton
Arthur Williams
Tom Williams

Taylor Brothers

William Bourn
Jack "Turk" Bridge
Graham Crowther
Ben D'Andrea
Gary Ellis
August Fuschberger
Peter Glover
Alex Goodfellow
Alan Haas
Paul Hornburg
Thomas Howell

Stewart Ims
Gareth John
Dean Khan
Michael Land
Charlie Lucas
Heather Mahoney
Trevor Manoel
Andrew McAllister
Alan McDonald
Adam McLea
Ivan Moy
Henry "Chook" Newman
Michael O'Brien
Sam Purdon
Martin Racket
John Rolls
Andrew Sampson
Bob Silberberg
R. W. R. "Mick" Smith
Athol Taylor
Donna Taylor
Geoff Taylor
Gregory Taylor
Jan Taylor
Norman Taylor
Phillip Taylor
Michael Winfield

Yacht Distributors

Lynette Denehey
Tim Jones
Theresa Kley
Tim Lovett
Greg Muir
Susan Muir
David Reeve
Duncan Wood

Synopsis

During the 20th century more than 12 commerical boat building yards were in operation along the Napoleon Street corridor of Battery Point. Combined, hundreds of men and women were employed and thousands of vessels were constructed. In addition to the building of new vessels, the yards were actively employed in the slipping, repair, refit, alteration, survey and/or overhaul of vessels. The 20th century also saw interstate delivery trips being made by boat builders, opening up another aspect of their businesses. All told, the waterfront area was a hive of activity and industry.

More than 470 wooden vessels are documented to have been built at Battery Point during the 20th century, including over 115 yachts; 70 motor launches, motor boats and motor cruisers; 44 fishing boats; 29 heavyweight and lightweight sharpies, 25 ketches; 22 cadet dinghies; 11 steam and motor driven ferries; and four schooners. Also manufactured were more than 3,000 fibreglass dinghies, 250 aluminium dinghies and ten fibreglass runabouts.

Regrettably many of the smaller vessels are likely not included in this tally. In general, tenders, punts, dinghies and lifeboats, et cetera, were not required to be registered nor were they routinely mentioned in the press. Thus estimates of the number of smaller vessels built at Battery Point during the 20th century are likely to be extremely conservative compared to the true number of boats built.

Of the larger vessels, the 153 ft schooner *Amelia J*, built by Henry Moore at Kennedy's shipyard, has the honour of being the longest vessel constructed at Battery Point during the 20th century. Launched in August 1919 to the order of Henry Jones and Company, the *Amelia J* was sadly lost, along with her crew, a year later while en route to Tasmania from New South Wales. Interestingly, the largest vessel constructed at Battery Point, in terms of tonnage, remains the 562 ton *Tasman*, built by Peter Degraves at a shipyard near the present day bottom of Finlay Street. Launched in 1847, it was Degraves' intention to build the largest vessel yet constructed in Tasmania. 170 years later, he still holds the record for the largest vessel built at Battery Point.

Like any industry there were peaks and troughs; influenced by the economy, world wars and advances in new technologies. Though World War I and the years immediately following saw a lot of vessels installed with auxiliary engines, they were lean years in terms of new commercial builds. The decline in the building of commercial vessels continued into the 1930s, coinciding with the Depression, with road transport becoming increasingly competitive, and Tasmania's timber trade suffering a downturn. During this period many ketches were converted to fishing vessels. The building of yachts, however, to compete in local and regional races and regattas continued, as did the building of recreational motor boats, launches and cruisers. The boat builders were also buoyed by Tasmania's successes at the Forster Cup for 21 ft restricted class vessels and the Stonehaven Cup for cadet dinghies.

The 1930s, and the many decades that followed, saw Battery Point's boat builders augment their income with delivery trips, particularly of vessels to and from the mainland. These journeys allowed the likes of Percy Coverdale, Jock Muir, Max Creese, amongst others, to become some of the country's most experienced deep-water helmsmen.

The onset of World War II resulted in many of Battery Point's boat builders involved in war efforts, either deployed overseas or working at Purdon and Featherstone. The period coincided with a diversification in the type of vessels built, including harbour defence patrol launches and sea ambulances, the first of their kind to be built in Australia.

The 1940s through to the 1970s saw several of Battery Point's boat builders become national leaders in the building of cruising yachts, including for state, national and international blue water races like the Maria Island Ocean Race, the Sydney to Hobart Yacht Race, the One Ton Cup, the Admiral's Cup and the Trans-Tasman Race. Up until this point, Australia's longest ocean race was the Royal Yacht Club of Tasmania's Bruny Island race. Not only did Battery Point's boat builders participate in and, in many cases win these events, but the opportunity also gave them a chance to showcase their designs, their craftmanship and themselves to national and international audiences. Their successes led to new orders from new customers, particularly from the mainland.

It was not all smooth sailing, however. In 1951 the federal government's overnight increase of the sales tax on boats from 10 to 33 per cent had a major impact on the boat building industry at Battery Point and across the country. Though later reduced, the short-sighted gain in the federal tax base led to a long-term decline in the industry. Those yards that survived had to become innovative and flexible. In 1952 Jock Muir installed a new slipway, thereby providing an additional source of income for his yard. Over 60 years later the slip is still in operation, as is Taylor Brothers' slip.

The post-1950 period saw Battery Point's boat builders continue to diversify the types of vessels they built and the projects they took on. Jock Muir and Max Creese complemented their yacht building efforts by building commerical fishing boats and designing vessels to be built elsewhere. Rainbows, cadet dinghies and sharpies were also built for their own children and other youngsters eager to take to the water. Taylor Brothers moved on to other projects, fostering the company's diversification into local engineering and construction activities.

The 20th century also saw the evolution of the craft of boat building and the way in which boats were built, including at Battery Point, spurred by the advent of power tools and other advances in technology, as well as with new types of materials such as fibreglass, resins, plastics, steel, aluminium and plywood. At one yard or another, these new ideas were tried and tested, and in many situations proved a success.

All told, over 180 years since the first commercial shipyard was established at Battery Point, several of the area's boatyards remain in active operation. These stand testament to the extraordinary amount of innovation, high degree of craftmanship and sheer passion of the workers whose hands have collectively built thousands of vessels, and whose sweat and dogged achievements are personified in the many vessels that today ply the rivers and coastal corridors of Tasmania, Australia and beyond. These are vessels that are beloved by their owners, custodians of a tangible fragment of our maritime history.

Crescent

Colville St

Trumpeter St

Marine Terrace

Sloane St

Derwent Ln

Cromwell St

Napoleon St

Terrace

Battery Point Boat and Ship Builders (1830s - 2000s)

Tom Pilkington (1946 - 2000)

Mackay and Cullen (1851 - 1870)
James and David Mackay (1870 - 1878)
James Mackay (1878 - 1890s)
James Mackey and Henry Featherstone (1890s - 1902)
Purdon and Featherstone (1903 - 1973)
Bayes Brothers (1907 - 1916, 1920s)
Neave Brothers (1920s)

Purdon Brothers (1951 - 1962)

Jacob Chandler and family (1847 - 1908)
Tom Purdon and family (1910s - 1937)
Royal Yacht Club of Tasmania (1937 - 1962)
Purdon Brothers (1962 - 1984)

Joseph Risby (1846 - 1858)
Charles Miller (1858 - 1889)
Joseph Clinch (1889 - 1895)
Tucker Abel (1897 - 1938)
Fred Saunders (1946 - 1947)
Max Creese (1948 - 1990)

Remains of John Ross' patent slip

John Ross (1865 - 1871)
John Lucas (1872 - 1884)
Robert Kennedy & Sons (1885 - 1923)
John Dalgleish (1912)
Fred Moore (1913)
Henry Moore (1919)
Muir Marine/Powercraft Marine (1966 - 2000s)

Jock Muir (1948 - 1987)
Muir Boatyard (1987 - present)

John Watson (1839 - 1856)
John Lucas (1856 - 1872)
John Bradley (1872 - 1875)
William Tilley (1880 - 1890)
Charlie Lucas (1899 - 1936)
Taylor Brothers (1936 - present)

Robert Inches (1880 - 1904)
William Lucas (1904 - 1914)
Percy Coverdale (1914 - 1963)
Bill Foster (1963 - 1968)

Batt family (1870 - 1970s)

Finlay Street
William Williamson (1835 - 1848)
Peter Degraves (1846 - 1853)
John Watson (1848 - 1851)
John Ross (1851 - 1865)
Whitehouse Brothers (1874 - 1883)
Lark Macquarie (1875 - 1885)
William Bayes (1880 - 1896)

Still Going Strong

Of the more than 470 wooden vessels documented to have been built at Battery Point during the 20th century, significantly over 115 are still in existence. These vessels stand as a testament to the quality and craftmanship of their builders, as well as the passion and commitment of their custodians.

~~~~~~

While many vessels built at Battery Point have journeyed beyond the waters of the River Derwent, thankfully there exists a yearn by owners to bring these boats back to their native place. The journey from Perth, Western Australia, made by the Charlie Lucas-built one-design yacht *Canobie*, for example, to participate in the 2017 Australian Wooden Boat Festival, is a tribute to her owner Owen Stacy. The recent transfer of the Percy Coverdale-built yacht *Chloe* back to southern Tasmania from Sydney marks another notch in the motivation of vessel owners to return these vessels home. The celebrated 21 ft restricted class yacht *Tassie Too*, built by Charlie Lucas and Chips Gronfors in 1927, made a triumphant return to the Royal Yacht Club of Tasmania in September 2017 after many decades spent in Melbourne.

Mike Strong, owner of the Percy Coverdale built *Landfall*, is another example of a passionate and committed vessel owner. Of his yacht's journey up the River Derwent in the final stage of the 2016 Sydney to Hobart Yacht Race, Mike said that he deliberately chose to sail up the western side of the river though it was not the quickest way to the finish line. Instead, he felt a sense of bringing his beloved yacht home and that a sail past the Battery Point boatyards, where *Landfall* had been launched 81 years prior, was a necessary step towards completing the event.

Whether for a visit or more permanently it is a credit to the drive, energy and passion of these owners to return the vessels to the Derwent. Moreover, with the advent of social media, and the staging of wonderful events such as the Australian Wooden Boat Festival in Hobart, the connections between past and present owners, past and present boat builders, and Tasmania's and Australia's maritime history more generally, are only being strengthened.

I would like to thank members of the "Battery Point Boat and Ships" Facebook group in helping develop the following list of 20th century Battery Point built vessels still in existence, particularly Graeme Broxam, Colin Grazules and Greg Muir. I would also welcome any updates or additions. These can emailed to: nicmays@gmail.com

"Every boat had its own soul, even those with almost the same specifications".

Jock Muir (*Maritime Reflections*).

Year	Name	Type	Builder	Location
1899	Caprice	Yacht	Charlie Lucas	Sydney, NSW
1900	Fairlie II	Yacht	Robert Inches	Sydney, NSW
1902	Fairlie III (Nanoya)	Yacht	Robert Inches	Italy
1904	Diamond	Yacht	Charlie Lucas	Northern TAS
1905	Palmer	Motor launch	Charlie Lucas	Gippsland Lakes, VIC
1906	Florence May	Yacht	Percy Coverdale	Southern TAS
1910	Aone	Fishing boat	Charlie Lucas	Northern TAS
1910	Eva Blanche	Motor launch	Tucker Abel	Southern TAS
1910	Pandora	Yacht	Charlie Lucas	Southern TAS
1910	Spindrift (Weene)	Yacht	Charlie Lucas	Sydney, NSW
1911	Curlew (Culwulla IV)	Yacht	Charlie Lucas	QLD
1911	Gannet	Yacht	Charlie Lucas	Sydney, NSW
1911	Vanity	Yacht	Charlie Lucas	Southern TAS
1912	Brooke	Motor launch	Ernest Bayes	Southern TAS
1912	Canobie	Yacht	Charlie Lucas	Perth, WA
1912	Cartela	Steam ferry	Purdon & Featherstone	Southern TAS
1912	Risdon (Kyeema)	Motor boat	Charlie Lucas	Southern TAS
1913	Sealark	Motor boat	Charlie Lucas	Southern TAS
1914	Hermione III	Motor launch	Charlie Lucas	Queenscliff, VIC
1914	Waterloo	Motor launch	Tucker Abel	Northern TAS
1915	Curlew	Fishing boat	Charlie Lucas	Southern TAS
1915	Tuna	Motor boat	Percy Coverdale	Southern TAS
1915	Vera	Motor launch	Tucker Abel	Southern TAS
1916	Ethel (Diane B)	Fishing boat	Charlie Lucas	Southern TAS
1917	Rowella (Nancy)	Motor launch	Tucker Abel	Southern TAS
1919	Diana (Rata, Bronzewing)	Yacht	Charlie Lucas	NSW
1922	Grayling	Yacht	Thomas Neave	Southern TAS
1923	Eveline May (Premier)	Ketch	Percy Coverdale	Southern TAS
1924	Latura	Motor boat	Ernest Bayes	Southern TAS
1925	Moani	Motor boat	Charlie Lucas	Sydney, NSW
1925	Storm Bay	Fishing boat	Percy Coverdale	Sorrento, VIC
1927	Tanda (Esmeralda, Lady Margaret)	Motor cruiser	Percy Coverdale	Gippsland Lakes, VIC
1927	Tassie Too	Yacht	Charlie Lucas	Southern TAS
1928	Allara (Aralla)	Patrol boat	Thomas Neave	QLD
1928	Gnome	Yacht	Percy Coverdale	Southern TAS
1928	Pixie	Yacht	Percy Coverdale	Northern TAS
1929	Anitra	Yacht	Charlie Lucas	Southern TAS
1929	Wanderer	Motor boat	Charlie Lucas	Southern TAS
1929	Windward (Windward II)	Yacht	Percy Coverdale	Melbourne, VIC
1930	Elfin	Yacht	Taylor Brothers	Southern TAS
1930	Margaret	Yacht	Charlie Lucas	Southern TAS
1931	Ninie	Yacht	Percy Coverdale	Southern TAS
1932	Adina (Seawind, Maskee)	Yacht	Percy Coverdale	Perth, WA
1934	Sjo-Ro	Yacht	Percy Coverdale	Sydney, NSW
1935	Landfall	Yacht	Percy Coverdale	Sydney, NSW
1936	Saona	Yacht	Charlie Lucas	Southern TAS
1937	Westwind	Ketch	Jock Muir	Cairns, QLD
1938	Chloe	Yacht	Percy Coverdale	Southern TAS

Weene on Sydney Harbour.
Courtesy Ben Stoner.

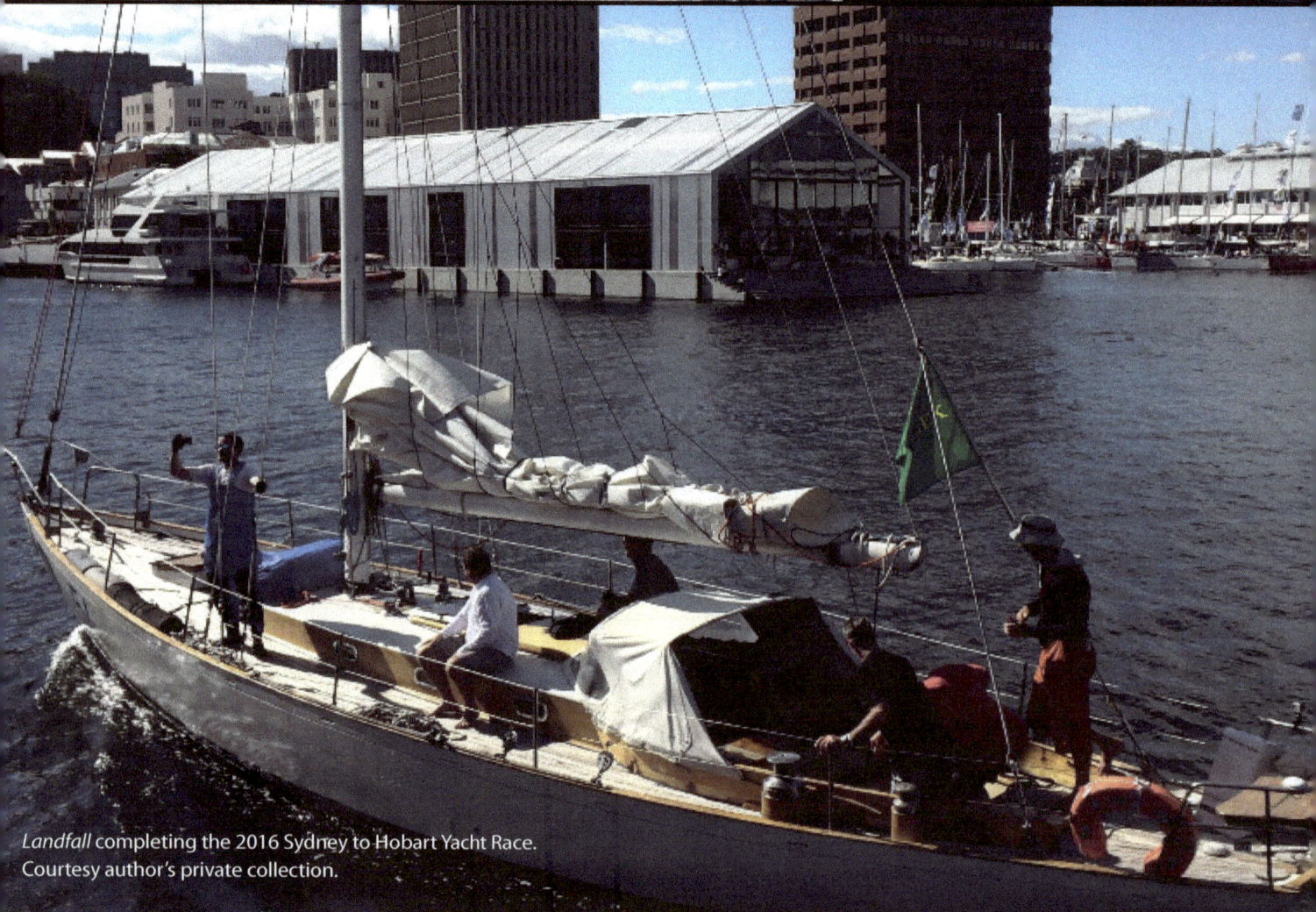

Landfall completing the 2016 Sydney to Hobart Yacht Race.
Courtesy author's private collection.

Year	Name	Type	Builder	Location
1938	Lewan	Yacht	Percy Coverdale	Wangaratta, VIC
1938	Sirocco	Yacht	Taylor Brothers	Southern TAS
1939	Toute Suite	Dinghy	Skipper Batt	Southern TAS
1939	Gumnut III	Cadet dinghy	Skipper Batt	Southern TAS
1941	Egeria	Motor launch	Purdon & Featherstone	Southern TAS
1943	HMAS HDML 1321 (Rushcutter)	Patrol launch	Purdon & Featherstone	Darwin, NT
1944	Kalua	Cruiser	Don McAllister	French Polynesia
1946	Ben Boyd (Ronnell)	Fishing boat	Taylor Brothers	Northern TAS
1946	Janus	Yacht	Jack "Turk" Bridge	Southern TAS
1946	Novar	Rowing boat	Percy Coverdale	Gippsland Lakes, VIC
1947	Awittaka	Motor launch	Purdon & Featherstone	Southern TAS
1947	Westward	Yacht	Jock Muir	Southern TAS
1948	Lass O'Luss	Yacht	Jock Muir	Sydney, NSW
1948	Sandra	Yacht	Max Creese	Sydney, NSW
1948	White Cloud	Yacht	Percy Coverdale	Florida, USA
1948	Yleena	Yacht	Purdon & Featherstone	Southern TAS
1949	Erica J	Yacht	Max Creese	UK
1950	Patsy (Patsy of Island Bay)	Yacht	Jock Muir	Sydney, NSW
1950	Skimmer	Sharpie	Bill Foster & Don Muir	Southern TAS
1950	Snowgoose	Yacht	Max Creese	Melbourne, VIC
1951	Jason	Yacht	Purdon & Featherstone	QLD
1951	Lahara	Yacht	Jock Muir	Sydney, NSW
1951	Terra Nova	Yacht	Max Creese	Lakes Entrance, VIC
1952	Shamrock	Yacht	?	Melbourne, VIC
1952	Van Diemen	Ketch	Jock Muir	Sydney, NSW
1953	Frayja (Sailmaker)	Ketch	Percy Coverdale	Sydney, NSW
1953	Sabre	Sharpie	Don Muir	Southern TAS
1954	J Lee M	Motor launch	Jim Jones/Jock Muir	Southern TAS
1955	Mistral VI	Yacht	Jock Muir	Southern TAS
1956	Captain Mackenzie	Pilot launch	Jock Muir	VIC
1958	James Mackey	Workboat	Purdon & Featherstone	Southern TAS
1958	Molly Ann	Yacht	Max Creese	Southern TAS
1958	Maris	Yacht	Jock Muir	Sydney, NSW
1958	Sandra II	Yacht	Max Creese	Gippsland Lakes, VIC
1959	Jabiru II	Sharpie	Purdon Brothers	Southern TAS
1950s	Chloe II	Open boat	Percy Coverdale	Southern TAS
1960	Seaman (Seaman of Pittwater)	Yacht	Max Creese	Sydney, NSW
1962	Acacia	Motor launch	Makepeace family	Southern TAS
1962	Thomas Piety (Charlotte Rose)	Motor sailer	Tom Pilkington	Southern TAS
1962	Salacia	Yacht	Jock Muir	Sydney, NSW
1963	Alert	Police launch	Muir boatyard	Southern TAS
1963	Con Moto	Yacht	Max Creese	Sydney, NSW
1963	Venom	Cadet dinghy	Ross Muir & Bruce Darcey	Melbourne, VIC
1964	Gwynne-B	Fishing boat	Jock Muir	Southern TAS
1965	Balandra	Yacht	Jock Muir	Southern TAS
1965	Huon Lass	Yacht	Max Creese	Sydney, NSW
1965	Kittiwake II	Cadet dinghy	Jock Muir	Melbourne, VIC
1966	Mistral IX	Yacht	Max Creese	Sydney, NSW
1967	Bradypus	Ketch	Bruce Thompson	Southern TAS
1967	Guiding Star	Cadet dinghy	Bill Foster	Southern TAS

Year	Name	Type	Builder	Location
1968	Leillateah	Fishing boat	Max Creese	Triabunna, TAS
1968	Barameda	Yacht	Purdon Brothers	Southern TAS
1969	Lady Nelson	Yacht	Jock Muir	Boston, USA
1970	Maria	Yacht	Max Creese	Southern TAS
1971	Trevassa	Yacht	Jock Muir	Southern TAS
1972	Ruma (Canopus, Van Dieman)	Motor sailer	Tom Pilkington	Eden, NSW
1972	Toheroa	Motor cruiser	Max Creese	Southern TAS
1973	Astrolabe	Yacht	Jock Muir	Southern TAS
1973	Nike	Yacht	Max Creese	Sydney, NSW
1975	Alkira	Yacht	Max Creese	Southern TAS
1975	Kittiwake III	Cadet dinghy	Jock Muir	Southern TAS
1975	Jantina	Motor cruiser	Max Creese	Southern TAS
1975	Lantara	Motor cruiser	Max Creese	Southern TAS
1975	Ruby	Motor boat	Tom Pilkington	Southern TAS
1981	Ramping Lion	Pulling boat	Max Creese & George Burrows	Sydney, NSW
1982	Tata	Fishing boat	Max Creese	Canada
1984	Tradition	Yacht	Max Creese	Southern TAS
1985	Ellen	Dinghy	Bill Foster	Southern TAS
1980s	Pindy Wira	Motor cruiser	Tom Pilkington	Southern TAS

Top (Right): *Ninie* at Cygnet. Courtesy Colin Grazules.
Bottom (left): *Jabiru II.* Courtesy Terry Lean.
Bottom (right): *Westward* and *Lahara* at Sandy Bay. Courtesy Greg Muir.

References & Bibliography

Archives and Indexes

Australian Dictionary of Biography

Australian Electoral Rolls

Australian Register of Historic Vessels

Australia, Tasmania, Civil Registration, 1803-1933

Mori Flapan: Register of Australian and New Zealand Ships and Boats

National Archives of Australia

Register of British Ships: Port of Hobart

Royal Hobart Regatta Programmes

Tasmanian Archive and Heritage Office

Books and Journal Articles

Barrett N (2015). Perce Coverdale: Yachtsman and Battery Point Boat Builder. Maritime Times of Tasmania; Autumn (March) 2015.

Broxam G (2006). Those That Survive. Vintage & Veterans Boats of Tasmania. Navarine Publishing, Australian Capital Territory.

Broxam G and Nash M (2013). Tasmanian Shipwrecks. Volume 2: 1900 – 2012. Navarine Publishing, Tasmania.

Cannon J (2013). Unpublished manuscript. Courtesy Maritime Museum of Tasmania.

Geeves M, Griggs G, Honeysett J & Johnson R (1980). Sailing On: A History of the Royal Yacht Club of Tasmania. Royal Yacht Club of Tasmania, Tasmania.

Graeme-Evans A & Wilson P (2005). Built to Last: The Story of the Shipwrights of Port Cygnet, Tasmania and their Boats 1863 – 1997. Regal Publications, Tasmania.

Hudspeth A & Scripps L (1990). Battery Point Historical Research. A. Hudspeth, Tasmania.

Kerr G (1987). The Tasmanian Trading Ketch: An Illustrated Oral History. Mainsail Books, Victoria.

Kerrison & Johnson (2006). Ebbs and Flows: A Short History of the Derwent Sailing Squadron, 1906-2006. Derwent Sailing Squadron, Tasmania.

Mays N (2014). Skilled, Spirited and Determined: The Boat and Ship Builders of Battery Point: 1835-1935. Self-published, Tasmania.

Norman G (1988). Yachting and the Royal Prince Alfred Yacht Club. Child & Associates, New South Wales.

Norman L (1938). Pioneer Shipping of Tasmania: Whaling, Sealing, Piracy, Shipwrecks, etc. in Early Tasmania. J. Walsh & Sons, Tasmania.

Muir, Hudson & Fogagnolo (1991). Maritime Reflections. E. J. Muir, Tasmania.

Parsons R (2008). Shipping Losses and Casualties concerning Australia and New Zealand. Vol. I and II. R. Parsons, South Australia.

Sims P (1985). The Abel Family. Quoiba, Tasmania.

Webster EH and Norman L (1936). A Hundred Years of Yachting. J. Walsh & Sons, Tasmania.

Newspapers and Periodicals

Advocate; Bairnsdale Advertiser and Tambo and Omeo Chronicle; Barrier Miner; Bucks County Courier Times; Circular Head Chronicle; Critic; Daily Post; Daily Telegraph; Evening News; Gippsland Times; Huon and Derwent Times; Huon Times; Newcastle Morning Herald and Miners' Advocate; Oakland Tribune; Portland Guardian and Normanby General Advertiser; Redlands Daily Facts; Referee; Saturday Magazine; Seacraft; Sporting Globe; Tasmanian Mail; Tasmanian News; The Advertiser; The Argus; The Australian Women's Weekly; The Cairns Post; The Canberra Times; The Clipper; The Cornwall Chronicle; The Examiner; The Hobart Gazette; The Mercury; The Newcastle Sun; The North Western Advocate; The Register; The Sun; The Sunday Herald; The Sunday Tasmanian; The Sydney Morning Herald; The Weekly Courier; Townsville Daily Bulletin; World; Zeehan and Dundas Herald.

Personal Communication

John Allport

Kenn Batt

Mary Brewer

Graeme Broxam

John Colquhoun

Peter Creese

Mori Flapan

Bill Foster

Colin Grazules

Terry Lean

John Lucas

Robyn Mays

Greg Muir

John Muir

Michael Muir

Philip Muir

Ross Muir

Graeme Norris

Andrew Perkins

Russell Pocock

Mick Purdon

Sam Purdon

Suzanne Rex

Gordon Stewart

Ben Stoner

Andrew Tait

Jan Taylor

Jane Tompson

Rob Virtue

Barry Wilson

Sandra Wilson

ENTERING PORT DAV

Jock Muir in December 1940 entering Port Davey aboard *Westwind*.
Courtesy Jock Muir Family Collection.

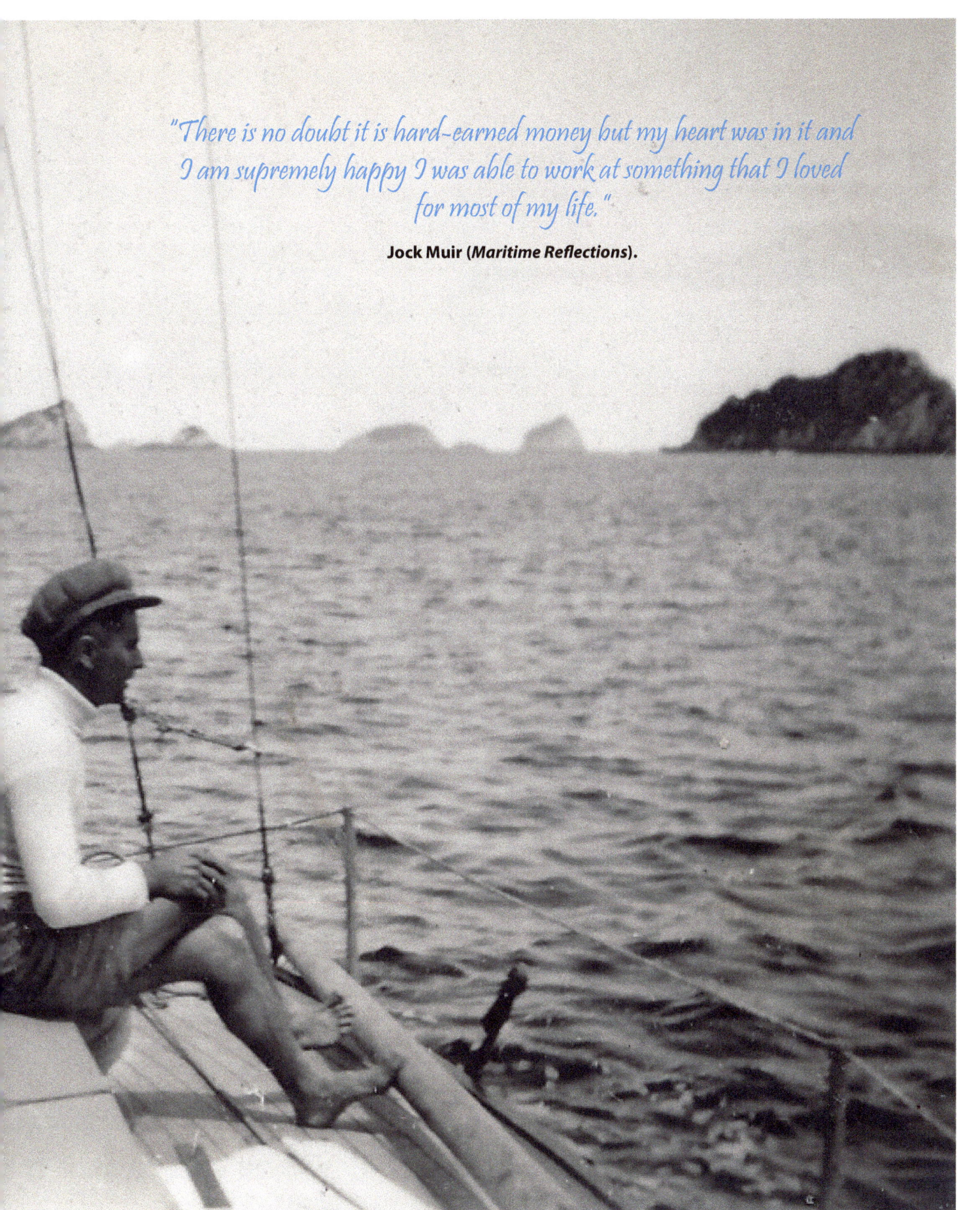

"There is no doubt it is hard-earned money but my heart was in it and I am supremely happy I was able to work at something that I loved for most of my life."

Jock Muir (*Maritime Reflections*).

Index

About the Author

Nicole Mays was born and raised in Hobart. After completing a Bachelor of Science at the University of Tasmania, Nicole moved to Washington D.C., USA, where she worked for a scientific research and policy organisation on Capitol Hill for over a decade. In 2012 Nicole returned to live in Australia, establishing a home in Adelaide, South Australia, with her husband and two young children. Since this time Nicole has been employed as a scientist and is currently working for a university based overseas.

With an interest in family history established in her teens, Nicole's first book, published in 2011, was on her great-great-great grandfather Jacob Bayly Chandler who was a boat builder of Battery Point between 1847 and 1901. This book was followed in 2014 by *Spirited, Skilled and Determined: The Boat and Ship Builders of Battery Point (1835-1935)*. In 2016 Nicole was involved in the publication of Mike Swinson's *Blood, Sweat & the Sea*, the biography of John Muir and the company he established (Muir Engineering). Nicole has also published several articles in the Maritime Museum of Tasmania's quarterly newsletter, *Maritime Times*.

In addition, Nicole serves as a committee member of the "Friends of Tassie Too" not-for-profit organisation and is the founder and administrator of the "Battery Point Boat and Ships" Facebook group.

Saona.
Courtesy Guy Rex Collection (Suzanne Rex).

www.ingramcontent.com/pod-product-compliance
Lightning Source LLC
Chambersburg PA
CBHW040315100426
42811CB00012B/1452